I.O. Evans Studies in the
Philosophy & Criticism of Literature
Number Four
ISSN 0271-9061

I0160481

THE SOCIOLOGY OF SCIENCE FICTION

Brian M. Stableford
University of Reading

BORGO PRESS / WILDSIDE PRESS

www.wildsidepress.com

Library of Congress Cataloging in Publication Data:

Stableford, Brian M.
  The sociology of science fiction.

  (I.O. Evans studies in the philosophy & criticism of litera-
ture ; v. 4)
  Bibliography: p.
  Includes index.
  1. Science fiction—History and criticism.   2. Science fiction—
Social aspects. I. Title. II. Series.
PN3433.5.S8 1987   809.3'876   81-21607
  ISBN 0-89370-165-3 (cloth)
  ISBN 0-89370-265-X (paper

First Edition——April, 1987

CONTENTS

ACKNOWLEDGMENTS

I am indebted to many people who have taken an interest in this project and who have offered help and encouragement, particularly Andy Tudor, Chip Delany, Barry Malzberg, Peter Nicholls, Bill Russell, Leonard Rivett, Anne Akeroyd, Tony Sudbery and Patrick Parrinder. I am also much indebted to Tina Ayres for her help in preparing the manuscript, and to the Science Fiction Foundation for the loan of some research materials.

INTRODUCTION

This book is the text of a doctoral thesis submitted to the University of York in September 1978. The degree was conferred the following July. I worked on the project, on and off, for about seven years, beginning when I first joined the sociology department at York as a postgraduate student in 1972. My interest in the sociology of literature arose from the fact that I was at the time supporting myself by writing science fiction novels, and was thus readily fascinated by questions about why people read, why they choose to read the things they do choose to read, and what effects their reading has upon them.

Curiously, there is a certain resistance by readers (and writers) to the asking of such questions. If you suggest to someone that his choice in reading-matter—or the mere fact of his choosing to spend his time reading—requires explanation, you are likely to find yourself face to face with a defiant antagonist. Similarly, if you suggest to a writer or a literary critic that what writers choose to write about, and the way that they go about doing so, is to some extent explicable in terms of their social situation and of various social pressures to which they are subject, you are likely to meet with a hostile response.

This resistance against the sociological investigation of literature and its consumers requires explanation itself. The fact that people are defensive about their reading habits reflects the widely-held opinion that what people choose to read reveals a great deal about them. When you ask a man what he reads, his image is at stake, and many people feel that it is injudicious to give an honest answer. People who read books which are of low prestige-value are often embarrassed about admitting it, and sometimes become aggressive, as if challenging you to disapprove if you dare. There is a suspicion that if someone were to come along and *explain* why they read what they do read, the explanation might be distinctly unflattering. Thus, the asking of such questions puts them at risk.

The defensive posture of writers and critics is not dissimilar. For them, literature tends to be seen as something sacred. It is to be discussed in terms of esthetics—in terms of value-judgments. Writers and critics might disagree fiercely with one another about which works are to be highly-valued and why, but they can present a surprisingly united front in the slightly eccentric acceptance of the belief that to account for the features and concerns of literary works by reference to factors outside and beyond the author is to *de*value the author's efforts and achievements. It is as if the writer's right to be God within his own private cosmos is being denied—a *prima facie* case

5

of blasphemy.

In the past, I have tended to respond with resistance to the kind of inquiry which is here carried out by reassuring people that there is no threat—that my work is in no way subversive and that it need not threaten the justifications which readers have for reading science fiction, which writers have for writing it, or critics for applauding it. I am, however, now more disposed to accept Howard Becker's dictum that any good piece of sociology will make people angry, because if it is to be good it must reveal that they are harboring illusions of some kind. Sociology which merely confirms what everybody already knows has little intellectual utility. For most of the last ten years I have been worried by the fact that expression of my ideas has led people to fulminate against me; now, however, I have fallen prey to the contrary anxiety: what frightens me is the prospect of not annoying anyone because caution has led me to be too tentative. It is my earnest hope, therefore, that dedicated followers of the science fiction field (in whatever capacity) should not only be reluctant to recognize themselves in this analysis of it, but should react in a spirit of pure paranoid horror.

Despite this hope, my intention in this work has been modest. I have tried to locate science fiction as a *genre* of popular literature, within its appropriate social context. I have asked what devoted readers get out of it. I have asked what kind of messages are transmitted by it. I have asked what features of the broader historical situation it is responsive to, and what forms its responses usually take. In order to provide sensible answers to these questions I have been forced to engage certain preliminary questions about fiction in general, and about reading behavior in general.

My primary interest in this particular work has been the development of a publishing category and the audience which it serves. I have therefore paid attention almost exclusively to work which was marketed under the science fiction label, referring to other futuristic and imaginative works mainly for purposes of comparison. Elsewhere I have tried to set the work done for the science fiction magazines and for the demarcated sector of the paperback book market in a wider literary context; interested readers should refer to my article "Science Fiction Between the Wars" (in the second edition of *Anatomy of Wonder*, published by Bowker in 1981), and my recently published book, *Scientific Romance in Britain*.

Throughout this inquiry I have followed the mildly controversial policy of ignoring questions of literary merit. I have attributed particular significance to some individual works on the grounds of their great popularity with readers; in other cases where I have used works as examples, I have done so on the grounds that they contain in a particularly clear or striking fashion notions which are typical of their time. This refusal to make value-judgments arises out of my conviction that one need not refer to matters of literary merit for the purpose of attempting to explain the existence and popularity of individual literary works or common themes in fiction. This should not be taken to imply that I believe that the business of making literary value-judgments is not a legitimate and valuable enterprise where other purposes are concerned. In most of my writing about science fiction I try to play the roles of sociologist and literary critic simultaneously, though I do not believe that they can be fused—the questions which they deal with are so very different.

In some ways, what follows is a rather unusual exercise in the sociology of literature. Most sociologists of literature have interested themselves in works which are "realistic"—which seem to reflect and pass judgment upon the actual social world. Imaginative fiction has generally been held to be less interesting sociologically; it has often been interpreted in an entirely negative way, as evidence of a retreat from confrontation with social reality—a pathological symptom of disenchantment. I have tried to argue that it is wrong to think of imaginative fiction in this way, and that even where charges of "escapism" are justified, the strategies of escape may themselves be of considerable sociological interest. I have also tried to argue that because science fiction deals so frequently with images of the future and with alternative modes of social organization, that it may actually be more revealing of people's attitudes to social change than fiction dedicated to the description and evaluation of contemporary social situations. I have tried to do this without being too credulous in accepting the claims made on behalf of the *genre* by its most enthusiastic adherents.

In the years since I completed this thesis I have become slightly dissatisfied with certain aspects of the analysis of themes and trends to be found in Chapter Five, but I still accept the conclusions to which I came as a result of it. I think that the analysis might have been a little more elaborate, and I have tried to be slightly more ambitious in the one similar exercise I have carried out in the same vein—my essay on "Man-Made Catastrophes," which appeared in *Foundation* 22 and in a book entitled *The End of the World*, published by the Southern Illinois University Press.

Brian Stableford
Reading, England

I
APPROACHES TO THE
SOCIOLOGY OF LITERATURE

1. LITERATURE AS A PRODUCT

It is the task of the sociologist of literature to relate the experience of the writer's imaginary characters and situations to the historical climate from which they derive. He has to transform the private equation of themes and stylistic means into social equations. [1]—Leo Lowenthal

This statement of Lowenthal's may stand as representative for a whole school of critical and sociological thought which examines literature primarily as a product. This is not to say that the tradition forgets or ignores that books are read as well as written, but simply that it puts the emphasis very much on the author as creator and the literary work as the product of a creative process. The questions asked in this tradition tend to be about the nature of the creative process, and when they are asked by sociologists rather than by literary critics they tend to be about the social factors influencing (and perhaps determining) the creative process. For the sociologist of literature who approaches his task from this direction the problem of connecting the literary work with its social context presents itself in the kind of terms Lowenthal uses. The questions which he meets on this particular road are: "Why has the author chosen this particular subject material?" and "Why has he chosen this particular technique of presentation?"

This approach, with its corollary emphasis, is readily understandable when it is associated with writers *on* literature who are themselves writers *of* literature. Many of the names prominent in this tradition of thought as literary critics are themselves writers or aspiring writers. Their primary interest, necessarily, is the creative process. The approach is not so common among critics who are *not* writers, and who therefore are more interested in what works have to say to them as readers. *These* critics tend to be associated with the alternative tradition, which approaches literature primarily as a medium of communication.

Psychologists of literature have, like writers, tended to be most interested in literature as a creative process, and literary works as products. Freud discussed literature under the heading of "The Paths to Symptom Formation" [2], and represented literary production as an expression of neurotic tendencies. He and his disciples produced a number of "case studies" of famous artists and writers, psychoanalyzing the men through their works, and discovering the well-springs of creative inspiration in the repressed desires inhabiting the unconscious mind. Given the importance accorded by psychoanalysts to fantasies and fantasizing, this emphasis is not surprising.

What *is* surprising is that so many sociologists of literature should have adopted this approach and its emphasis, preferring to study literature much more as a product than as a medium of communication. It is surprising not because the questions associated with this tradition are of no sociological interest, but because they are not the only ones which might interest sociologists, and perhaps not the ones which they might find most interesting. The psychologist and the *littérateur* have a special interest in the creative process, but the sociologist who similarly restricts his attention may be a little narrow-minded, for who else but the sociologist is likely to investigate questions about the social functions of literature as a medium of communication? At present we seem to be in the odd situation that the people who have been most interested in literature as a medium of communication have been a group of literary critics, while sociologists of literature have usually confined themselves to the more limited mode of thoughts. The reasons for this are largely historical.

Madame de Staël described the task which she undertook in her book *De la littérature* (1880) as the examination of "the influence upon literature of religion, custom and law." Much of what she actually wrote did not, in fact, have much to do with this prospectus, being concerned with drawing naive but picturesque metaphors connecting the literature of various nations with the prevalent climate, but she was definite in seeing literature primarily as an *expressive* phenomenon. Like a number of her contemporaries, including Herder and Hegel, the main connection she drew between literature and its social context was between individual works and a general "spirit of the nation" (*volksgeist*) or "spirit of the age" (*zeitgeist*).

Hegel spoke [3] of each "age" preserving its own prevailing mental attitude and characteristic world-view, and he saw literature as being an expression and an embodiment of this attitude and world-view. Though he did not indulge in the metaphorical elaborations of de Staël, he saw literature in much the same way.

In this view of literature the individual artist tends to become a vehicle whose work is the articulation of something that belongs to society in general—indeed, something which is a property of society in general. The writer may represent the spirit of his age well or badly, but this is all the latitude he has because that is all that there is for him to do. This is a rather presumptuous attitude to literature, but because it is so very vague and elastic it is hardly open to falsification. It explains nothing because it really asserts nothing; but what it does do is to point out a perspective—a direction of approach—and in this way it has been influential in determining the methods of several modern sociologists of literature. A direct line of transmission extends from Hegel through Georg Lukacs to Lucien Goldmann, perhaps the most prestigious of twentieth century sociologists of literature. Marxist sociologists have in general tended to adopt the Hegelian mode of approach, though they have modified his concept of *zeitgeist*, replacing it with collective consciousness based on social class.

The most sophisticated version of this mode of approach is Goldmann's, and its key concept is the notion of a "world vision." The term itself is borrowed from Lukacs, but Goldmann makes a much more determined effort to clarify the concept and to state exactly how it can be used. He claims that:

> The history of philosophy and literature can become scientific only when an objective and verifiable instrument has been created which will enable us to distinguish the essential from the accidental elements in a work of art; the validity of this method will be measured by the fact that it will never proclaim as accidental works which are aesthetically satisfying. In my view, such an instrument is to be found in the concept of the *world vision*....
> What is a *world vision*? It is not an immediate, empirical fact, but a conceptual working hypothesis indispensable to an understanding of the way in which individuals actually express their ideas. Even on an empirical plane, its importance and reality can be seen as soon as we go beyond the ideas of work of a single writer, and begin to study them as part of a whole....
> What I have called a "world vision" is a convenient term for the whole complex of ideas, aspirations and feelings which links together the members of a social group (a group which, in most cases, assumes the existence of a social class) and which opposes them to other social groups....
> In a few cases—and it is these which interest us— there are exceptional individuals who either actually achieve or who come very close to achieving a completely integrated and coherent view of what they and the social class to which they belong are trying to do. [4]

At a later stage in his career Goldmann became more definite about the nature of the homology between society and literary works, coopting the vocabulary of structuralism:

> The collective character of a literary creation derives from the fact that the *structures* of the world and the work are homologous with mental structures of certain social groups or is in intelligible relation with them, whereas on the level of content, that is to say, of the creation of the imaginary worlds governed by these structures the writer has total freedom. [5]

In this view literary works "crystallize" the social relationships which exist in the world, their basic structures modelling the essential features of those relationships.

One of the most striking features of Goldmann's procedure is the extent to which it narrows down the field of interest—it rejects a great deal of work as being of no sociological interest. In *The Hidden God* Goldmann is concerned with sorting out the "essential" from the "accidental," implying that a considerable number of whole works, and certain features of all works, belong to the latter category. In *Towards a Sociology of the Novel* all of the "content" of all works has become uninteresting, and all that remains for the sociologist to work with is a single basic structure common to a handful of works. Goldmann's ostensible justification for choosing these particular works is simply that they are the ones which contain the structure which he interprets as the one appropriate to modern society (the atomized society of "crisis capitalism"). He does not, therefore, study literature in the hope of discovering anything (though he does claim extra justification for *The Hidden God* on the grounds that he *did* discover something), but simply to confirm that what he expects to find there can be identified. The fact that he can only identify it in a very small number of literary works does not worry him—he has already declared that the author who manages to articulate correctly the world vision of his group is an "exceptional individual."

Another curious feature of Goldmann's comments in *The Hidden God* is his claim that further justification for his *modus operandi* will be provided by the fact that his method will never identify as accidental works which are esthetically satisfying. Here he seems to be on very dangerous ground, in that he must exclude so much in order to fulfill his prospectus. One presumes that this argument must become circular in order to cope with any claim that any critic might make regarding the esthetic merits of works outside Goldmann's chosen range (or, of course, the esthetic demerits of works within it).

This approach is basically unproductive. It commits the sociologist to rejecting as uninteresting the great majority of literary works—all those, in fact, which do not conform to a rather narrow-minded set of preconceptions about what literary works ought to be. It hardly needs pointing out that few, if any, writers would accept Goldmann's analysis of what they are doing.

Neither Lukacs nor Goldmann had any real interest in attempting to come to terms with the profuse products of twentieth century literature, for both regarded it as necessarily degenerate. Lukacs believed that it had become impossible for anyone to write "great literature" in his own time because of the absence of a coherent socialist consciousness which might restore "totality" to the modern vision of the world. He was optimistic that such totality would be recovered in time, but Goldmann was less convinced of its imminence. The Marxist theorists are virtually unanimous in considering that twentieth century literature had lost both its power and its purpose in "becoming a commodity." For this reason they have been quite uninterested in trying to map the connections between modern life and modern literature except insofar as the literature illuminates the desolation and the hopelessness of life in capitalist society. It is hardly to be expected, therefore, that the Marxist sociology of literature will offer useful tools for the sociologist who does want to map these connections.

It is not only the intellectual descendants of Hegel and Marx who have tended to emphasize literature as a product and to concentrate their attention upon the social forces and influences presiding over literary creation. Hippolyte Taine, a follower of Comte and the "positive philosophy," was dogmatic in his insistence that this is the approach befitting the scientific study of literature. His *History of English Literature* (1863) is devoted to an examination of social factors as *causes* of literary production. Again we find the writer reduced almost to the status of an automaton, merely serving as a focussing device for the spirit of his nation and the spirit of his age. Again we find the corollary reliance on the notion of the great artist as the individual who manages to achieve perfect articulation, so that other writers may be dismissed as uninteresting because they are making the wrong connections, or making the right ones incompetently.

Taine, however, does go further than this into a consideration of "literary taste," and speaks of audience reaction as an important force in the generation and evolution of literary kinds. He speaks of literature *adapting* itself to the taste of those who can appreciate and pay for it. The invocation of the concept of adaptation is not surprising in view of the fact that the notion had been brought into vogue in science by Lamarck earlier in the century. In one of the subsequent developments of this line of inquiry, *Évolution des genres dans l'histoire de la littérature* (1890), Ferdinand Brunetière produced a quasi-Darwinian theory of the evolution of literary *genres*, seeing therein a kind of natural selection as those *genres* which are "fitter" in the sense of meeting the demands of an audience survive and thrive while others fail or decline. The falseness of the analogy was sternly criticized by Levin Schucking, who attempted to provide a less ambitious account of changes in literary taste in *The Sociology of Literary Taste* (revised ed. 1931).

There is not sufficient coherence about this series of inquiries to warrant calling it a tradition, but this additional mode of approach to the problem of explaining the pattern of literary production has continued to recur in sociological writing. In modern times Robert Escarpit has attempted to come to terms with the way that the writer and his audience interact and with accurate description of the literary marketplace. His method, however, consists largely of gathering statistics concerned with book production, and his main concern is with the book as a commodity rather than as a communiqué. His work remains quite disconnected from the analytical sociology of literature as practised by the Marxists, and also from any kind of literary criticism. We thus find a rather peculiar situation in the sociology of literature, in which there are two major directions of approach which are both highly selective in the data which they propose to study, and neither of which seems to have the intention—or even to provide the possibility—of coming to grips with the everyday social functions of literature in circulation in modern society.

Whatever the merits these approaches may have, it would surely be ridiculous to claim that they exhaust the possibilities for the sociological study of literature. It seems to me, in fact, that if the sociology of literature is to be confined by such approaches as these it is likely to remain essentially sterile. Unless we can consider literary works not only as things created and sold, but also as communications, we will surely run the risk of misunderstanding their real nature. Works of literature are not only written but intended to be read. They are not simply expressive, but also—and perhaps more importantly—communicative. And, while a statistical study of book production and the economics of the book marketplace may be helpful (or essential) to an understanding of the network of literary communication, we must surely be prepared at some stage to go beyond that to an examination of the communiqués themselves.

2. LITERATURE AS A MEANS OF COMMUNICATION

If literature is to be regarded as a means of communication, then we must ask what kind of communication is involved. The questions which we are likely to meet as we approach the problem from this direction are: "What *special* functions are performed by literature which differentiate it from other media of communication?"; and "Are the differences between various kinds of literature accountable in terms of different kinds of communicative function, or simply in terms of different communiqués?" Because sociologists have so far, for the most part, failed to interest themselves in questions like these, it is necessary to turn to other sources in search of useful suggestions as to what to look for.

The first theory of the social functions of literature was advanced by Aristotle, who saw the explanation of its existence in terms of a "delight in imitation." He saw the function of poetry as primarily didactic, but invoked as a further function for drama the notion of *catharsis*, proposing that by evoking within us the emotions of pity and terror drama might allow us to be purged of tensions and leave us with "calm of mind." The communicative function suggested here is both ·an affective one and an instructive one. Opinions, however, have varied as to whether drama really does permit the release of emotional tension or whether it simply creates it. Plato contended that tragedy and comedy "nourish and water our emotions when we ought to dry them up." This still recognizes an affective function for literature but evaluates its social usefulness rather differently.

As previously noted it is in the writings of literary critics who are not themselves authors that the notion of literature as communication predominates—it is members of the audience rather than writers who tend to dwell on the issue of what purpose is being served by the dramatic performance or by the act of reading, and what purpose *ought* to be served thereby. It is only to be expected that opinions on these points will vary, in that there is no logical necessity for the same function to be served by every act of reading.

The modern critic who has developed most extensively the notion of literature as a medium of communication is I. A. Richards, primarily in his *Principles of Literary Criticism* (1924). Because he is aware that writers themselves have a rather narrower interest in the creative process, he takes some pains to establish the validity of his approach, and he justifies it as follows:

> That the artist is not as a rule consciously concerned with communication, but with getting the work, the poem or play or statue or painting or whatever it is, "right," apparently regardless of its communicative efficacy, is easily explained. To make the work "embody," accord with, and represent the precise experience upon which its value depends is his major preoccupation, in difficult cases an overmastering preoccupation, and the dissipation of attention which would be involved if he considered the communicative side as a separate issue would be fatal in most serious work ....But his conscious neglect of communication does not in the least diminish the importance of the communicative aspect....The very process of getting the work "right" has itself...immense communicative consequences. Apart from certain special cases...it will, when "right" have much greater communicative power than it would have had if "wrong." [6]

Richards declines to consider the question of whether effective communication is an "unconscious motive" on the part of the writer, but is content to claim as an observation the fact that what is for the writer effective expression is for the writer *and* reader effective communication. He moves quickly on to a set of proposals regarding the proper function of the arts:

> The arts are our storehouse of recorded values. They spring from and perpetuate hours in the lives of exceptional people, when their control and command of experience is at its highest, hours when the varying possibilities of existence are most clearly seen and the different activities which may arise are most exquisitely reconciled, hours when habitual narrowness of

interests or confused bewilderment are replaced by an intricately wrought composure...without the assistance of the arts we could compare very few of our experiences, and without such comparison we could hardly hope to agree as to which are to be preferred. [7]

In this view the great artist is again an exceptional individual, but for what is almost the opposite reason to that proposed by Goldmann. He is exceptional because of his uniqueness, his ability to discover new possibilities, not for his ability to become the voice of a social class or the spirit of an age. Actually, the presumed roles are not so very different, but Richards' exceptional people are discovering and creating what Goldmann's are reflecting and articulating.

Richards' goal is to justify the value-judgments which literary critics habitually make by claiming that in judging the value of works of art they are in some way judging the value of human experiences. What his argument actually does is to transform the value-judgment regarding the esthetic merit of a work of art into a value-judgment regarding a "way of life"—a judgment passed upon society. Instead of regarding the difference between "good art" and "bad art" as a matter of style or symmetry he characterizes bad art as communication which does not simply fail, but also corrupts. In this view, people who are able to appreciate great art are, in a perfectly literal sense, better people, and people who cannot are degenerate:

> The basis of morality, as Shelley insisted, is laid not by preachers but by poets. Bad taste and crude responses are not mere flaws in an otherwise admirable person. They are actually a root evil from which other defects follow. No life can be excellent in which the elementary responses are disorganized and confused. [8]

For Richards, bad art—including mass-produced literature—is not merely art which fails to fulfill its function but which is actually dysfunctional. It *does* have a communicative effect, but one which is bad:

> At present bad literature, bad art, the cinema, etc., are an influence of the first importance in fixing immature and actually inapplicable attitudes to most things....
> The losses incurred by these artificial fixations of attitudes are evident. Through them the average adult is worse, not better, adjusted to the possibilities of his existence than the child. He is even in the most important things functionally unable to face facts: do what he will he is only able to face fictions, fictions projected by his own stock responses. [9]

Richards is, of course, primarily interested in justifying his value-judgments, but in order to do this he has to make hypotheses about the way in which literature actually functions within society; and it is these hypotheses which may provide initial guidelines for the sociological study of literature.

Richards' lead has been followed enthusiastically by a series of literary and social critics, including F. R. Leavis and Richard Hoggart, both of whom were attracted by the notion that bad art is actually "harmful" and a threat to social well-being. A slightly more moderate and much more thoughtful extension of Richards' line of thought is also apparent in the work of Raymond Williams.

Leavis took Richards' case to extremes in developing the notion of a tiny esthetic elite alone capable of appreciating literature and life, surrounded and in imminent danger of eclipse by Yahoos. The culmination of his thesis is the claim that:

> The minority capable not only of appreciating Dante, Shakespeare, Donne, Baudelaire, Hardy (to take the major instances) but of recognizing their latest successors constitute the consciousness of the race (or of a branch of it) at a given time. [10]

Here, again, we are back to the spirit of the age, save that in this view it is literary appreciation which defines it rather than literary production which is defined *by* it.

In the work of Hoggart and Williams the emphasis shifts from the passionate need to establish the superiority of great literature and its devotees to the attempt to investigate much more closely the role played by literature (good *and* bad) in affecting—or in helping to constitute—society. Williams' inquiry is the more detailed, and focuses upon the ambiguity in the word "culture," which can be used with reference either to art or to society. In *Culture and Society, 1780-1950* (1958) Williams tracks the changing implications of the word as used by commentators on literature and society. In his view the word comes ultimately to mean "a whole way of life," and literature-as-communication is an active force in creating, reconstructing, and maintaining it. This position is summarized and further developed in *The Long Revolution* (1961), where we find the following comments on the social functions of art:

> Art cannot exist unless a working communication can be reached, and this communication is an activity in which both artist and spectator participate. When art communicates, a human experience is actively offered and actively received. Below this activity threshold there can be no art.
>
> The nature of the artist's activity, in this process, may be further defined. The artist shares with other men what is usually called the "creative imagination": that is to say, the capacity to find and or-

ganize new descriptions of experience....The special nature of the artist's work is his use of a learned skill in a particular kind of transmission of experience. [11]

We cannot say that art is a substitute for other kinds of communication, since when successful it evidently communicates experience which is not apparently communicable in other ways. We must see art, rather, as an extension of our capacity for organization: a vital faculty which allows particular areas of reality to be described and communicated. [12]

Thus our descriptions of our experience come to compose a network of relationships, and all our communication systems, including the arts, are literally parts of our social organization. The selection and interpretation involved in our descriptions embody our attitudes, needs and interests, which we seek to validate by making them clear to others. [13]

Leavis' development of Richards' perspective is to make it into a weapon for social (and sometimes personal) criticism. In Leavis' hands the transformation of esthetic value-judgments into social ones make the study of literature into a vast series of arguments *ad hominem*, and ultimately renders it sterile. Williams, by contrast, retreats from the impulsive value-judgments to develop the hypotheses regarding the nature and functions of art, and makes constructive suggestions as to what the student of literature might expect to find there. He is wary of accepting the arrogant stance of Richards' attack on bad literature as a corrupting force (an arrogance which becomes hatred in Leavis and patronization in Hoggart). Williams approaches the problem of mass-produced art and its badness in a more cautious spirit:

We are faced with the fact that there is now a great deal of bad art, bad entertainment, bad journalism, bad advertisement, bad argument. We are not likely to be diverted from this conclusion by the usual diversionary arguments. Much that we judge to be bad is known to be bad by its producers....

But this is said to be popular culture. The description has a ready-made historical thesis. After the education act of 1870, a new mass-public came into being, literate but untrained in reading, low in taste and habit. The mass-culture followed as a matter of course. I think always, when I hear this thesis, of an earlier one, from the second half of the eighteenth century. Then, the decisive date was between 1730 and 1740, and what had emerged, with the advance of the middle classes to prosperity, was a new middle-class reading public. The immediate result was that vulgar phenomenon, the novel. [14]

He goes on to observe that to concentrate on the badness of popular culture is to ignore the fact that good books as well as bad now circulate far more widely than at any previous period of history, and then adds a much more important observation:

> Secondly, it is important to remember that, in judging a culture it is not enough to concentrate on habits which coincide with those of the observer. To the highly literate observer there is always a temptation to assume that reading plays as large a part in the lives of most people as it does in his own. But if he compares his own kind of reading with the reading-matter that is most widely distributed, he is not really comparing levels of culture. He is, in fact, comparing what is produced for people to whom it is, at best, minor. To the degree that he acquires a substantial proportion of his ideas and feelings he will assume, again wrongly, that the ideas and feelings of the majority will be similarly conditioned. But, for good or ill, the majority of people do not yet give reading this importance in their lives; their ideas and feelings are, to a large extent, still molded by a wider and more complex pattern of social and family life. There is an evident danger of delusion to the highly literate person, if he supposes that he can judge the quality of general living by primary reference to the reading artifacts. [15]

Williams remains, throughout his work, preoccupied with the problem of making prescriptions for a better society, but he is not prepared to make popular culture into a scapegoat for his dissatisfaction with the way things are. Because of this his attempt to use literature as a means to the end of a better understanding of society seems far more objective than the attempt made by Richards to evaluate society through its sensitivity to literature.

In *Culture and Society, 1780-1950* Williams discusses literary works in terms of what he calls their "structure of feeling," seeing the works as dramatizations of emotional conflict which not only express the conflicts but also attempt some kind of resolution. In this view a novel becomes a kind of exemplar in which the attitudes of the writer are ultimately "justified" by the outcome of the imaginary situation. When such exemplars become stereotyped, giving a common pattern to a number of literary works (Williams refers to the 19th century "industrial novels") then we are presumably dealing with an attitude common to (and perhaps characteristic of) a social group or class. The analogy with Goldmann's world vision or his literary structures is clear, but Williams' tool of analysis is on the one hand more flexible because it is not constrained by such dogmatic preconceptions, and on the other hand more powerful, in that it is actually creating or reconstructing the structure of feeling within society at large, not merely reflecting it.

Goldmann's notion of the world vision offers little hope for an inquiry into the sociology of popular literature, because it is fundamental to Goldmann's case that only great literature can be expected to present a coherent and fully-formulated world vision. Bad fiction may still contain an incoherent and badly articulated vision, but it is difficult to imagine how one would be able to identify and characterize it. Williams' notion of the "structure of feeling" seems potentially more useful, in that one might expect to find some structure of feeling even in popular fiction, albeit simplified and lacking in subtlety. However, we must heed Williams' own warning regarding the danger of the assumption that popular culture is simply a crude and stupid version of elite culture. We must not simply take it for granted that popular culture is fulfilling the same communicative function as elite culture, even if we are prepared to assume that the function credited to good literature by Williams is, in fact, the correct one.

3. THE FUNCTIONS OF LITERATURE

As we have seen, the recent growth of concern regarding the communicative functions of literature is associated with an anxiety regarding the "misuse" of those functions by the mass media, including mass-produced popular fiction. The reaction of men closely associated with elite culture to the products of the mass media is inevitably condemnatory, but it is at least possible that they overreact. It is therefore worth looking at another direction of approach to the problem of communication and its functions—that adopted by a group of media sociologists.

One of the most surprising things about the sociology of the mass media is that many people working within the field have simply imported the condemnatory attitudes of elite culture, devoting themselves not so much to analysis of the situation as to criticism of it. Nevertheless, sociologists in this field have been disposed to look much more closely at the supposed corruptive effects of media content, in order to find out *how* it influences its consumers. [16] A certain amount of empirical research has been done with the aim of discovering what kind of gratification the audience get from the content of the mass media and how they use that content. From considerations of this kind a more complicated picture of the kinds of communication which might take place through the medium of art (good *or* bad) has grown up.

In *Communication and Social Order*, (1962) Hugh Dalziel Duncan identifies three probable categories of literary communication. [17] He distinguishes between "literature as great art," "literature as magical art," and "literature as make-believe." He sees the function of "literature as great art" in much the same terms as Richards and Williams:

What we mean by "originality" is not that a writer is able to create great numbers of fantasies (madmen do this just as well) or that he can invoke profound traditions out of the past (sacred writings do this far better) but that he presents new actions, or phases of social action, which give us, as we say, a new life. Our self-consciousness is raised to new intensity because we are able to enter into great undertakings on a symbolic level among characters whom we would know nothing of in our ordinary life. In this sense great literature is not an appeal to the passions or a vehicle for community daydreaming. It is the exploration through symbolic action of how men *can* act when they act freely in human society. [18]

When literature functions as "magical art," according to Duncan, its purpose is to maintain attitudes and values and to help in the preservation of norms:

Popular literature maintains sentiments requisite for success within the society and transmits these from one generation to another through embodiment in symbolic works which are easily accessible....We use such literature not to weigh ends and means but to charge objects and experiences with sentiments useful to communal practical action. Literature of this kind is close to daily life because it takes its standards of achievement from the powerful institutions of the community. [19]

The third function of literature suggested by Duncan recalls Aristotle's theory of catharsis, seeing art as an aid to some kind of release from desires which must be repressed in everyday social intercourse. Here the release is obtained by imaginative wish-fulfillment:

Make-believe literature...removes us from practical action by dissipating emotions which, if developed into action (as in the use of magical art) or into conscious rational experience (as in the use of great art) would be a threat to those in control of the society....whether it is a child reading from Grimm...or a sophisticated adult following the daily horrors of sex crimes in the daily press, they are making use of forms of expression which are approved by their society and which are one means by which they learn to satisfy their instinctual drives....
Make-believe allows us to elaborate desire through imaginative symbolic forms developed in time as traditional forms of wishing. On this level our wishes are no more unique then our clothes, which may be individual but never an arbitrary expression of the self.

Our wishes, too, are limited to a culturally determined range of make-believe forms. [20]

These proposed communicative functions are no more than hypotheses, but they seem plausible for two reasons. On the one hand, they offer a potential explanation for the repetitiveness of much popular fiction and its standardization. On the other hand, they recall categories which are clearly recognizable, both in the content of popular literature and in the ways we habitually talk about it. The third function proposed by Duncan is little more than an elaboration of the common notion of "escapist" reading.

A tripartite classification similar to that of Duncan, though couched in a rather different jargon, is suggested by Gerhardt Wiebe in a paper dealing with "The Social Effects of Broadcasting," in which he attempts to identify the socializing effects of the mass media. He distinguishes between three different species of communiqués (or, as he calls them, messages) [21]:

> *Directive* messages come from authority figures. They command, exhort, instruct, persuade, and urge in the direction of learning and new understanding that represent progress in the estimation of authority figures. Directive messages call for substantial and conscious intellectual effort on the part of the learner.
> *Maintenance* messages include all the every-day messages sent and received in the customary business of living. They call for relatively little conscious intellectual effort on the part of the learner.
> *Restorative* messages, including individual fantasies, are those with which the individual refreshes himself from the strain of adapting, the weariness of conforming. They provide an interim for the reasserting of impulse. The child, seemingly with perverse precociousness, articulates his restorative messages as he screams, complains, jeers, taunts, defies, says forbidden words and gleefully plays out cruel and destructive fantasies. [22]

Wiebe goes on to apply these general categories of communicative function to the way that the content of mass media is used by the audience. Although this classification is not identical to Duncan's, it shares a great deal with it—one could quite well apply the labels *directive*, *maintenance* and *restorative* to the three kinds of function which Duncan discusses under the headings "literature as great art," "literature as magical art," and "literature as make-believe."

Similar categories crop up elsewhere, sometimes as part of more extensive classifications. In *What Reading Does to People* (1940), Waples, Berelson, and Bradshaw attempt an analysis of the kinds of effects which reading may produce, distinguishing five categories. Those which correspond roughly to the Duncan/Wiebe categorization are: the *instrumental* function, in which reading serves to gather information for use in coping with practical and personal problems; the *re-enforcement* function, in which support is sought for attitudes and beliefs already held; and the *respite* function, in which reading is used for "forgetting worries," "having a good laugh," or "killing time." The other two functions mentioned are reading for self-esteem or prestige, which might well be reckoned a sub-category of the re-enforcement function, and reading "for enriched aesthetic experience," which is in the Duncan/Wiebe classification not distinguished from the instrumental or directive function.

These systems provide potentially-useful hypotheses which may help to resolve some of the problems which arise from assuming that the function identified by Richards and Williams is *the* function of literature, which individual literary works fulfill either well or badly. They also provide what the Marxist sociologists clearly do not—a conceptual framework which will allow us to put *any* literary work into some kind of social context, with the hope of establishing some kind of connection between the work and society. The question still remains, however, as to whether these hypotheses are, in fact, true. Can we, in fact, distinguish between three (or more) categories of communicative function which are habitually served by reading fiction? Are there observations which support the contention?

One significant observation which has been made more than once with regard to the problem of the communicative functions of popular literature is that its consumption actually involves a rather different kind of reader behavior. One clear statement of this particular observation forms the starting point for C. S. Lewis's book, *An Experiment in Criticism* (1961):

> In this essay I propose to try an experiment. Literary criticism is traditionally employed in judging books. Any judgment it implies about men's reading of books is a corollary from its judgment on the books themselves. Bad taste is, as it were by definition, a taste for bad books. I want to find out what sort of picture we shall get by reversing the process. Let us make our distinction between our readers or types of reading the basis, and our distinction between books the corollary....
> In the first place, the majority never read anything twice. The sure mark of an unliterary man is that he considers "I've read it already" to be a conclusive argument against reading a work. We have all known women who remembered a novel so dimly that they had to stand for half an hour in the library skimming through it before they were certain they had once read it. But the moment they became certain they rejected it imme-

diately. It was for them dead, like a burnt-out match, an old railway ticket, or yesterday's paper; they had already used it. Those who read great works, on the other hand, will read the same work ten, twenty or thirty times during the course of their life.

Secondly, the majority, though they are sometimes frequent readers, do not set much store by reading. They turn to it as a last resource. They abandon it with alacrity as soon as any alternative pastime turns up. It is kept for railway journeys, odd moments of enforced solitude, or for the process called "reading oneself to sleep." They sometimes combine it with desultory conversation, with listening to the radio. But literary people are always looking for leisure and silence in which to read and do so with their whole attention. When they are denied such attentive and undisturbed reading even for a few days they feel impoverished.

Thirdly, the first reading of some literary work is often, to the literary, an experience so momentous that only experiences of love, religion or bereavement can furnish a standard of comparison. Their whole consciousness is changed. They have become what they were not before. But there is no sign of anything like this among the other sort of readers. When they have finished the story or the novel, nothing much, or nothing at all, seems to have happened to them.

Finally, and as a natural result of their different behavior in reading, what they read is constantly and prominently present to the mind of the few, but not to that of the many. The former mouth over their favorite lines and stanzas in solitude. Scenes and characters from books provide them with a sort of iconography by which they interpret or sum up their own experience. They talk to one another about books, often and at length. The latter seldom think or talk about their reading. [23]

Lewis contends that the literary elite and the masses use books in entirely different ways. His thinking is reminiscent of Richards insofar as he divides the world into "us" (superior) and "them" (inferior), but he has taken heed of Williams' warning about making assumptions too readily about the way in which the masses use literature. He is condescendingly sympathetic to the people who, though they understand the symbols on the page, still cannot read *properly*:

Literature...admits us to experiences other than our own. They are not, any more than our personal experiences, all equally worth having. Some, as we say, "interest" us more than others. The causes of this interest are naturally extremely various and differ

24

from one man to another; it may be the typical...or the abnormal...it may be the beautiful, the terrible, the awe-inspiring, the exhilarating, the pathetic, the comic or the merely piquant. Literature gives the *entrée* to them all. Those of us who have been true readers all our life seldom fully realize the enormous extension of our being which we owe to authors. We realize it best when we talk with an unliterary friend. He may be full of goodness and good sense but he inhabits a tiny world. In it, we should be suffocated. The man who is content to be only himself, and therefore less a self, is in prison. [24]

Lewis is undoubtedly too sweeping in his generalizations, and the patronizing self-satisfaction of the second quote may help us to understand the curious blind spot which results in one major false generalization. What Lewis has observed is two different kinds of reading behavior, and his characterization of the two kinds, is apt. The inference which he has taken from this—that there are two kinds of people in the world, the literary and the unliterary—is over-ambitious. In making an essentially similar observation Robert Escarpit is careful to note that he is distinguishing two kinds of reading behavior which are effectively available to anyone, and which might actually both be present in a particular act of reading. His distinction is between "connoisseur reading" and "consumer reading":

The role of the connoisseur is to "go beyond appearances," to perceive the circumstances which surround literary creation, to understand its intentions, to analyze its means. For him, there is no such thing as ageing or death of a work, as it is possible at any given moment to reconstruct in his mind the system of references which restores to any work its aesthetic nature. This is an historical attitude.

The consumer, on the contrary, lives in the present, albeit the present may have its origins in a rather distant past. He has no active role, merely an existence. He tastes what is offered him and decides whether or not it pleases him. The decision has no need of being explicit: the consumer reads or doesn't read. This attitude in no way excludes intellectual lucidity on his part, nor does it rule out someone's examination of the reasons for his preference which demands more perspicacity than simply justifying it.

The two orders of value can and must co-exist; sometimes they even coincide. Their apparent incompatibility is only an effect of the social and cultural structures which we have described and, in particular, of the isolation of the cultured circuit. In fact, whatever that pattern of the reader's intellectual and emotional reaction, the act of reading is a whole and must be considered as an entity. Like the act of literary creation which is at the other end of the chain, it is a free act influenced by the circumstances within which it occurs. [25]

This modification of Lewis's position is crucial, for it liberates us from the trap of having to assume that any particular literary work has only one possible function, or the equally difficult assumption that any particular reader can only use literature to serve one or other of the possible functions at one time. Escarpit's view accepts the more reasonable opinon that individual literary works may be differently used by different readers, and that different communicative functions may be served simultaneously. This is a much more complex situation than the one Lewis imagines, and one which is bound to create problems for the analyst who wants to determine what is happening in any particular act of reading; but it is surely in better accordance with our ordinary experience of reading.

What is being observed here is a range of possible relationships between the reader and text which vary according to the degree of *disposability* with which the text is treated. Both writers refer to the common metaphor of "taste" in talking about the reader-experience, and I think that we may extend this metaphor a little here in order to illustrate the implications of this notion. What Lewis and Escarpit are suggesting is that what is primarily of interest in "consumer" or "unliterary" reading is the "taste-sensation" associated with the text, whereas the focus of interest in "connoisseur" or "literary" reading is the "food for thought" which, as it were, ultimately nourishes the mind. Just as all the food we eat has some taste and some nutritional value all reading involves us, at least potentially, with taste-sensations and food for thought. But the reasons we have for indulging in different texts may be as different as the reasons we have for indulging in different foodstuffs. Some may be light and pleasant while others are solid and nutritious. (We do sometimes hear works designed specifically for consumer reading described as "literary confections.")

The most important distinction between connoisseur and consumer reading dramatized by the observations made by Lewis and Escarpit is that consumer reading, concerned with "taste-sensations," tends to be important only while the reader-experience is actually happening. Thus experience is essentially transient. In connoisseur reading, by contrast, though the reader-experience may still be satisfying, what is more important is the contribution which the book may ultimately make to the readers' knowledge or attitudes. (Thus it sometimes happens that we may encounter books that require a determined effort to read, but which we are subsequently glad of *having read*.)

It is the transience of the experience of consumer reading which Lewis deplores, for he cannot see how the momentary pleasure of taste-sensations is any substitute for mental and spiritual nourishment. The likely answer is that it is not a substitute at all, and we can perceive the importance of the distinction drawn by Lewis and Escarpit if we refer back to the categories of communicative function drawn up by Duncan, Wiebe, and Waples *et al..* The *directive* function, to use Wiebe's terminology, is concerned with information which is intended to remain with the recipient of the literary message—to be, in some sense, incorporated into his consciousness. Here we are clearly dealing with food for thought and connoisseur reading. The *maintenance* function is, however, rather different. Here we are involved with little more than a continual series of ephemeral reassurances which provide support for everyday thoughts and actions. Because the maintenance function is concerned with knowledge and norms already internalized their importance is superficial. Messages of this type are important only while they are being received, though they may need to be repeated or renewed more-or-less constantly. Obviously, this function could be served perfectly well by consumer reading.

The case of the restorative function is more interesting, because this category of function is concerned with "resting" or "escaping" from, as Wiebe puts it, "the strain of adaption, the weariness of conforming." Here again it is the taste-sensations which are important, but we may make the additional observation that it is *essential* that this function should be served by consumer reading. Because the content of this kind of message is strategically opposed to reality it must necessarily be transient and must not make any lasting impression on the mind (at least, no lasting impression in the sense that directive material is held to affect the individual's consciousness of the world and attitudes to it). If the "messages" appropriate to this kind of communicative function were to be internalized as information about the real world, or as material that could shape attitudes to the real world, then the result would very probably be incongruous and possibly harmful.

It is precisely because "literary people," who think of reading entirely in terms of "connoisseur reading," jump to the conclusion that material which is intended to serve the restorative function is being consumed directively that they see mass culture and popular fiction as corruption. The bitter attacks launched by Richards and Leavis on mass-culture and the ongoing debate concerning the effects of television are all haunted by this assumption, which is probably false. Its probable falseness is apparent in the fact that none of those who attack the media on these grounds ever claim that they themselves have internalized false information or perverted values—they merely worry on behalf of others, particularly children. It is at least possible that other people—including children—are just as adept at unthinkingly discriminating between fact and fantasy as the critics. It still remains to be demonstrated that people do not have the ability to sort out directive messages from restorative messages and use each according to its function. If we are not, for the most part, capable of this discrimination, it is difficult to explain how "escapist" fiction manages to exist at all. The very fact that we can recognize its nature and—usually, at least—know it when we encounter it suggests that we are using restorative messages in fiction "correctly." The existence of tabloid newspapers and their characteristic style of reportage suggests that if extensive "misreading" does go on it tends to be the other way round—ostensibly directive material is consumed in service of restorative function.

Relatively little empirical research has been done to investigate the uses and gratifications which are associated with popular fiction and the mass media. There are difficulties involved in simply asking people why they read, or why they read the things they do read, or what rewards they get from reading, because the answers to these questions are not readily available to the people themselves. They read what they read because they enjoy it, and often cannot analyze what their enjoyment consists of. There is a danger that an interviewer who asks his respondents to choose from a list of possible gratifications those important to them will simply provide a set of convenient rationalizations which may be grasped eagerly for the purpose of framing a reply. Nevertheless, a certain amount of attention needs to be paid to what the users of popular fiction actually say when they are asked about their reasons for devoting time to it. An interesting early survey in this field was Herta Herzog's investigation of the gratifications obtained from radio soap operas in the early Forties. From the replies derived from a hundred intense interviews with soap opera "addicts" Herzog isolated three main types of gratification:

> Some listeners seem to enjoy the serials merely as a means of emotional release. They like "the chance to cry" which the serials provide; they enjoy "the surprises, happy or sad." The opportunity for expressing aggressiveness is also a source of satisfaction. Burdened with their own problems, listeners claimed that it "made them feel better to know that other people have troubles too."
> On the one hand, the sorrows of the serial characters are enjoyed as compensation for the listeners' own troubles....
> On the other hand, in identifying themselves and their admittedly minor problems with the suffering heroes and heroines of the stories, the listeners find an opportunity to magnify their own woes. This is enjoyed if only because it expresses their "superiority" over others who have not had these profound emotional experiences.
> A second and commonly recognized form of enjoyment concerns the opportunities for wishful thinking provided in listening. While certain people seem to go all out and "drown" their troubles in listening to the events portrayed in the serials, others use them mainly

to fill in the gaps of their own life, or to compensate for their own failures through the success pattern of the serials....

A third and commonly unsuspected form of gratification concerns the advice obtained from listening to daytime serials. The stories are liked because they "explain things" to the inarticulate listener. Furthermore, they teach the listener appropriate patterns of behavior. "If you listen to these programs and something turns up in your own life, you would know what to do about it, is a typical comment." [26]

The echoes here of Duncan's classification of literary functions are clear. What is also clear is the simultaneity of the three functions. Emotional release and advice, apparently, can be obtained from the same source at the same time.

A survey done in England by Peter Mann involved sending out questionnaires to those readers who received by mail a catalogue of books published by Mills & Boon Ltd., who specialize in "romantic fiction." Some 2,800 replies were analyzed by Mann and his conclusions concerning the gratifications obtained by the readers were published in *The Romantic Novel: a Survey of Reading Habits* (1969). Mann discovered that his respondents were mostly young married women with small children, many of whom had worked in secretarial or similar jobs and had a reasonable standard of literacy. He seems to have been slightly surprised by the readiness with which most of the respondents referred to their reading as escapist, and observed that:

It was clear in written comments that these women recognize the "fairy story" aspect of their reading and enjoy the books because of their unreality. [27]

The common assumption that many readers of romantic fiction considered the books to be an honest representation of the world is undermined by Mann's survey, which suggests that the gratification involved (at least for this admittedly biased sample) is mainly restorative.

Empirical investigations of this type, therefore, seem to provide a certain amount of support for the basic framework laid down by Duncan and Wiebe. It does seem that more than one communicative function is involved, and that the classification into three main categories is reasonably apt. If we are to adopt this hypothetical framework, however, a certain caution is necessary in its use. It is probable that the categories are capable of further subdivision, and there is no necessity to assume that, broad as they are, they exhaust the possible communicative functions available to literature. Their validity as a research tool must be established by their usefulness in allowing us to explain aspects of popular (and perhaps elite) literature which other approaches are not competent to deal with.

One further point which might be made here is that if we are to adopt this framework we must be careful of the kind of value-judgment made by Lewis in assuming that the directive function is somehow much more laudable than the disposable functions of literature. All three of these kinds of communication are necessary to our well-being. We cannot get by in life without any of them. In no sense is literature the *sole* provider of messages which meet any one of these needs. In all three cases, however, literature is potentially useful, and may even be uniquely useful in respect of certain messages or to certain individuals. It seems a little unreasonable to maintain that literature ought to serve one function and that when it serves others its writers or readers are guilty of a kind of moral treason. Without in any way denying the value of the role attributed to "great literature" by Richards and Williams I think it is reasonable to suggest that popular literature too may make a significant contribution to social well-being. This judgment, however, lies outside the scope of the inquiry, whose aim is simply to investigate —without passing moral or esthetic judgments—the communicative functions performed by one particular *genre* of popular literature.

II
THE ANALYSIS OF COMMUNICATIVE FUNCTIONS

1. USING THE FRAMEWORK

If we are to try to apply the perspective developed in the previous chapter we are faced with a number of practical problems relating to procedure. What is our investigation to consist of? What kinds of information do we need about science fiction in general, and how are we to go about the task of analyzing particular texts?

The first important point to be made is that a straightforward content analysis of texts, however it is carried out, is inadequate on its own to an understanding of the communicative functions of the *genre*. It is not enough to discover what the characteristic preoccupations of the *genre* are and how they change with time. We must make some attempt to distinguish different categories of social function, and to do this we must make some attempt to investigate the patterns of reader demand. Unless we are in a position to estimate what kind of use is being made of various aspects of the fiction we run the risk of mistaking the significance of these aspects. One might expect that a *genre* like science fiction, which deals by definition with the unreal, exists solely to serve the restorative function; but as we shall see, there are certain features of the *genre* which do not lend themselves to interpretation in this light, and in any case the assumption is illegitimate because it begs the question.

It may well be that once we are aware of the different kinds of communiqué that might be found in science fiction we shall have no difficulty in sorting out different kinds of content into the different categories. But we cannot approach the task guided only by intuition. There must be rational criteria which we can apply.

The first thing which needs to be done is to look closely at the kind of requirement which readers of science fiction have. What do they actually demand of the fiction? One way to attempt to discover this is by direct Inquiry—the kind of survey carried out by Herzog or Mann. Such methods, however, always run the risk of "creating" the data which they are attempting to discover; and there is another way to investigate the kinds of demands which science fiction readers make and the ideas they have regarding what science fiction *is* and what it ought to be. Science fiction was, when it was first labelled as a distinct species, a *genre* featured by the American pulp magazines. There have always been at least half a dozen science fiction magazines in existence ever since then. Most of these magazines carry letters from readers. In addition, there has always been a good deal of writing *about* science fiction on the part of writers and readers alike, some of it in the professional magazines, but the greater part in amateur magazines produced by science fiction fans. All of this writing provides a remarkably rich resource for the investigator who wants to find out what readers of science fiction get out of their reading, and what they expect from this particular *genre* as opposed to others, or to fiction in general. I have therefore based my estimates of the kind of communicative function which users of science fiction demand on an analysis of this material. The results of this part of the investigation are summarized in Chapter Four.

The investigation of reader demand—which reveals the ways in which readers of science fiction use it and obtain gratification from it—is, however, only a preliminary to the content analysis of texts. Hopefully, with the aid of some knowledge of what science fiction readers use various aspects of the fiction *for*, we will be able to sort out the directive content of the *genre*, and the maintenance content from the restorative content. Some supplementary observations on the ways in which this can be done are made below. Only when we have done this sorting can we hope to draw connections between the fiction and its social context. The different kinds of connection appropriate to each communicative function are also discussed below.

The form of the content analysis also proposes problems, largely because there are decisions to be made about its degree of generality. Put crudely, the basic question is whether it is better to single out a few particular texts for exhaustive analysis or to investigate themes and ideas that are common to a large number of texts. This decision depends, at least to some extent, on what kind of thing we are looking for. Directive content must, by its nature, be unfamiliar to the reader, and thus we can hardly expect to find directive material by looking for that which is common to hundreds of texts. The reverse is true of maintenance material, which *must* be familiar in order to lend support to attitudes and convictions already held. The issue is more complex with reference to restorative material, which does tend to become stereotyped, though it is not wholly necessary that it should. For these reasons, the method of content analysis adopted is certain to prejudice the inquiry because it will lend itself more to the identification of some kinds of material than others.

The choice which I have taken in this matter is to attempt to track predominant themes through large numbers of texts—to identify what is common to many rather than unique to each. My principal reason for choosing this alternative is that it is the one which has been neglected by other writers. There is a good deal of orthodox literary criticism which deals with the most prestigious texts of science fiction as unique entities, analyzing in depth what each has to say. Much of this work already points to connections between the texts and their social contexts, and though some of it is more interesting to sociologists than the rest, I do not think that there is a neat boundary to be drawn between literary criticism and the sociology of literature insofar as the directive functions of literature are concerned. Where there *is* a sharp distinction between the concerns of the literary critic and those of the sociologist, is with respect to the other categories of communicative function; for where these functions are being served the literary critic is content to declare his lack of interest, if not his contempt. In my view, the sociologist ought not to be disinterested, let alone contemptuous of these alternative functions, and therefore I have directed my inquiry primarily toward their elucidation.

2. INVESTIGATION OF THE DIRECTIVE FUNCTION

Of the three categories of communicative function identified in Chapter One, the one which Wiebe calls "directive" poses the most difficult problems for the sociological analyst. (Though I shall adopt Wiebe's labels, I do not wish to be bound too strictly by the working of his definitions, and thus I shall use the word "directive" to cover any communiqué which has a lasting effect on its recipient, giving him new information or affecting his attitudes or dispositions—i.e., any non-disposable communiqué.) The basic problem is that a directive effect is so difficult to identify, especially when we are dealing with attitudes or dispositions rather than simple information. Some material which is *intended* to be directive can be easily identified in texts, but even where such material is effective (at least with reference to some readers), it is virtually impossible to specify exactly what the effect is likely to be.

This places severe limitations on the kind of statement which the sociologist is likely to be able to make as a result of his investigation of directive material in literature. They are, alas, condemned to be vague and rather uncertain. This is the kind of situation in which sociologists often find themselves, but it is never a comfortable one.

There are, of course, one or two ways by which this harsh conclusion may be avoided, but to my mind they are unjustified, in that they simplify the situation at the cost of misrepresenting it. There is a temptation to copy the literary critic in concentrating on one particular (hypothetical) ideal reading of the text which may never (or very rarely) occur in reality. This strategy tends to divorce the text from its actual readers—and often from the real intentions of the author—in order to concentrate on the kind of communiqué which can, after exhaustive analysis, be shown to be possible *via* the text. This is by no means a sterile pursuit, as the function of literary criticism is (presumably) to help readers to make the most of the texts which they read, both by pointing out the special features of particular texts and by training the faculties of the reader. It seems to me, however, that the sociologist should be more concerned with what actually happens in the ordinary course of affairs rather than with what *ought* to happen in an ideal situation, or with the attempt to change the real situation so as to bring it a little nearer to that ideal.

A second strategy which minimizes the problems which the sociologist has in dealing with this kind of material is that which condemns much of the work to be studied as uninteresting —or, to use Goldmann's term, "accidental." By this narrowing of the field of attention to some core or essence of the work, the sociologist can reduce his data to a point where they become fairly clear and not too difficult to handle. The chief difficulty attendant upon this strategy is that it requires certain acts of faith. In the first place, one must accept on trust that whatever one is casting away as uninteresting really is "accidental" or unimportant. Secondly, one must take on trust that there really is a core or essence of the work which can be laid bare by this procedure. The risks are easy to see—one is that the baby must be thrown out with the bathwater, the other that the metaphor of baby and bathwater may be inappropriate. It should be noted that Goldmann eventually had to reject the whole content of even those literary works he considered to be worth studying, with the exception of some hypothetical skeletal structure submerged deep within the text. A sociologist who (unlike Goldmann) has not made up his mind in advance exactly what kind of thing he was going to find "inside" a text would inevitably have extreme difficulty in applying a method of this kind. He would also find himself completely at odds with most literary critics, who would find the value of a text in its wholeness and its uniqueness, not in terms of some inner structure homologous with the relationships of men in society.

It seems to me that the attempt to distinguish between the "essential" and the "accidental" *so far as directive communication is concerned* is mistaken. This criticism applies not only to Goldmann's work but also to Lowenthal's "decoding of equations," and to those writers who attempt to separate "content" from "style" in order to explain the "meaning" of each as if they were two independent variables. (We find, for instance, Vytautas Kavolis claiming that "The main sociological function of artistic *style* is the shaping or emotional reinforcement of general tendencies to perceive situations of action in certain structural ways....artistic *content* has the function of helping man to develop an emotional involvement with the objects of his social and cultural environment." [1] Ayn Rand makes a similar claim: "The subject of an art work expresses a view of man's existence, while the style expresses a view of man's consciousness." [2] When we are trying to say something about the directive potential of a text such attempts to reduce it to its "constituent parts" are hazardous, because they misrepresent the way we learn, and therefore the way that directive messages are likely to affect us. When Thomas Kuhn, in *The Structure of Scientific Revolu-*

34

tions, defines the notion of a paradigm, he makes the point that we do not simply learn theories as sets of regularity statements; we learn them in connection with exemplary instances of their application. [3] He maintains that textbook examples *embody* ways of thinking rather than simply providing instances of essentially abstract principles. If this applies even to scientific ways of thought, then it surely applies much more to unanalytical, everyday ways of thinking.

All this is not to say that we must not abstract from works of literature statements of particular importance, or that we cannot offer synoptic accounts of what a book is "about." But it *is* to insist that these abstractions and synoptic accounts do not constitute the "essence" of the book, or that what they leave aside is "accidental" or superfluous. They remain statements *about* the book. In my view, texts cannot be dissected in the same way that cadavers can, and the sociologist should not attempt to define his task as if they could.

It must be stressed that to assert the uniqueness of a text is not to imply its autonomy from its social context, but simply to say that the connections are likely to be complex, and that the set of connections which exists between the directive content of a text and its social context is likely to be unique, though it may have certain aspects in common with other sets. Where texts are contemporary and written by authors in similar social circumstances we would expect them to have many connections in common, but this does not mean that these connections are the only ones which are essential, or that any others are accidental or uninteresting. Indeed, the reverse may be the case, for the power of a work to influence the minds of readers, and perhaps to alter their awareness of their social situation (and thus, implicitly, the social situation itself), may well depend upon its novelty and its uniqueness. Where directive content is duplicated it runs the risk of functioning for many of its readers as maintenance material.

What all of this implies is that the task facing the sociologist if he wishes to deal exhaustively with the directive functioning of texts is certainly no easier than that of a literary critic, and might well be regarded as an elaboration of it. Certainly, the most determined attempts to tie texts into their social context have been carried out by writers who came to the task from literary studies rather than from sociology. The best example is probably Ian Watt's book, *The Rise of the Novel* (1962), which provides commentaries on several individual texts as well as an attempt to relate the emergence of the novel as a species to the social context of eighteenth century England. Although Watt is able to generalize in the latter case, there is no question of an attempt to distill some kind of essence common to all novels which alone provides the key to their social function, or which represents the extent to which they are socially determined.

One more point which needs to be made is this; the fact that, in this view, the sociological study of literature (insofar as it is concerned with directive functions) comes to resemble the work of the literary critics more than it resembles the equation-hunting activity of the physicist, does *not* mean that it is somehow "less scientific" than it might be. It is the nature of the data which forces us to adopt such procedures, not our own lack of scientific integrity. It is surely thoroughly scientific to prefer a complex and cumbersome explanation to one which is false or to one which assaults and distorts the phenomenon for the sake of convenience.

3. INVESTIGATION OF THE MAINTENANCE FUNCTION

It is important to remember that what was said in the last section applies only to the investigation of the directive content of literature, or rather to the content of literature insofar as it is *used* directively by its readers. When we move on to the problems involved in analyzing literary works in terms of the maintenance and restorative functions, we find that they are quite different. We have already noted that when these functions are being served literature is being used *disposably*—the experience of the reader is transient. When books are read entirely in this way they make little impression upon the memory, and what impression they do make tends to be superficial. The experience does not become paradigmatic in the sense that it influences the reader's knowledge of the world or his attitudes to it. The uniqueness of the text, which is the main difficulty facing the analyst of directive content, is therefore of little consequence in terms of the maintenance and restorative functions.

Insofar as the maintenance function—by which I mean communiqués used by the reader simply to lend support to ideas and attitudes which he already has—is concerned the utility of the text is determined by the extent to which it *reiterates* what is already present in the mind of the reader. (It does not matter whether what is being reiterated was originally implanted *via* literary communication or not.) For this reason the extraction of common images, common themes, and common structures becomes central to the analysis of texts as maintenance messages. In this case it really does make sense to speak of these common features as essential. It is essential to the performance of the maintenance function that the messages performing the function are repeated. The need for ideas already held to be supported in this way obviously varies considerably, but in some cases it is more-or-less continual and does not diminish with constant supply.

Maintenance messages may operate in different ways—confirming notions about what happens in the world by repeating information or multiplying examples, justifying opinions and value judgments, either by echoing them or building them into anecdotes as "morals" (in the literary meaning). The last of these examples is clearly uniquely suited to literary communication. It seems probable that the most important aspect of the maintenance function in literature is that it can lend emotional support to moral judgments, value judgments, and convictions about the way that facts relate to one another. It does this by providing an extensive series of exemplars which are emotionally charged by virtue of the reader's "identification" with the fictional characters.

A great deal of literature which is described as didactic (for example, the moralistic fictions produced under the auspices of nineteenth century religious tract societies) is presumably consumed in service of the maintenance function rather than directively. We recognize in the moral of a story not a revelation but something already familiar, and the satisfaction which we gain from it is the satisfaction of confirmation, a sense of appropriateness. Esthetic satisfaction can, to a considerable degree, be associated with the maintenance function. In *Art as Experience*, John Dewey talks about esthetic sensibility in the following terms:

> There are two sorts of possible worlds in which esthetic experience would not occur. In a world of mere flux, change would not be cumulative; it would not move towards a close. Stability and rest would have no being. Equally it is true, however, that a world that is finished, ended, would have no traits of suspense or crisis, and would offer no opportunity for resolution. Where everything is already complete, there is no fulfilment. We envisage with pleasure Nirvana and a uniform heavenly bliss only because they are projected upon the background of our present world of stress and conflict. Because the actual world, that in which we live, is a combination of movement and culmination, of breaks and reunions, the experience of a living creature is capable of esthetic quality. The live being recurrently loses and reestablishes equilibrium with his surroundings. The moment of passage from disturbance into harmony is that of intensest life. In a finished world, sleep and waking could not be distinguished. In one wholly perturbed, conditions could not even be struggled with. In a world made after the pattern of ours, moments of fulfilment punctuate experience with rhythmically enjoyed intervals. [4]

This relates primarily, of course, to the directive function: great literature is that which shows us new harmonies, discovers new resolutions. But it also relates to the maintenance function and to the way in which literary works constantly remind us about the modes of resolution which are provided socially as goals, norms, and values. Indeed, it not only reminds us of them but reinforces them by underlining their value and propriety. The kind of *feeling* which is associated with "the moment of passage from disturbance into harmony" is produced not only by the first discovery of a particular passage, but by the reiteration of it.

It is, of course, a banal observation that at any one time in a particular culture literature tends to feature a fairly narrow range of characteristic resolutions. We often hear it argued that there are only three basic plots (the number varies somewhat), and what is meant by this is that there are only a few basic harmonies into which plots may ultimately be resolved. There are, of course, corresponding anti-plots in which the resolutions are deliberately subverted or withheld, but these rely for their emotional power on the fact that we are aware of the harmony which is being refused (tragedies tend to employ "anti-plots" of this nature).

Basically, modern plots are usually "success stories." In the heyday of the novel in the nineteenth century the vast majority of books combined the financial success story with the romantic success story, and ended with a happy marriage and the prospect of an economically secure future for the main characters. This became so standardized as to be virtually compulsory for any novel which aspired to find a welcome with the public at large; and when circumstances and the novelist withheld this conclusion, the sense of tragedy could be quite extreme and desperately exaggerated (as, for instance, in *Wuthering Heights*). The main variant on the theme—which became increasingly important as the reading habit spread to the working class—was the resolution asserting that money wasn't particularly important as long as romantic success was achieved.

The endless repetition of this formula in literature (and there is still a great deal of popular literature which is identifiable as a *genre* by virtue of its endless repetition of it) should not be seen as evidence that anyone thought (or thinks) that this is the way the world actually is. Many complaints about the supposed *naivety* of this kind of fiction emerge from precisely that false premise. What the constant repetition actually amounts to is a series of affirmations of the principle that this is the way an ideal world *ought* to be. It helps to maintain a set of beliefs about values, social goals, and motives, not about the way the world really is. Sometimes, it seems, people do make mistakes and acquire illusions about the way of the world that are more in accordance with the mythology of romantic fiction—but the very fact that the mistake is easily recognizable and can be so readily derided, is testimony to the fact that it is a mistake most of us do *not* make.

There are, of course, other characteristic patterns of resolution which have come to be identified with particular species of literature. At the end of a detective novel the puzzle is solved and the detective discovers the murderer. At the end of a "western" the hero fights a duel with the villain and shoots him dead. In all these cases the ingenuity of authors tends to be entirely involved in the business of constructing and circumventing obstacles which delay the characters reaching these prescribed destinations, thus building up tension.

All mass-produced fiction works according to this kind of

formularization. It is *because* of the formularization that it *can* be mass-produced, and it is because literature is useful in serving a maintenance function that formularization is possible. In America, the home of mass-production, mass-market publishers quickly became aware of the "rules" which determined the success of maintenance fiction. The Scott Meredith literary agency, one of the agencies which supplied the American pulp magazines, evaluated stories according to a fixed and clearly-articulated set of principles:

> Meredith took full page back-cover ads each month in the *Writers' Digest*...which...encouraged writers to send us their mss. for evaluation....The first letter to a new client always began by explaining that his story was unsaleable because it did not follow the Plot Skeleton. The letter went on to enumerate the parts of the Plot Skeleton, viz: 1. A sympathetic and believable *lead character*; 2. an urgent and vital *problem*; 3. *complications* caused by the lead character's unsuccessful attempts to solve the problem; 4. the *crisis*; 5. the *resolution*, in which the lead character solves the problem by means of his own courage and resourcefulness. [5]

This plan is still extensively used by various "schools" of creative writing, and Scott Meredith is still a successful agent. Literary critics tend to react to this scheme with horror and fury because it represents, in their eyes, a betrayal of the *real* purpose of literature. But it works, because it is actually gearing literary works to serve a different function—the maintenance function.

New patterns of resolution emerge continually. The big success of the twentieth century has been the intellectual/spiritual success story, which ends on a vague note of triumphal hope as the hero conquers his sense of alienation. Some version of this has been introduced by many of the major writers of the century as a directive message. We find it in Sartre, Hesse, Lawrence, Mailer, and many others, sometimes entangled with other kinds of success-story, but nevertheless quite distinct. There are, of course, many different versions of the story, but the vital message is that it *can* be done. The first encounter with this kind of novel is, of course, directive (provided that the reader takes the conclusion to heart), but the continual proliferation of fictions of this general nature is plainly associated with the service of the maintenance function.

In analyzing a particular literary *genre* in terms of the maintenance function, therefore, what we are looking for is its characteristic variants of a particular kind of resolution: a repeating pattern which affirms some particular formula for bringing order out of chaos and harmony out of frustration. I shall attempt to show in due course that science fiction is remarkable among the *genres* of mass-produced fiction by virtue of its multiplicity of characteristic resolutions, and the rapid pace at which variants thereof come into being and decline.

It is something of a relief, after contemplating the difficulties which the sociologist must face in trying to come to terms with literature as directive communication, to discover that dealing with the maintenance function is so much easier, at least in terms of analytical methodology (there may still be difficulties involved with linking changes in patterns of resolution to the social context). It is so much easier, in fact, that we must remember not to claim too much for the products of the analysis. It is possible to get a much clearer picture of the kind of communication that is taking place *via* literature in respect of this function than it is with respect to either of the other functions, but we should not permit this to mislead us into attributing too great a role to the maintenance functions of literature. Reference to the maintenance function may, indeed, allow us to explain a great deal, but there are many features of literature in general and of specific literary works which still remain to be explained.

4. *INVESTIGATION OF THE RESTORATIVE FUNCTION*

The function of restorative communiqués is to engage the mind of the recipient in such a way as to "release" him or allow him to "rest" from his confrontation and negotiation with the real world. Literature serving this function is usually described as "escapist." The term is often used in a derogatory way, but apologists for popular literature often reply with the claim that *all* reading—or, at any rate, all reading for pleasure— is escapist. There is, in any case, every reason to suppose that this need for release from constant confrontation with reality is universal, and that in serving it literature geared to this function is meeting a genuine need. The derogatory overtones are often associated with accusations of *over*-indulgence in escape, implying that the individual concerned is unwilling to face reality with a stout heart.

The difficulties of connecting the restorative content of fiction with its social context are perhaps less complex than those concerned with connecting the directive content, but they are quite different in kind. The connections between social reality and the directive and maintenance functions of literature are presumably direct. But when we come to ask questions about the reasons people have for their preferred modes of escape from reality, we are looking for connections which are definitely *not* direct. The question may be made clear by the admittedly oversimplified idea that books offer "fantasy worlds" into which people may escape. If we want to know why people chose one fantasy world rather than another we can hardly begin with the expectation that these fantasy worlds will be reflections (however distorted) of the situations from which the people are escaping. Rather, one might expect them to be some kind of "inversion" or "negative image" of reality, whose elements are justified by virtue of their opposition to the way things are in the real worlds.

As with the maintenance function, the design of literature to cater to the restorative function involves a degree of stereotypy. The kinds of fantasy-worlds provided by popular fiction tend to fall into certain patterns. It is not immediately apparent, however, why these particular patterns are preferred. It is certainly not immediately obvious that the explanation will be a sociological one. One might argue that an individual's choice of fantasy-world is likely to depend on psychological quirks—perhaps not enduring ones, but ones which first give a reader a taste for a particular species of popular fiction which is later maintained, either by habit or by the fact that readers prefer to return to fantasy-worlds which are already (at least in their standardized features) familiar to them.

What *is* certain is that a great many readers are extremely loyal to the kinds of fiction they habitually consume. In some cases this loyalty might be explicable with reference to the maintenance function in that different species of fiction tend to have different resolutions, but we see the same loyalty manifested *within genres* when readers are particularly devoted to a single author, and in some cases *genres* have *subgenres* which use different *milieux* (the *genre* of romantic fiction, for instance, may be subdivided into contemporary and historical romances, and Harlequin/Mills & Boon does, in fact, categorize their output in this way.) The power of long series of works featuring the exploits of a single character or group of characters to attract and hold readers is well-known in mass-market publishing, and many of the most prolific writers of the century have sustained themselves very largely by series work.

I think it is probable that the explanation of restorative stereotypy is to be sought largely in psychological terms, and particularly in terms of developmental psychology. It hardly needs pointing out that our reading preferences tend to change markedly as we move from childhood into adolescence and from adolescence into adulthood. The kind of fantasy-world which children find suited to their needs is very rarely the kind of fantasy-world which appeals to adults; and it is a difference in restorative content which, more than anything else, tends to distinguish children's literature from adult literature. However, I think there is also a good deal of scope for sociological explanation of at least some of the patterns of stereotypy which we see in adult literature. I think it unlikely, for instance, that the very marked difference between much popular literature written specifically for women and much written specifically for men reflects innate psychological differences between the sexes rather than differences in social roles and social situations.

In virtually all popular fiction the restorative and maintenance function are served simultaneously, and they collaborate in governing the substance of the text. While the maintenance function determines characteristic patterns of resolution and plot structure, the restorative function governs the *environment* of the story—the literary "decor." This collaboration is, in a sense, slightly uneasy in that the maintenance function works to sustain the norms and values of the real world, whereas the restorative function affords relief from it. The two functions, however, are by no means incompatible, and there is no real conflict of interest. (It is worth noting that the fiction which is furthest removed from reality—outright fantasy in the vein of *The Lord of the Rings*—often tends to be the most rigidly and overtly moralistic.)

The nature of the alliance between the maintenance and restorative functions is perhaps easiest to see in romantic fiction of the most stereotyped varieties. Peter Mann's survey suggests that a significantly large number of readers of Mills & Boon romances are young married women. It is not too difficult to guess what kind of frustrations typical of their social situation might generate tensions requiring release through escapism. But it is important to remember that the release sought is intrinsically transient—it is temporary relief, not escape in the literal sense. It is significant, therefore—and probably a matter of necessity—that the alternate world in which the housewife submerges herself is one which *both* affords escape from the immediate situation *and* confirms the set of values which maintain her in it. Thus, the housewife typically escapes not into a world where the myths that bind her into her real situation are inapplicable, but, on the contrary, into one where they are especially and in an exaggerated sense *meaningful*.

Feminists often rail against romantic fiction because they see it as an enemy, creating and maintaining the restrictive world-view which, as it were, chains women to their social role. For instance, Germaine Greer compares the mythology of romantic fiction to religious mythology, and goes on to claim that "Sexual religion is the opiate of the supermenial," and that "If female liberation is to happen....this sterile self-deception must be counter-acted." [6] She is probably wrong to describe what is happening as "self-deception," for she is assuming that the restorative content of romantic fiction is being consumed directively and then maintained. However, there is a sense in which she is right—while women prefer to escape to a world from which they can return refreshed and re-armed for the struggle to live *within* their situation, rather than to a feminist Utopia from which they might return armed with a determination to *change* their real situation, the prospects for wholesale liberation may be slim. The problem, however, is not to persuade the readers of romantic fiction that the fiction is pure fantasy, for they know that already, but the rather more difficult one of persuading them that it is an inherently undesirable fantasy.

It must be stressed that no one has to *believe* in fiction in order for it to be effective in terms of the maintenance function, not even in the special sense that we sometimes credit great literature with being "true," though it deals with fictitious events. Even in such extreme cases as people writing to the inhabitants of *Coronation Street* as if they were real, it seems probable that this is not the same kind of belief they have concerning the existence of real people and real streets. It is as though they have accorded the fantasy worlds the status of "parallel realities," with their own integrity, but nevertheless distinct from reality. (Although science fiction has largely taken over the notion of parallel worlds, the archetype still remains the land of Faerie. Legend and literature manifestly attribute this property of "parallel existence" to their imaginary countries.)

We see, therefore, how it is that popular literature can and does serve the maintenance and restorative functions simultaneously, and that by virtue of the combination literary experience can not only provide release from confrontation with reality, but also a kind of preparation for reentering into that confrontation.

It seems to me that what the sociologist must do in trying to find explanations for the stereotyped restorative fantasies in popular fiction, is to see them as responses to particular kinds of frustration arising from social circumstances. This will not always be possible, because the explanation for the existence of a particular pattern that persists through time may be psychological rather than sociological. Where such patterns change with time, however, waxing and waning in their predominance, there seems to be hope that a sociological hypothesis will, in fact, provide the best explanation. This is what I shall try to do in attempting to map the changes in the characteristic imaginary worlds of science fiction.

5. A NOTE ON "MISREADING"

Wiebe, having categorized media messages into the three functions, is much concerned with the question of "misreading." He alleges that we often mistake the kinds of influence that television has or is capable of having because we assume too readily that its communiqués are consumed by the audience in the way that is intended by their producers. He claims that much material which is intended to be informative (and hence directive) fails because most consumers simply ignore it—it makes no impact on their consciousness; and where it is used at all it will be used as maintenance material by those people who already know or believe what the program producers are trying to tell them. This is a problem with such media as television and radio largely because of their inherent nature. They are particularly suited to disposable material because they transmit in "real time," and whenever attention wanders what is missed is irrevocably lost. A book can be put down temporarily. Difficult passages can be read slowly and re-read. The material remains perpetually available. The television picture, by contrast, is inherently transient, and the medium is therefore particularly suited to those kinds of message which are themselves inherently transient. "Good" television programs are difficult to make, and they are unpopular because they demand an effort of concentration over a sustained period of time which a great many people are unwilling to make.

To some extent this applies to popular literature too. Most people like most of their reading to be light, undemanding of extreme concentration. As Lewis observed, the reading of popular literature can sometimes be combined with desultory conversation or listening to the radio. When we examine popular literature, therefore, we must be doubly careful. We must be careful on the one hand to remember that much of the material therein is not designed to serve the directive function. We must *also* remember, however, that even where the author clearly *intends* that his material should serve a directive function (carry a "message" in the special use of the word), this is far from being a guarantee that it will be consumed directively. Indeed, we would probably be justified in assuming that in the majority of cases it will certainly *not* be consumed directively, but will be either refused or "misread." (This is, of course, a perennial source of frustration and dissatisfaction among authors.)

It is not beyond the bounds of possibility that other misreadings may occur. We all begin as naive readers, and it is in fiction—often crude and routine fiction—that we first encounter many ideas that surprise and delight us. Even the most banal hackwork has the capacity to fulfill a directive function if it happens to be the first work of its kind encountered by a reader. There is also some potential for mistaking directive content for restorative content—this is sometimes the fate of allegories and satires. *The Pilgrim's Progress* and *Gulliver's Travels* are read today primarily by children as exotic adventure stories, and so are the myths of the Greeks and the Norsemen. I do not think, however, that there is any serious danger that we will make foolish mistakes in attempting to explain the content of popular literature today if we ignore the latter problem. The former will require some special comment with reference to science fiction, because a first contact with science fiction very often seems to be an experience which can only be described as a revelation.

It is, of course, true that two readers can occupy themselves with the same text and yet have very different experiences. Sometimes this is due to the refusal or misinterpretation of directive material. By and large, however, the differences of impact are attributable either to differences in preference for particular kinds of restorative fantasies, or to differences in allegiance to the values and attitudes involved in the maintenance function of the text. For these reasons, I do not consider the kind of "misreading" which preoccupies Wiebe to be a particularly important factor in the present inquiry.

III
THE EVOLUTION OF SCIENCE
FICTION AS A PUBLISHING CATEGORY

The most awkward problem facing historians of science fiction has always been that of finding a place to start. Different concepts of what science fiction is or ought to be have led different writers to different points of origin. If one sees science fiction as a series of fantastic tales dependent upon a prolific imagination, then one is likely to claim an ancestry for the *genre* which dates back to the *True History* of Lucian of Samosata—a second century skit on travellers' tales featuring an absurd trip to the moon. If one sees it in a slightly more sober light as a mythology of the modern age, then one is likely to favor the *Odyssey* as an appropriate fountainhead. One who considers that science fiction is a primarily didactic medium, popularizing the ideas of science and attempting to awaken dull minds to the wonderful imaginative vistas opened up by scientific ideas, might point to the didactic poem, *On the nature of the Universe*, by Titus Lucretius. A historian who sees the beginnings of modern scientific thought in the cosmological speculations of the seventeenth century, would probably begin his account of science fiction with John Kepler's attempt to popularize the Copernican theory through the medium of fiction in the *Somnium*. A sociologist interested in science fiction's construction of hypothetical societies is more likely to look to the tradition of Utopian literature developing from Plato's *Republic*. The etymologically-minded critic might well claim that the term loses its meaning if we try to project it back in time beyond the point at which "science" and "fiction" acquired their modern meanings, and he is likely to settle for the rather conservative designation of *Frankenstein* (1818) by Mary Shelley as the first significant work of science fiction. [1] The science fiction fan of the Thirties and Forties, however, who knew science fiction only through the medium of the pulp magazines, would trace its history back to the founding of *Amazing Stories* in 1926.

If we characterize science fiction according to what its stories are usually about—the future, fantastic inventions, journeys to other worlds, etc.—we can find isolated examples conforming (more or less) to the description throughout literary history. Not until the late nineteenth century, however, did fiction fitting this description begin to be produced in any great quantity; and not until the final years of the century was it acknowledged that stories like this were a recognizable *kind*, allowing some kind of category distinction to be made which would label them. The first such label in popular use was "scientific romance," which is most familiar in association with the fantasies of H. G. Wells.

If we trace the syncretic process by which this category of stories came into being, we see that there were four basic imaginative stimuli which gave rise to speculative fictions in the latter part of the nineteenth century. These were: the revolution in transportation; the theory of evolution; the socialist movement; and the anticipation of large-scale war. It was not so much the actual logical and social implications of these developments that were important, but the effect they had on the popular imagination. They gave rise to what were, initially, quite distinct varieties of speculative fiction, which gradually came together because of the cross-fertilization of ideas and the gradual realization that they had something significant in common.

The revolution in transport was important because the steam locomotive was the first major product of the industrial revolution to intrude into the world of the middle classes and display the potential of technology in remaking everyday life. The advent of railways and steamships meant that the world "shrank" rapidly in terms of its apparent scale, and the main literary response to this was the novel of imaginary tourism, whose most popular exponent was Jules Verne. In his books Verne visited every corner of the globe, the bottom of the sea, a world inside the earth, the moon, and (in *Hector Servadac*) outer space. His archetypal works are the ultimate tourist story, *Around the World in Eighty Days* (1873), and the langorous dream of being cast away on *The Mysterious Island* (1875).

The theory of evolution as propounded by Lamarck and revised by Darwin had a considerable impact on the popular imagination because of its implications for the image of man and his place in nature. Speculation concerning man's relationship with Creation opened up great vistas in time to the literary imagination, encouraging the development of the prehistoric romance and the romance of the far future. The most significant contributors to these species of evolutionary fantasy were the French writers Camille Flammarion and J. H. Rosny *aîné*, and the British writers H. G. Wells, J. D. Beresford, and Olaf Stapledon.

The importance of the socialist movement was that it was largely responsible for a change in the pattern of Utopian fantasy. With one or two exceptions Utopias designed before the mid-nineteenth century had all been set in distant places. They were visions of society as it might be—standards for comparison inviting readers to think about the quality of their own lives. The notion of social progress which emerged in pre-revolutionary France and which was ultimately taken up by the socialists, however, stimulated a new kind of Utopian model—an ideal society situated in the future, which thus became a vision of society as it *might become*, a social goal rather than a simple standard of comparison. The great success story in this type of fiction was Edward Bellamy's *Looking Backward* (1888), which became a phenomenal best-seller and provoked many replies in kind from all quarters, including William Morris's *News from Nowhere* (1891).

The war-anticipation story grew out of a British political movement following the consolidation of the German Empire after the Franco-Prussian war of 1870. The potential of technology to remake war was already suspected because of the innovations introduced during the American Civil War, and Germany was already rearming and remodelling her army. Britain, however, was very slow to undertake any steps in this direction. One of the proponents of reorganization and rearmament, Sir George Chesney, sought to aid his cause by publishing an account of "The Battle of Dorking" in *Blackwood's Magazine.* This novelette told the story of a German invasion which caught England quite unprepared, and provoked such urgent debate throughout the land that Gladstone had to make a speech against "alarmism." The coming Anglo-German war became a favorite topic for popular writers and remained so until 1914. What contribution this prolific literature made to the readiness of Britons to go to war against Germany when the time actually came is open to conjecture.

I have gone into some detail elsewhere [2] on the matter of the overlap between these varieties of fiction and the way in which they gradually came to be seen as a *genre.* Suffice it to say here that a number of popular writers—notably George Griffith, H. G. Wells, and Conan Doyle—built an early reputation on the originality of their work, originality in this case meaning that they produced new and exciting speculative ideas. These were among the first generation of writers who found that they could make a reasonably good living writing fiction for mass-market magazines (*Pearson's*, *The Strand*, *Pall Mall*, etc.), and all three—Wells in particular—cultivated their reputations by deliberately going in search of more bizarre and provocative notions. They became quite eclectic in their choice of imaginative material and imaginative *milieux.* All three, of course, wrote a good deal of fiction that was not in this category.

From Britain the *genre* spread rapidly to America. America took mass-production very seriously, and had already begun producing fiction in vast quantities aimed at the "lowest common denominator" of the potential audience. These were the dime novels, which had first been produced to keep the Union Army amused during the Civil War, but which had become almost a national institution. They had more in common with the British "penny dreadfuls" than with the magazines—and, indeed, many were reissued in Britain in that form. In the last decade of the nineteenth century, though, the dime novels went into a rapid decline as they were superseded by the pulp magazines, which took over their role as principal suppliers of mass-produced fiction as well as capturing the rather more "upmarket" audience corresponding to the British magazines. Because relatively few books were produced in America (as compared with Britain), the pulp magazines won a virtual monopoly over the market for popular literature, and held that dominance for forty years.

The pulp fiction magazines published a great many "scienti-

romances" between 1890 and 1920, but these appeared alongside all other kinds of fiction. In the twenties, however, pulp magazines began to specialize in a big way. There already were detective pulps, westerns, and romance pulps, but there was a sudden proliferation which ultimately produced such bizarre experiments as "yellow peril" pulps, oriental adventure pulps, foreign legion pulps, and even *Zeppelin Adventures*, plus such curious hybrids as *Spicy Detective Stories*. In 1919 there appeared a magazine called *The Thrill Book*, which specialized in fantasy fiction with a slight bias toward scientific romance and otherworldly exotica rather than toward the more conventional ghost and horror stories. This experiment proved short-lived, but it was followed in 1923 by the founding of *Weird Tales*, ultimately to become a straightforward horror-fantasy pulp, but which in its early years featured a considerable amount of scientific romance. The founding of a straight "scientific romance pulp" seemed logically inevitable, but what actually happened was rather more complicated than that. The magazine which actually appeared to provide the manifesto of science fiction was not an experiment in pulp fiction specialization at all, but an experiment of quite a different kind, at least so far as its ambitions and pretensions were concerned.

Hugo Gernsback was an inventor who came to America from Luxembourg in 1904 after being refused a patent for a new kind of battery in Germany. He was passionately interested in electricity and in radio, and in 1908 he founded a magazine called *Modern Electrics* to popularize developments in these fields, and to spread the gospel of the wonders of technological progress. Gernsback believed that technology would remake the world as a Utopia, and he was extremely enthusiastic about the possibilities of the coming "Atom-Electronic Age" or "Age of Power Freedom," as he like to call it.

In *Modern Electrics* he occasionally featured fiction about marvellous inventions and the technological miracles of the future. In 1911 he wrote a novel called *Ralph 124C41+: A Romance of the Year 2660* for serialization in the magazine. It was little more than a catalog of wonders, with an extremely crude plot that might have been taken from a silent movie melodrama, involving a villain who kidnaps the heroine and has to be pursued by spaceship. English was not Gernsback's first language and his command of it left something to be desired, but his principal interest was didactic. He regarded the literary framework and the plot as a kind of "sugar coating" to make the science and the technological speculation in his story more palatable. He tended to read other scientific romances in the same way, regarding Verne, Wells, and even Edgar Allan Poe simply as popularizers of science whose principal value was determined by the nuggets of scientific information and inventive inspiration which lay buried in their works.

Gernsback went on to publish *The Electrical Experimenter*, which changed its name to *Science and Invention*, and in 1923 he experimented by publishing an entire issue of "scientifiction." Three years later he founded a new magazine called *Amazing Stories*, subtitled "The magazine of scientifiction." It was a companion to *Science and Invention*, carrying similar advertisements and promoting essentially the same product [1], an enthusiastic attitude to technology. Because of this strange kinship *Amazing Stories* did not much resemble the mass-market pulp fiction magazines. It was considerably larger, printed on paper that was somewhat stouter, and had trimmed edges which made it look neater and less ephemeral than the ragged-edged fiction pulps. In his introductory editorial, Gernsback offered the following prospects for "scientifiction":

> It must be remembered that we live in an entirely new world. Two hundred years ago, stories of this kind were not possible. Science, through its various branches of mechanics, electricity, astronomy etc., enters so intimately into all our lives today, and we are so much immersed in this science, that we have become rather prone to take new inventions and discoveries for granted. Our mode of living has changed with the present progress, and it is little wonder, therefore, that many fantastic situations—impossible 100 years ago—are brought about today. It is in these situations that the new romancers find their great inspiration.
>
> Not only do these amazing tales make tremendously interesting reading—they are always instructive. They supply knowledge that we might not otherwise obtain—and they supply it in a very palatable form. For the best of these modern writers of scientifiction have the knack of imparting knowledge, and even inspiration, without once making us aware that we are being taught.
>
> And not only that: Poe, Verne, Wells, Bellamy, and many others have proved themselves real prophets....New inventions pictured for us in the scientifiction of today are not at all impossible of realization tomorrow. Many great science stories destined to be of historical interest are still to be written, and *Amazing Stories* magazine will be the medium through which such stories will come to you. Posterity will point to them as having blazed a trail, not only in literature and fiction, but progress as well. [3]

Gernsback thought of science fiction as an essentially directive medium. Its purpose was to teach science and to inspire enthusiasm for technology—its entertainment value was only a means to this end. Gernsback fully expected that the fiction would justify itself by its prophecies regarding the scientific miracles of the future, and through these prophecies and its inspirational effect on its readers it was to make a real contribution to progress.

Science fiction failed to live up to this prospectus. In a

speech delivered at M.I.T. in October 1963 Gernsback blamed this failure on the fact that the medium had betrayed his high ideals. It had become so polluted by pure fantasy that very little of it really deserved the name of science fiction. Right from the very start, however, it was plain that what the readers found to enjoy in *Amazing Stories* was not quite what Gernsback intended for them to find.

Gernsback's first recourse in filling the pages of *Amazing Stories* was to his literary heroes, and he reprinted all the major scientific romances of Verne and Wells, together with all the Poe stories with any hint of scientific flavor. These reprints included a good deal of what was, by his standards, pure fantasy (e.g., Poe's "The Facts in the Case of M. Valdemar" and Wells' "The Man Who Could Work Miracles"). For other material to reprint he turned to the pulp magazines. He found a certain amount of fiction there which fit his prospectus relatively well—a few stories by the astronomer Garrett P. Serviss, for instance—but most of what he picked up was the most extravagant of exotic romance. He obtained a new novel from Edgar Rice Burroughs for the only issue of the *Amazing Annual*, and reprinted several works by A. Merritt, Ray Cummings, and George Allan England. Merritt's work consisted entirely of gaudy fantasies set in wholly imaginary worlds, and was primarily remarkable for its purple prose. Cummings specialized in "microcosmic romances," which were basically Burroughsian romances set in worlds within single atoms. England was a socialist writer who wrote a number of novels about the coming defeat of capitalism, but whose most famous work was a trilogy of fantasies set in a world following the decline of civilization and the reversion of the bulk of humanity to barbarism. In none of this fiction was there any real scientific content.

Gernsback did slightly better with one or two other writers whom he recruited. He obtained work from the mathematician Eric Temple Bell, who had published several novels as "John Taine." Bell had a truly prolific scientific imagination, and wrote some remarkable evolutionary fantasies for *Amazing Stories Quarterly* based on the discovery that radiation caused genetic mutations. A new writer "discovered" by Gernsback was David H. Keller, a doctor who had taken up the practice of psychiatry. Keller, too, had a prolific imagination and a reasonable knowledge of science, though his prose was extremely amateurish. Gernsback was also able to find a number of scientific romances in French and German which suited his requirements very well, and which he had translated for his magazines.

An essential part of Gernsback's vision of the future was man's conquest of space. He was confident in predicting that the moon would be reached before the end of the century and that spaceships would be carrying men to the planets shortly thereafter. Interplanetary romances were by no means uncommon in the pulp magazines, and a good many had been written in Europe before the end of the nineteenth century. Nothing symbolized the wondrous future better than the vision of rockets blasting off for other worlds, and this was an image that Gernsback and his illustrators exploited to the full. To many of its readers and to the majority of onlookers "scientifiction" became almost synonymous with "space fiction," and it was in this area that Gernsback's *Amazing Stories* made its deepest impression. In 1928 it began serialization of *The Skylark of Space* by Edward E. Smith—the first pulp space adventure story which went beyond the solar system, making the whole universe into a gigantic playground with the aid of an extravagant, pseudoscientific jargon. This took pulp romance into hitherto unknown territory, discovering a scale of action vaster than anything previously imagined. This was something new—and because it broke through the previous horizons of the popular imagination it was something that many readers and writers found very exciting. The new-style space adventure was quickly adopted by such writers as Edmond Hamilton, John W. Campbell Jr., and Jack Williamson as their standard product.

In 1929 Gernsback lost control of *Amazing Stories* when his entire magazine chain was declared bankrupt. The magazine continued in its new ownership virtually uninterrupted, with Gernsback's assistant editor T. O'Conor Sloane in charge. There was no change in its declared editorial policy, but Sloane was not nearly so passionate in his own personal advocacy of the coming glories of technocracy as Gernsback had been. He was already in his eighties and extremely suspicious of progress, but his editorials still relayed the latest in science news, he still insisted that the stories he published should contain some nuggets of information, and he still pretended that scientifiction had legitimate claims to being a prophetic medium. He was extremely careless of the quality of the scientific components of his stories, permitting a great many impossibilities and absurdities, but it cannot really be said that he was significantly worse in this respect than Gernsback.

Gernsback founded a new publishing company within a matter of months, having discharged his debts very quickly. His new science fiction magazines (which carried the label in its modern form) were *Air Wonder Stories* and *Science Wonder Stories*, combined in 1930 to form *Wonder Stories*. The new title was quickly supplemented by a quarterly companion in imitation of *Amazing Stories* and *Amazing Stories Quarterly*. These magazines were still distinct in appearance from the standard fiction pulps.

In January 1930, however, one of the pulp fiction publishers, William Clayton, decided to extend his chain—which was already highly differentiated—by producing *Astounding Stories of Super-Science*. *Astounding* was the brainchild of Harry Bates, who apparently suggested that the chain should branch out into science fiction, as an alternative to Clayton's proposal that the new magazine should be called *Torchlights of History* and feature historical romances. Bates, of course, had no intention of adopting the pretensions of *Amazing*, but simply wanted to use the imaginative decor of science fiction for standardized pulp adventure fiction. In an introduction to Alva Rogers' *A Requiem for*

Astounding, which traced the history of the magazine from its inception until it became *Analog* in 1960, Bates described *Amazing* as "Packed with puerilities! Written by unimaginables! Cluttered with trivia!" [4]   The puerilities and trivia to which he referred were the fruits of Gernsback's didactic intentions. Bates intended that *Astounding* should feature nothing but entertaining adventure stories, adapted straightforwardly to the restorative function of pulp fiction.   The main question was whether there was yet a large enough potential readership with a taste for space adventure.   Both *Amazing* and *Wonder* paid their contributors a pittance—a quarter of a cent a word was Sloane's standard fee, and Gernsback had never been prepared to offer more than half a cent per word.   *Astounding*, by contrast, offered the standard word-rate applicable to the whole chain—two cents a word. [5]   Thus, despite the cheaper format, *Astounding* was more expensive to produce per issue.   Despite the high word-rate, however, Bates had trouble finding suitable fiction.

He commented:

> My biggest difficulty, and a never-ending one, was the obtaining of suitable stories....We could think of fewer than half a dozen fair-to-good pulp writers who had ever written stories of the kind we wanted, but never doubted that some of my adventure writers could produce them.   However, I at once found myself locked in a continuing struggle with nearly every one whom I induced to try.   Most of them were almost wholly ignorant of science and technology, so most of what eventually got into their stories had in one way or another to be put there by myself....I did very much rewriting....When I dared, I sent stories back to the writers....this required the sending of long letters of detailed instructions....The time all this took!   And the little return! [6]

Although he had abandoned Gernsback's pretensions, Bates was obviously willing to pay lip-service to the essential "ethic" of science fiction—that it should be based on scientific speculation and should not (at least without reasonable excuse) violate the presumed limits of what was physically possible.   Bates was apparently quite clear in his own mind that this was what made science fiction different from supernatural fantasy and fairy stories, in which the impossible was subject to the whim of the writer and a few ill-formulated conventions.

Astounding never quite managed to break even, but—according to Bates—had almost established itself as a paying proposition when the entire Clayton chain went bankrupt in 1933.   It is difficult to obtain accurate estimates of the circulation figures of the various science fiction magazines in this period (the word of editors is not always reliable in this respect), but it seems that in the very early days *Amazing Stories* sold somewhere between 60,000 and 100,000 copies per issue. *Astounding* probably never reached 100,000, but almost certainly sold better than *Wonder Stories* or *Amazing* (which had lost about half its readers by 1933). By the end of 1935 *Amazing Stories* was said to be selling only 20,000 copies, *Wonder Stories* about twice that, and *Astounding*, which had been revived by Street & Smith under the editorship of F. Orlin Tremaine, in the region of 70,000. [7]

Both *Wonder Stories* and *Amazing* were forced in 1933 to revert to a cheaper production format which brought their appearance in line with the other fiction pulps. Their quarterly companions became extinct; *Wonder Stories* tried hard to court its fans by starting the "Science Fiction League," offering a focal point to the burgeoning science fiction community. Devotees of science fiction were mostly in their teens, and tended to be so profoundly affected by their first contact with the mythology of science fiction that it became their sole reading matter and their principal hobby. They already had some kind of a voice by virtue of the letter-columns of the magazines, which allowed them to make their views known; and they soon began forming local groups and corresponding with one another. During the Thirties several groups and individuals began producing amateur magazines featuring fiction, articles, and letters. The hobbyist aspect of science fiction reading has remained one of the most remarkable features of the *genre*—and is still thriving. There are numerous conventions every year in the U.S.A. and several more in Europe, and the number of "fanzines" now runs into the hundreds, with circulations ranging from less than ten to over three thousand. The early consolidation of the science fiction community into a loosely-knit and widely-dispersed whole owed a considerable a-mount to the sponsorship of the Science Fiction League by Gernsback and his assistant editor, Charles Hornig.

The revived *Astounding* set out to capitalize on the sound start given to it by Clayton and Bates. Tremaine's first attempt to excite new reader interest was a declaration in the December, 1933 issue of his intention to present in every issue of the magazine a "thought-variant" story. What he meant by this was a story based on a novel and exciting idea. Bates had never really asked his writers to be innovative, and much of the fiction he had published was remarkably pedestrian in its use of the concepts of science fiction, many of which had been rendered banal with astonishing rapidity. After a mere seven years of life science fiction already appeared to many of its readers to have settled into dull routines. The letter columns of the magazines of 1933 are full of complaints regarding the uniformity of the stories and demanding the injection of new ideas. Early in 1934—not necessarily in imitation, but in response to the same stimulus—Hornig also announced that *Wonder Stories* would attempt to promote "new plots." *Amazing* made no announcements, but Sloane also began to make claims about the exciting new ideas in stories scheduled for future issues. This new emphasis brought to the fore such writers as John W. Campbell Jr. and Stanley G. Weinbaum, both of whom were well-educated in science and could combine ingenuity with, in Campbell's case, adventure on a titanic scale, and, in Weinbaum's case, exotic otherworldly scenarios. The demand that writers should search for novel notions produced some extremely eccentric stories (Edmond Hamilton's "The Accursed Galaxy," for instance, suggests that the reason the universe is expanding is because all the other galaxies are fleeing from ours because it is "infected" with the disease of life), but it also produced some ideas which were later to prove very useful to science fiction writers (for instance, the idea of worlds parallel to Earth which had "alternative histories," adopted into science fiction by Murray Leinster in "Sidewise in Time").

Tremaine, in *his* introduction to *A Requiem for Astrounding*, offered his own view of the unique merits of science fiction:

> I believe we can safely call the years 1933-37 the first golden age of science fiction. It came alive in those years and laid a foundation for much of its present popularity as a story medium. But, more important, the individual enthusiasm of its supporting fans has not lessened. I have had reason to be proud of the large number of young men whose interest has been maintained while they became substantial citizens, moving into the current of modern life without confusion because *they knew what was coming* in the scientific field.
> Science fiction has enabled many of us, who have followed it through the years, to maintain an untroubled poise in what is too often referred to as a "troubled world." And as newer generations grow up within the circle of our fictional forecasts of things to come they learn to feel the serenity which comes from knowledge.
> The mysterious doors of nature's secrets are being opened to us one after another in real life, and the population at large finds these revelations a little terrifying. But to those of us who rode jet spaceships to those planets in our stories many years ago, there is no surprise in the actuality of jet planes. To those of us who have lived through interplanetary wars, there is no particular reason for surprise at the H-bomb. [8]

Tremaine is not echoing Gernsback's claim that science fiction would justify itself through its prophecies but is making a point that is a little more subtle. His claim is that by opening minds to a great range of wonders science fiction prepared its readers for sweeping changes in the world in which they lived, acting, as it were, as a "cushion" against what Alvin Toffler has characterized as "future shock." It is doubtful that Tremaine considered science fiction in this light while he was engaged in editing *Astounding*—the opinion is clearly the result of hindsight—but he did take the *genre* seriously, trying to maintain at least the pretense of fidelity to known science while promoting new perspectives. The most significant action which he took, however, was the hiring as assistant editor of *Astounding* one John W. Campbell, Jr., who took over all his duties from September 1937.

The science fiction market suffered a general upheaval during the last few years of the Thirties. *Amazing Stories*, in a hopeless financial situation, was acquired by the Ziff-Davis chain of magazines, and was given a companion magazine named *Fantastic Adventures*. Both were edited by Ray Palmer, a devoted science fiction fan who adopted some rather imaginative strategies in trying to recover the magazine's lost circulation. The Ziff-Davis pulps operated with a chain of "house writers" who produced vast amounts of material under a variety of pseudonyms for a whole range of specialist pulps—most of it extremely crude and formularistic. While relying on these writers for much of his material, Palmer also took work from some established science fiction writers, and persuaded Edgar Rice Burroughs to write a series of novelettes for him. During the Forties he discovered a crank named Richard S. Shaver who believed that the world was being run by an evil race living in caverns beneath America, and who wrote prolifically in the attempt to "expose" this conspiracy. Palmer promoted the "Shaver Mystery" vigorously for some years in the pages of *Amazing Stories*, and built up a considerable following on the lunatic fringe. Palmer claimed that under his editorship *Amazing*'s circulation reached 200,000, but this figure seems rather dubious. [9]

Wonder Stories also failed, and was acquired by Better Publications, who modified its title to *Thrilling Wonder Stories* and founded a companion called *Startling Stories*. These were initially under the editorship of Mort Weisinger (who was later to be extremely successful as a comic book publisher, guiding the careers of Superman and Batman). The two magazines were slanted at the teenage market, dropping all Gernsback's science features and paying no more than the merest lip service to his ideas of what science fiction ought to be. For three years there was a third companion magazine called *Captain Future*, which was the first science fiction pulp built around the exploits of a single character. Every issue carried a novel in which Captain Future and his supporting team (a robot, an android, and an aging scientific genius) saved the solar system.

Several new magazines appeared on the market before 1940 but most were short-lived. So keen were some science fiction fans to make a contribution to the *genre* that Donald Wollheim approached a pulp publisher and volunteered to edit two science fiction pulps without any salary or editorial budget, gathering stories from an enthusiastic group of amateur writers. The magazines— *Stirring Science Stories* and *Cosmic Stories*—lasted only a few issues. The writers who were fellow-members of this particular fan-group (which was known as "The Futurians") included Frederik Pohl, Cyril Kornbluth, Damon Knight, and James Blish, all of whom were to become leading names in the field after the war. Pohl also became an editor, of *Super Science Stories* and *Astonishing Stories*. His salary was very low, the theory being that he would augment it by writing much of the magazine's contents himself, thus co-opting most of the editorial budget. [10] *Super Science Stories* proved to be one of the more tenacious pulps—it was killed by the war but revived for a few years in the late Forties and early Fifties. Of all the new magazines started before the war, only *Planet Stories* lived through it (except for the companions of the established titles). *Planet Stories* specialized in colorful adventure stories set on other worlds, and presented what was essentially costume drama in space. It too was aimed primarily at a teenage market.

While the other magazines retreated from the Gernsbackian prospectus, however, Campbell tried to reformulate it as a policy for *Astounding*. When the other pulps presented formularistic melodrama, Campbell tried to break away from the pulp image altogether. He changed the title of the magazine from *Astounding Stories* to *Astounding Science Fiction*, and gradually shrank the first word while increasing the prominence of the others. In 1942 *Astounding* became a large-sized magazine similar to the original *Amazing* in format, and when the war and the paper shortage made this unviable Campbell made *Astounding* into a digest magazine.

Campbell kept the science that the other magazines threw out. His editorials concerned new developments in technology, and he published numerous science articles. He had a much more intimate knowledge of physical science than Gernsback had, and he kept in close touch with contemporary publishing in the journals. He was particularly interested in developments in atomic theory, and throughout 1939 and 1940 his editorials insisted that atomic power was imminent. His most vital contribution to the *genre*, however, was his notion of how science and fiction ought to fit together to make science fiction.

Gernsback had simply attempted to weld popular science and popular romance together, wrapping the one up in the other. In his view, the fiction was just gaudy wrapping-paper which made the package attractive. But Campbell thought that fiction could be used as a medium for "thought-experiments" in science. His primary interest was in the ways that technology would change society, and he knew full well that Gernsback's Utopian expectations were hopelessly naive. His expectations of science fiction are summed up in the following statement:

> Scientific methodology involves the proposition that a well-constructed theory will not only explain every known phenomenon but will also predict new and undiscovered phenomena. Science fiction tries to do much the same—and write in story form, what the results look like when applied not only to machines but to human society as well. [11]

56

He modified Gernsback's notion of science fiction as a prophetic medium by pointing out that it could only extrapolate from known data and that anticipations were no less meritorious for being invalidated by new and unexpected data:

> Any extrapolation whatsoever is, necessarily, based on the implied but unstated proposition, "If things go on as they have been...." The proposition is, right now, open to serious question...whenever science becomes engineering, it meets legislation made by man.
>
> The science writer is, therefore, faced with a simply stated problem. Taking off from the solid ground of known laboratory science, sighting along the backtrack of past experience, he launches into the future.
>
> But he may come down in a never-will-be future, because somebody harnessed telepathy, and threw civilization off on an entirely unexpected track. Or because the Supreme Court...has eliminated the institution of patents. Or because a new social theory has decided that no scientific advance should be permitted for 250 years.
>
> Nevertheless, science fiction can not only be fun, but extremely valuable experience. [12]

In Campbell's view of what science fiction should aspire to be, a much greater responsibility was placed on the fiction, which was no longer simply a vehicle but the actual experimental medium. This made him less tolerant of bad prose than Gernsback had been. More important, it made him suspicious of the formularistic plot-structures of pulp fiction.

Until this time science fiction had survived very largely on plots which involved some terrible menace threatening visitors to strange worlds, or the earth, or the whole universe. Usually this included a particular threat to the heroine, often necessitating such absurdities as lustful aliens or ravishing robots. In the formula used by *Captain Future* (most of whose adventures were written by Edmond Hamilton), there was a female lead who had no purpose save to get into one or more thorny situations per novel, and a hero who must be captured at least three times before finally escaping to save the solar system. Not all science fiction followed this pattern quite so scrupulously, but its elements were clearly recognizable more-or-less universally. Aliens, robots, and mad scientists filled the slot marked out for villains, while the heroes would have been perfectly at home in a . western or a thriller—and many, indeed, seemed to have wandered into a science fiction plot entirely by mistake. None of the other magazines of the period 1937-46 had any interest in changing this recipe. Even Tremaine, who was keen to import new speculative ideas into the *genre*, was not particularly interested in new approaches to the fictional component, though he did publish the stories of one "Don A. Stuart," whose plots arose naturally out of the ideas they contained rather than being grafted on. "Don A. Stuart" was a pseudonym used by John Campbell. Campbell-as-Stuart did not work entirely alone in this regard—one can identify a handful of short stories per year that paid only lip service to pulp formula—but it is worth noting that several of the best stories of the early Thirties did not find a paying market at the time. (Examples include: "What's it like out there?" by Edmond Hamilton, "The Creator" by Clifford Simak, and "The Titan" by P. Schuyler Miller.)

Campbell knew very well that the bulk of his audience consisted of pulp fiction devotees, but one of his aims was to seek out—and, if necessary, to create—a new audience. For this reason the demands which he made of his writers were rather different from those made by the Ziff-Davis group. He demanded more attention to the human element of the fiction, welcomed attention to political, sociological, and ethical issues, and was far more style-conscious than his competitors. The metamorphosis was slow, but gradually *Astounding* was quite transformed. In order to achieve this transformation Campbell recruited a whole school of writers. Within three years of his assuming control he had "discovered" Isaac Asimov, Theodore Sturgeon, Robert Heinlein, Lester del Rey, A. E. van Vogt, and L. Sprague de Camp. Already-established pulp writers began new careers under his aegis: Henry Kuttner and his wife C. L. Moore invented two new pseudonyms for their collaborative work in *Astounding*—Laurence O'Donnell and Lewis Padgett—while Jack Williamson invented "Will Stewart" and also produced some remarkable new work under his own name. A prolific pulp hack named L. Ron Hubbard also began to take his speculative ideas much more seriously with Campbell's encouragement (so seriously, in fact, that in due course he gave up writing to found a new school of psychoanalysis called "Dianetics," which he subsequently transmuted into a religion called "Scientology").

Many of the members of the Campbell school are still active, and some have become remarkably influential—particularly Asimov. Most have been vociferous in their support for the kind of science fiction which Campbell advocated, quite certain of its merit and its social value. Campbell completed the transformation of *Astounding* in 1960 when the magazine title was changed to *Analog*, with a subheading signifying the phrase: "science fiction is analogous to science fact." Its audience, by then, apparently consisted largely of scientifically-educated people in their late teens and early twenties. Its circulation soon climbed to 100,000 and has remained close to that figure ever since. [13] It is doubtful that it ever sold significantly more than that or significantly less, and though *Amazing* (if Palmer is to be half-believed) outsold it in the Forties and *Galaxy* certainly outsold it in the Fifties, it has been far more consistent and more durable than any of its rivals, and has certainly been the principal influence on the direction of development which the *genre* took.

Campbell's notion of the essential nature and the value of

science fiction was influential, in that most writers and editors were at least prepared to pretend that theirs was the same cause. To a large extent, however, it *was* a pretense and no more than that. Even Campbell, most of the time, was prepared to pretend that the work he published lived up to his prospectus. Perhaps that which has survived to remain in print at the present day (and a surprising amount of it *did* survive and *is* still available) fit his prospectus best, but even this is dubious. Edward E. Smith's "Lensman" series, which enjoyed an astonishingly successful revival in the early Seventies, is crude pulp fiction on a galactic scale whose superscience jargon is transparently ridiculous.

There is a curious, almost paradoxical element in the success of science fiction as a *genre*. The pretense that Campbell maintained seems to have been essential to that success, but not because it served to create a new fiction that left pulp conventions behind (one of the most striking features of the field is how well it retains its unity, with simple-minded space adventure selling alongside highly sophisticated literary works). What seems to have been essential is the *illusion* of fidelity to science and responsibility to the principles of logical extrapolation, probably because it is this illusion that permits—or at least facilitates—the suspension of disbelief which allows the reader to *participate* in the fiction by identifying with its endeavor.

Other promoters of science fiction than Campbell stressed different aspects of the fiction when they functioned as its apologists. Groff Conklin, introducing one of the first hardback anthologies of stories from science fiction pulps, *The Best of Science Fiction*, made the following comment:

> It is in its embroideries that the largest merit of science fiction resides...any branch of writing, no matter how incredible, which explores regions of man's imagination heretofore virgin to his interest is worth reading. If only because the stories included in this book are incredible, they may be said to have value... the fact that here are ideas and dreams which man has never before thought or imagined in the written history of the world gives these tales a certain permanence. [14]

What Conklin argues is simply that science fiction is valuable because it is mind-opening. In this view, it is not really very different from supernatural fantasy, but is simply more suited to the modern world-view. Supernatural fantasy obtains its plausibility by reference to ideas whose possibility was established by a religious world-view, or at least by the antiquity of the notions themselves. Science fiction, by contrast, obtains its plausibility by reference to the ideas of science—a strategy more appropriate to the twentieth century. There is undoubtedly some truth in this, because it explains the fact that in so very many cases the strategy of the science fiction writer amounts to little more than jargon-mongering in the service of creating an illusion. But this thesis in its simple form leaves out, however, the fact that this difference in strategy led to an entirely different series of imaginary worlds, and entirely different kinds of imaginary events. There *is* a good deal of science fiction which consists of horror stories or fairy stories with the symbols transposed, or of mundane fiction in a particular kind of fancy dress, but this is a minority and it has been a minority ever since 1946. From that date on, even the bulk of badly-written science fiction functioned in an imaginative space which was very much its own.

The significance of the year 1946 for science fiction was that it was the year after Hiroshima. The dropping of the first atom bomb was an event of tremendous significance for the science fiction community, because they saw it as a justification of the *genre*. Campbell said that "the science fictioneers were suddenly recognized by their neighbors as not quite such wild-eyed dreamers as they had been thought, and in many soul-satisfying cases became the neighborhood experts." [15] It is doubtful that many neighbors realized any such thing, but what was really important was the way that science fiction writers and readers felt. They felt entitled to shout "I told you so" to the world. Campbell had every reason to be elated, because it was largely due to his attention to the possibilities of atomic research and his urging that a significant number of stories on this particular theme had appeared. He was particularly delighted that at one point (following the appearance of Cleve Cartmill's atomic bomb story "Deadline"), his offices had been raided by security forces convinced that the Manhattan Project was not as secret as it should have been. (This anecdote becomes less impressive when one recalls that the FBI also caused two *Superman* comic books to be suppressed because of references to atomic bombs.)

After the war against Japan was brought to such a striking conclusion, however, science fiction suddenly seemed to have claims to be taken much more seriously. With the end of the war came the end of the paper shortage, and there was a veritable explosion in magazine publishing. In the post-war decade more than forty magazine titles appeared, most of which disappeared very quickly. The pulp magazines enjoyed a brief burst of new popularity and then died in the face of escalating paper costs. The digest format became standard, but during the changeover there was a period of economic chaos. Many publishers went bankrupt, very many new ones appeared to fight for the market, and a few survived with their policies completely transformed. *Astounding*, already a digest, was completely unaffected, Ziff-Davis survived, and *Amazing* became a digest too, but it suffered a spectacular loss of readership and by the mid-Fifties it was precariously balanced on the margin of survival—a position it has occupied ever since. [16]

The most important of the new magazines founded in the post-war period were *Galaxy* and *The Magazine of Fantasy and Science Fiction*. The former, edited by H. L. Gold, enjoyed rapid success and exploited a new generation of writers, most of whom had had budding careers interrupted by the war. Gold, unlike Campbell, had a sense of humor and encouraged a rather irreverent and sometimes satirical approach to the subject-matter of science fiction. While Campbell still liked the science in his stories to be of the nuts-and-bolts variety, with a heavy emphasis on mechanical engineering, Gold encouraged the use of ideas over a much wider spectrum. Stories in *Galaxy* tended to be more interested in alien psychology and sociology than in alien biology or technology. *The Magazine of Fantasy and Science Fiction*, by contrast, had the main aim of promoting fiction of a better standard than its competitors. Its editors, Anthony Boucher and J. Francis McComas, concentrated on short stories which were neat and sophisticated, and which owed more to the conventions of such magazines as *Saturday Evening Post* and *Atlantic Monthly* than to the pulps. They did not intend to distinguish between science fiction and any other kind of fantasy, but they discovered eventually that issues of the magazine with spaceships and robots on the cover sold significantly better than those with fantasy *motifs*, and the magazine's bias has always been toward science fiction despite its liberal editorial policy. [17]

The post-war decade saw the expansion of science fiction from the magazine medium which, until then, had been the *genre*'s only home. (A good deal of speculative fiction had, of course, appeared in book form during the Thirties and Forties, but none of this was labelled as science fiction, and some publishers actually tried to disavow the label in their promotional material. Some of this fiction was known to and read by the science fiction community, but it was not, at that time, recognized as "belonging" to science fiction. Only in the Fifties, when writers and readers began making broader claims for the value of their fiction, aimed primarily at the general literary audience, was there a serious attempt to co-opt this fiction and impose the label upon it.)

The *genre*'s first expansion was a relatively limited one. Numerous science fiction novels originally published in the magazines began to appear as hardbacked books. The great majority of these books were produced by small specialty publishing houses established by science fiction fans: Gnome Press, Fantasy Press, F.P.C.I., and Arkham House were the most notable. There was, however, some notice taken by large established publishing houses, who began to issue a number of science fiction novels and story anthologies under that label. Simon and Schuster were in the vanguard of this movement, but the most significant event was the establishment by Doubleday in 1952 of the Science Fiction Book Club (which is still thriving today).

Science fiction also became recognized in this period as a film *genre*. There had, of course, been films made previously whose content was science-fictional, but they had always been regarded as horror films. Now the new label was adopted. Many of the early science fiction films were monster movies, famous examples being *The Thing* (1951) and *The Beast from 20,000 Fathoms* (1953), but George Pal made a sober film about a trip to the moon—*Destination Moon* (1950), scripted by Robert Heinlein—and *The Day the Earth Stood Still* (1950) presented a visitor from outer space who came to moralize rather than to terrorize.

The most important change in the science fiction market, however, was the advent of paperback books. Two major publishers—Ace and Ballantine—began science fiction lines, issuing titles on a regular basis. Ballantine selected the cream of the contemporary work from the magazines, while Ace (paying somewhat lower advances) had a more extensive and more diverse range. Most of the early Ace science fiction came out as "Ace doubles" —paperbacks which featured two novels printed back-to-back—and these usually combined one new title with one reprinted from the magazines. The editor of this line was Donald Wollheim, whose encyclopedic knowledge of science fiction enabled him to pick up a good deal of old material from the Forties that was still marketable.

The advent of the paperbacks was highly significant, not because it had any direct impact on the nature or quality of what was being written (Campbell's notion of what science fiction should be was by now paradigmatic, if only as a pretense, and Ace was aiming directly at the pulp fiction audience); but because it greatly increased the amount of money there was to be made out of science fiction. A writer could now reckon that any novel-length work he placed with the major magazines was virtually certain to appear in book form, and there was now much more scope for writing in the novel length rather than in the shorter lengths preferred by the magazines.

Until the mid-Fifties science fiction writing was basically a hobby, except for the pulp fiction hacks who wrote for a wide range of pulp fiction outlets, and had not found it particularly profitable to write a great deal of science fiction. A large number of the leading names in the field were part-time writers. Now, however, the possibility of becoming full-time science fiction writers presented itself. Many took the opportunity, and so did a large number of young fans who had aspirations of becoming writers.

It was also in the post-war decade that science fiction spread from the United States to Europe. There was already a science fiction community in Britain, whose reading matter had been supplied by imported or reprinted American magazines; and now a number of new publishing ventures emerged to exploit this ready-made market. Several magazines, most notably *New Worlds*, appeared, and a number of paperback publishers began science fiction lines, including Scion and Hamilton (later Panther Books). Both of these operations were very much at the "bottom" of the market, dealing in mass-produced hack-work aimed at the same kind of audience as the Ziff-Davis pulps, but they provided something of a living for their house writers. A number of hardback publishers also began to issue science fiction books—

notably Sidgwick & Jackson and T. V. Boardman.

Over the last twenty years, since the original paperback lines became well-established, the readership of science fiction has expanded constantly. The original Ace doubles sold something in the region of a hundred thousand copies in their first printings, the Ballantine paperbacks slightly more. In those days, however, there were little more than fifty science fiction books being produced per year, as opposed to two hundred or so issues of various magazine titles. Today, though the average initial sale of most paperbacks is something between 20,000 and 50,000, there are over a thousand titles issued each year. [18] Numerous titles which have remained in print over the entire period have sold millions of copies apiece, and half a dozen new titles each year reach the bestseller lists.

Throughout the Sixties, Seventies, and Eighties science fiction increased its importance in books and in the cinema. In the latter medium spectacular successes were scored by *2001: A Space Odyssey* (1968) and *Star Wars* trilogy (1977-83). Science fiction now accounts for approximately 10% of new fiction titles produced in books and in paperback each year, and considerably more than that percentage of new films in production. Because of relatively expensive production costs, it has had little impact on television, despite the success in America of *Star Trek* and in Britain of *Doctor Who*. Nevertheless, new series are constantly being tried. Science fiction artwork has also become very popular, and both illustrations from the pulps and the work of contemporary artists are frequently used to provide material for "coffee-table" picture books.

Throughout this period there has been much argument within the science fiction community regarding the essential nature of the species and its appropriate goals. There has been a constant call for improvements in general literary quality, often opposed (sometimes zealously so) by factions which fear that if science fiction becomes too "literary" it will lose the mind-opening quality which is generally referred to by the clichéd phrase "the sense of wonder." Much fuel has been added to this debate by the fact that in the last fifteen years science fiction has begun to attract a good deal of academic attention. Most American universities now offer courses in science fiction as part of degrees in literary studies, and there has been an astonishing proliferation of historical and critical writing about the *genre*. Much of this writing, inevitably, deals primarily with works which were not initially labelled as science fiction, but which can now be so classified because of their content; and a great deal of criticism is scornful of the pulp heritage of the *genre* as it exists today. Many contemporary writers feel that the labelling of science fiction and the fact that it *is* a popular *genre* is detrimental to their chances of reaching a wider audience and achieving critical success. This school of thought tends to regard the founding of the label in the pulp subculture as a kind of "ghettoization" which has cursed the species with disreputability. Publishers, however, point out that only a handful of science fiction titles have a much better chance than other kinds of fiction of staying in print over a long period of time, and that the loyalty of the science fiction readership at least assures that few titles ever make a loss.

It is, for obvious reasons, difficult to discover the structure of the science fiction audience. It is relatively easy, at least today, to find out who is prepared to admit to reading science fiction, but not so easy to get a comprehensive picture of the audience as a whole. The science fiction community, though extremely vocal, represents a very tiny minority of the whole readership, and generalizing from the facts that are known about the hard core of science fiction fans is hazardous.

It seems clear that throughout its history as a publishers' category science fiction has been aimed at an audience consisting mainly of young people. It was the young that Hugo Gernsback attempted to inspire and to educate. Most of the pulp magazines of the Forties were deliberately slanted at teenagers. Science fiction written for older children (known in Britain as "juvenile fiction," in America as "young adult" fiction) has always done very well in hardback, and the same books usually do equally well if they are reprinted as standard mass-market paperbacks. (Virtually all the works of André Norton are published in hardbacks as juveniles and then reprinted as mass-market paperbacks. The juvenile novels of Robert Heinlein, Isaac Asimov, Lester del Rey, and others have enjoyed some success as ordinary *genre* paperbacks.) There is (now, at least) a large adult audience for science fiction, but virtually all these readers were probably "recruited" to the habit during their teens.

Science fiction magazines occasionally run surveys of their readership, but the results tend to be based on very small returns. *New Worlds* ran such polls regularly, and received 500 replies in 1958, 350 in 1964. A poll conducted by *Science Fiction Monthly* in 1975 received some 300 replies. The total sale of the magazine in each case was over 10,000 and probably nearer 20,000. A much higher percentage return is achieved regularly by a science fiction newspaper called *Locus*, which has a circulation of 5,000, and whose annual survey is completed by 20-30% of the readers. The circulation of the magazine is confined to the hard core of the science fiction community, but the statistics which it yields are nevertheless interesting. The average age of the subscribers is 27 (this figure did not alter over the years 1972-77), but the most striking figures emerge from the subsidiary question, "How long have you been reading SF?" Answers to this question revealed that the average age at which people began reading was 12. (This figure was given by the 1976 and 1977 surveys. The 1973 and 1975 surveys showed a mean age of 13, but 12 was both the median and the mode in all four cases.) In all four years that this question was asked the results showed that only 5-6% of the readers began reading science fiction after the age of 20. [19]

Publishers tend to look upon science fiction as a market

with a fast turnover—i.e., they assume that the audience is renewed fairly regularly, thus permitting them to reprint books regularly every five years or so, finding a new "generation" of readers each time.

The picture of the audience which emerges from this, therefore, is that the science fiction audience is at any one time predominantly a young audience. Readers seem to take up the habit, if they are ever going to, in their early or mid-teens. Some then abandon it after a period of a few years, while others maintain the habit much longer, and may never give it up at all. Informal observations of the fan community, whether in terms of attendance at conventions or in terms of activity in amateur publishing, seem to support this view. The average age of subscribers to *Locus* is probably somewhat higher than the average age of the audience as a whole largely because of its utility to writers and publishers. In 1977 14% of the respondents had sold work within the field, and 9% gave their profession as writer or editor.

A further point of interest concerning the structure of the audience is that for very many years it appears to have been almost entirely male. In *All our Yesterdays* (1969) Harry Warner claims that before 1940 there were no female fans at all, and that a small-scale census carried out by Wilson Tucker in 1948 revealed that 89% of fans were male. The surveys conducted by *New Worlds* show a similar figure. The *Locus* poll shows that between 1971 and 1977 17-20% of respondents were female, but the fact that these figures show no trend is a source of surprise to the editor and to some observers, because other evidence indicates that over the past ten years the sex-structure of the audience has altered dramatically.

One source of evidence for this supposition is the unusual number of female writers recruited to the *genre* within the last decade, the most notable being Vonda N. McIntyre, Joan Vinge, Octavia Butler, C. J. Cherryh, Marta Randall, and Alice Sheldon (alias James Tiptree, Jr.). Even more striking has been the shift in the kind of fiction written by female writers. When Alice Mary Norton began writing science fiction in the Fifties she adopted a male pseudonym (André Norton, sometimes Andrew North), and her first few published works contain no major female characters. Marion Zimmer Bradley attempted in the same period to use females as lead characters, but was forced to revert to the standard pattern in order to sell. Since 1970 there has been a boom in "feminist" science fiction, not only from new writers, but from established female writers as well. Writers suspected of male chauvinism have been subjected to fierce criticism in the *Forum* of the Science Fiction Writers of America (a professional organization which includes most science fiction writers who are regularly published in the U.S.A.). The editor of *Locus*, Charles N. Brown, commenting on replies to the 1977 survey, claims that the figure of 17% derived from respondents as an estimate of the percentage of female subscribers is about half the probable figure derived from random checks of subscriber lists. Richard

Geis, editor of *Science Fiction Review*, commented during 1977 that although most long-term subscribers to the magazine were male, approximately 50% of new subscriptions came from females.

If it is true that a significant change in the sex-structure of the audience for science fiction has taken place over the last ten years, then this has presumably had a profound effect upon the actual gross size of that audience—or at least upon its potential size. The apparent connection between this upsurge of interest among female readers and writers and the feminist movement is interesting.

When we come to consider the science fiction audience in terms of the employment of its members, we immediately find the task confused by the fact that the majority of readers are still within the educational system. Because the results of various surveys are based on such small sample sizes the number of respondents in each case who are in full-time employment is very low, and it would be reading too much into the figures to draw conclusions about the relative numbers of teachers, engineers, and manual workers. *Astounding*, when run by Campbell, was always slanted toward readers with a strong interest in technology, and when it became *Analog* it seemed to be very much a magazine for engineers; but it would be most unwise to take this appearance too seriously. (Westerns, it should be remembered, are not aimed at a target audience of gunslingers). The *Locus* survey presents an interesting breakdown of the educational areas in which its undergraduate respondents were working, and these do show a marked bias toward the sciences, but this is only to be expected. (The figures are: 31 out of 139 majoring in the natural sciences; 27 in the social sciences; 23 in engineering or technology; and a further 15 in mathematics. Only 18 recorded their major as English literature and only 9 as another arts subject. 16 did not declare their major subject.)

What is perhaps more interesting is the average level of education attained by respondents. In 1977 93% had attended college, 71% had graduated and 35% had an advanced degree. These results are undoubtedly biased because of the relative unreadiness of less well-educated people to respond to complex questionnaires but they are still surprisingly high. The *New Worlds* surveys revealed similar figures. In 1958 28 out of the 82 respondents in the appropriate age group had degrees (12 B.Sc., 3 B.A. and 13 "others," including M.A.s, M.D.s, etc). It has always been a common allegation that members of the science fiction community are, on average, significantly more intelligent than the population at large; but as the people alleging this have been the science fiction community, the claim can hardly be accepted in the absence of supporting evidence. It is true that an unusual number of highly intelligent and precocious teenagers tend to appear in the science fiction community, but it may well be that it is not the intelligence *per se* which governs the attraction to the medium, but its secondary effects in causing the individuals concerned to become alienated from their contemporaries. (The connection between the appeal of science fiction and the social isolation will be explored further in the next chapter.) There is, unfortunately, no reliable data concerning the average intelligence of science fiction writers or science fiction readers, and it is difficult to imagine how such data might be obtained. It is, however, a point worth noting that, whether the allegation is true or not, it is certainly a deep-seated conviction in the science fiction community. The egotism of several of the most famous people in the field is almost legendary.

This introduction to the evolution of the science fiction field, its markets, and its audience is necessarily slight. More detailed and elaborate historical information can be obtained from James Gunn's *Alternate Worlds* (1975) and Michael Ashley's *History of the Science Fiction Magazines* (4 Vols., 1975-78), and from sources noted in the text.

IV
THE EXPECTATIONS OF THE
SCIENCE FICTION READER

In order to determine what kind of communication is taking place *via* the medium of science fiction, it is necessary to look at its content from both sides. It is not sufficient for the sociologist to ask what is put into the communiqué by its author, or what there is in a particular communiqué for potential recovery by a suitably sensitized reader. He should also be prepared to ask what it is, ordinarily and habitually, that readers derive from their reading. In this chapter I want to make some assessment of what it is that readers expect from science fiction, and I want to approach that question in three ways. Firstly, I shall look at the kind of thing that readers say when they are enthusing about the *genre*, and what they say when they feel that they have been disappointed—when they feel that a story (or science fiction in general) has not lived up to their expectations. Secondly, I shall look at the numerous definitions of the *genre* which have been proffered, regarding them not so much as attempted descriptions of what science fiction stories characteristically contain as prescriptions for their composition. Thirdly, I shall look at some slightly more elaborate statements about the function and value of science fiction made by its writers and its apologists. I shall also make some supplementary remarks about the kinds of people for whom these expectations fulfill something of a craving, or perhaps even a need.

Just as in the last chapter my attention was directed primarily to the evolution of science fiction as a publishing category, so in this chapter my attention will be primarily directed towards people who might well bear the label "science fiction reader." This is not to say that I am ignoring the fact that a large number of readers read science fiction as part of a much more omnivorous literary diet, any more than I am ignoring the fact that there are a large number of books whose content invites the description of science fiction though they were never labelled as such. However, I do want to argue that there is an important difference between an act of reading in which a book is read *as science fiction* and an act of reading in which a book (whatever its content) is read *as a novel.* This distinction is to do with what we mean by the word "*genre.*"

Darko Suvin defines a literary *genre* as "a collective system of expectations in the readers' minds stemming from their past experience with a certain type of writing, so that even its violations—the innovations by which every *genre* evolves—can be understood only against the backdrop of such a system." [1] What this means is that the emblem which labels a work science fiction does not simply—or even necessarily—tell a reader what a book contains. It tells him something about *how it is to be read*. It invites the reader to provide a certain kind of context (a "backdrop," as Suvin has it) in which the new reader-experience is to be located. This can often be crucial to the work's success as a reader-experience, for it allows the writer to exploit certain conventions of *milieu* and vocabulary. All experience is, of course, compound. Without knowledge gained in the past we could not interpret the experience of the moment. This applies to artifical experience as much as it does to experience of the real world.

Once we are aware of this we need no longer be puzzled by such statements as: "It's good science fiction but a bad novel" (or its converse), and "I just can't stand science fiction." In the first case we are, as it were, balancing a work between two different sets of expectations which make different demands of the text. In the second case we are dealing with the instance in which a reader finds science fiction (or any other *genre*) so alien to his literary expectations that he finds the attempt to read it mildly disturbing. (C. S. Lewis used the metaphor of a phobia when referring to people who react to science fiction in this way—it is quite a common reaction.)

What I am attempting to investigate in this chapter, therefore, is the set of expectations which the reader brings to the reading of a science fiction text in order for it to function as science fiction—indeed, in order for it to *be* science fiction rather than simply fiction. It is not a simple task chiefly because there is no single, essential set of expectations which each and every science fiction reader has. There are, in fact, fierce disputes within the field as to what kind of expectations it is reasonable and/or best to entertain. I shall attempt to identify that which is common to most sets, but this should not obscure the fact that they do vary quite considerably, particularly on the awkward question regarding the extent to which it is legitimate or desirable to import into one's expectations of science fiction the expectations which one has of fiction in general.

Virtually all the pulp magazines gave space to letters written by readers commending or complaining about their content. The convention became less prevalent in the digest magazines which succeeded the pulps, and where letter columns survived they tended to occupy only two or three pages, whereas in the more indulgent pulps readers' letters might fill ten or fifteen pages. The reason for publishing so many letters was to give readers a sense of participation in the magazine. For many of them, having a letter published was something of an accomplishment, and for some of them writing letters to their favorite magazine became a habit—almost a hobby. This was particularly true of the science fiction community, who laid claim to a louder voice in the development of their favored fiction than the readers following any other *genre.* Among other things, this allows us to be sure that at least a substantial proportion of the letters published in the science fiction pulps were genuine. Many bore the signatures of people who were (and, for the most part, are) undoubtedly real.

The great majority of letters published, of course, consist of reactions to the stories published two or three issues previously. Insulting letters were frequently published, in the interests of supposed fairness. In most pulps this was virtually all there was to it, but in the early science fiction pulps there were also letters which discussed science rather than fiction. Errors were pointed out, clarification was asked. There were often fierce disputes about the possibility and plausibility of particular notions, with authors being invited to defend their conjectures against attack. Gernsback gave priority to this kind of material, and so did Sloane. When Campbell took over *Astounding* he separated out his letter-column into two sections, one headed "Brass Tacks," the other "Science Discussions" (though after a short period of favor the contents of the second column retired whence they had come, into the general melting-pot).

It is obvious that as a sample of the opinions of the readers the letter columns of the pulps are twice biased. On the one hand, the letter writers are not a random sample of the readership at large, and on the other, the letters published are not a random sample of those received. The editors—particularly those of *Amazing Stories,* and *Wonder Stories,* in the early days—selected the letters which seemed most relevant to their image and supposed purpose. Priority was given to the letters which contained lots of science for exactly the same reason that priority was given to stories which contained lots of science. Many of these letters came from people with some educational background in the sciences, and often from people whose work was concerned with some aspect of technology or theoretical science. Their presence and preponderance in the letter-columns of the magazines should not, however, be regarded as evidence that they were representative of the readership. Gernsback's primary aim was to educate and inspire the young, and his magazine was aimed chiefly at people who were ignorant of science. With Campbell it was a different matter—he hoped to appeal to readers who were already more-or-less sophisticated scientifically—but so far as Gernsback was concerned any readers who were already knowledgeable about science represented a kind of bonus. Their letters were often letters of complaint about poor science, but Gernsback accepted this as aid for his crusade and used them. He was *not* interested in changing his policies to meet their requirements. It is highly likely that the only advice editors ever took from their readers' letters was advice on such minor policy matters as whether to run serials or not. On the few occasions that they did listen to complaints the results were unsatisfactory, presumably because the complaintants represented a small minority, while the silent multitude tended to be silent largely because they were satisfied. (A very common early complaint addressed to

Amazing concerned the lurid covers. At one time—for a few months in 1933—Sloane instituted a change in policy, replacing the garish action-scenes with covers in pastel shades featuring more emblematic motifs. Within a few months he cancelled the change and thereafter replied to people who complained that it had had an immediate and unfortunate effect on sales.)

For this reason there is no point whatever in attempting any kind of quantitative survey of the kinds of demands made in readers' letters. Figures would signify nothing. What I have tried to do, therefore, is to obtain some kind of overview of the occasions which the readers found for enthusiasm, and of the reasons for their dissappointments; and I shall illustrate the main points by reference to letters which seem to me to represent particular points of view. The letters quoted are far from typical, but tend instead to be over-articulate and to exaggerate the points which I want to make. They thus constitute "ideal types" in one of the several senses in which Weber used the phrase.

This is a letter from the September, 1928 issue of *Amazing Stories*:

> I am so enthused over the *Amazing Stories* that when I received a letter giving me a chance to read more of the kind of stories that are issued through the best magazine in the world I immediately filled out the card without looking what I was buying. I know that *Amazing Stories* would give me stories not only thrilling in fiction but full of education. I think now that I can look the world in the face and say "I know you and your secrets, and if you have secrets unsolved I will try and solve them in some of my wild dreams." Is it not "Extravagant Fiction Today....Cold Fact Tomorrow"; yes, old world, you cannot fool me today: "There is a reason for everything." I am just a 15-year-old amateur scientist with some wild ideas and funny actions. But if my parents and neighbors call me crazy, "goofey" and any other popular nickname I know some people that will stand by me, they are the devout readers and editors of *Amazing Stories*. I feel no enmity or fear toward them because the age is fast coming where truth will dominate. And personal things will be everyday talked about, and I have also realized after reading Wells' *Research Magnificent* that fear is "the first limitation of man." So you see, truth is fast becoming dominated. If you do not understand what I mean, read this last paragraph through slowly.
>
> I am making up a story, a scientifiction story that shows my ideas vividly and truthfully, it deals with the future of the Universe, nearly all of the planets are involved. I base it on my own life. I tell the misfortunes and tryings of my younger life, what I

think now, and the many wildest dreams to what I might do, and what is possible for me to do in the future, and how I save my earth from the most complicated and inexplicable scheme ever thought up by a villain mind. I do not know whether I will make it of book-length or into a group of short stories sequeling each other.

I am very interested in the new Science Club, and hope that the age limits are lowered.

Amazing Stories shall not discontinue. It has proved my place in this world, and as long as there is life in me I will not see the best magazine in the world go to pieces. I say this simply and truthfully for what good is there keeping something secret that is useful and truthful to the world?

Yours for a bigger and better *Amazing Stories*.
—Thaddeus Whalen.

To which the editor added the comment: "This letter tells its story so well that we can add little or nothing thereto." [2]

There was, in fact, little for the editor to add. Here we see a fully-fledged convert to the Gernsbackian cause—a convert in the sense that he has undergone a quasi-religious conversion-experience. He now sees the world in a new way. It will not matter if others think him mad, for he has seen the light. He has been introduced to a vision of the future, and he is convinced that it is, in some sense, *the answer.* The emphasis on *truth* is significant, and the sense of having penetrated a secret.

The sense of "breaking through" to a new way of seeing the world (and oneself) is common in the autobiographical comments of the science fiction fans of the Thirties, almost all of whom discovered the Gernsback magazines, having previously encountered nothing like them. It is understandably less common among the fans of today, who are extremely unlikely to fail to make contact with science fiction even when very young. It is not possible today for a thirteen-year-old to "discover" science fiction in quite the sense that many young readers of *Amazing Stories* did. Science fiction no longer comes as such a devastating surprise, though it may come to seem particularly significant at one particular time, after which it tends (temporarily or permanently) to drive out all other kinds of reading matter.

What is important here is a shift in perspective, analogous to the "gestalt shift" by which an ambiguous drawing can suddenly shift in the mind of the observer from one of its appearances to the other. It is a breakthrough to new concepts, which allow a new interpretation of the perceived world by setting "today" in a new context which extends far beyond yesterday and tomorrow to hitherto unsuspected imaginative horizons.

This perspective shift is one of the most vital elements in the expectations of the science fiction reader. He looks for great vistas in time and space, not necessarily made explicit, but at least suggested. He will read stories about the present only if there are alien instrusions which remind him of a vast universe of possibility beyond the everyday. He may read stories of the distant future more readily than stories of the very near future, and will often measure the value of the latter according to the magnitude of the possibilities opened up. It is highly significant that several of the most popular science fiction stories ever written are stories *about* perspective shifts of this kind. Isaac Asimov's "Nightfall" and James Blish's "Surface Tension" are among the cardinal examples. [3]

The essence of the perspective-shift is the focal point of a short essay written by a reader of *Wonder Stories* in connection with a "test" set for the members of the Science Fiction League. The title proffered was: "Why do you read Science Fiction?" The essay gives the following answer:

> The common people of the world have been noted for their obsolete views concerning the advancement of science; despite persuasion, they will not swallow anything that is beyond their infinitesimal brains. But science-fiction changes that—the sheer power of magnificence that will leave the reader vainly wondering what he is on this wee tiny Earth. The force of science-fiction can never be equaled by any other type of story. When I finish a science-fiction yarn, I feel overwhelmed with thoughts that surge in my brain. Can it ever be true? Will such things ever come to pass? The glorious heights that the reader soars to make one realize why there are such active fans. Science-fiction makes one think—to ponder on the whole universe. Is it a wonder that science-fiction is an opiate?—to feel that exuberant thrill course through your body; to feel your sense rise and your pulse beat stronger. Ah, deep is the love....Science is stupendous. The huge thoughts that we humans try to understand, to analyze, are great. Science-fiction has the ability to grasp me and to whirl me up—up—up into the realms that dominate the cosmos. A fiction that gives fact, food for thought, and yet contains exciting adventure, is indeed a marvelous fiction. It is a fiction that is intelligent and that educates, not toward the bad or immoral things, but for the future advancement of the people of the world. Why do I read science-fiction? Ah! Feeble are the words to express such a great subject! [4]

The writer of the essay was David A. Kyle, who is still a prominent member of the science fiction community. He founded one of the specialty publishing houses of the post-war decade, penned several novels, and wrote a history of science fiction that was published in 1976. At a science fiction convention in Britain in 1976 he was a guest of honor, and gave a speech condemning modern science fiction for betraying the kind of ideal set out in the essay, by becoming pessimistic and permitting the expression of immoral ideas.

Perhaps the most striking thing about the essay is its use of metaphors of size. It is the *bigness* of science fiction's scale of action which is primarily attractive. The earth becomes tiny and the perspectives of ordinary people are rejected by the contemptuous reference to "infinitesimal brains."

A rather more eloquent, if no less extravagant, comment on the excitement of discovering science fiction and of its special perspectives is offered by Isaac Asimov in his introduction to James Gunn's *Alternate Worlds*:

> There was a time, forty years ago, when I was not one of the great seminal influences of contemporary science fiction. I was only a kid, reading science fiction and experiencing in it an extreme of joy beyond description.
>
> I envy that kid, for I have never known such joy since and I never expect to. I have known other joys —the sales of stories, the discovery of sexual love, the earning of advanced degrees, the sight of my new-born children—but none has been as unalloyed, as all-persuasive, as *through and through* as reaching out for a new issue of a science fiction magazine, grasping it, holding it, opening it, reading it, reading it....
>
> It was such a different joy because there was no other reading like it, no other worlds like those it described, no other dangers like those it lived with. It was such a private joy because there was no one else you knew who read it, so that all its universe was yours alone. It was such an intense joy because it was tied to the calendar; because longing built and built within you until it reached a kind of ecstatic pain by the time that emerald moment came when the new issue arrived.
>
> I have a montage of memories of stories that shone before me in my boyhood with a great luminous flame that out-glamored the sun. [5]

Most of this tells us only that ten is an impressionable age, but the final reference to the glamor of science fiction is striking. This quotation follows Asimov's complaint that the best science fiction story ever published (his own "The Last Question") had not been mentioned in *Alternate Worlds*. In a footnote Gunn admits to not having read it, but adds that he remedied the omission promptly, and though declining to confirm Asimov's estimation of its status says that it is "an ideal example of what science fiction is all about: a big, brilliant mind-expanding concept that could only be told as science fiction, a story which concerns the end and beginning of the universe...." [6]

Another striking metaphor, albeit one which does a certain violence to the English language, is used by Donald Wollheim in his own reminiscences of a lifelong affair with science fiction.

74

Of the early science fiction fans he says: "We lived in an atmosphere of infinite horizons that could not be communicated to most of the grim and haunted world of the Depression around us." [7]

It was this sense of a world with "infinite horizons" populated by concepts which "out-glamored the sun" that marked the attitude of the early science fiction reader, and constituted the "sense of wonder" to which he was wont to make continual, awed reference.

Two points need to be made in this connection. The first is that this perspective was something that was reached *through* stories rather than found *in* them. Some stories were undoubtedly more effective than others—the two most popular stories in the early *Amazing*, if response in the letter column can be trusted, were A. Merritt's *The Moon Pool*, the gaudiest of all his odysseys in exotica, and Edward E. Smith's *The Skylark of Space*, the first interstellar adventure to appear there—but almost *any* story could strike the right note as long as it was lurid enough. Subtlety was a positive disadvantage, as was careful writing—what made the impact on the teenage mind were bold strokes of the imagination coupled with melodramatic purple prose. The perspective itself was necessarily vague, something that gave the reader some hint of the *immensity* of the universe which, implicity, his mind could not quite handle. The stories, individually, were largely heuristic devices. The second point is that, once experienced, this perspective inevitably began to lose its newness. Through many recapitulations induced by the reading of a hundred or a thousand science fiction stories it became, inevitably, familiar. In some cases, it became banal, or came to seem meaningless, and so some readers abandoned the *genre* like any other fad. The real strength of the sensation, however, was its vagueness and its lack of formulation. Because it remained always indistinct it had the potential to remain always mysterious. In every case the excitement became muted, and in very many cases it was discovered in a much less spectacular fashion and was much less dramatic in its claim upon the imagination.

The effect which the discovery of science fiction had upon Whalen, Kyle, and Asimov is clearly a directive effect. It showed them imaginary worlds they had not dreamed of, and it gave them an attitude to the real world that was new. This directive effect may be associated with the age of the people involved. New imaginary worlds can be very exciting to a child of twelve who is only just beginning to discover the power of his imagination, in the sense that he is only just becoming self-conscious about it. In particular, one might expect that special value should be attributed to a perspective-shift which reduces the world, previously seen as a vast and complex place within which the child is very vulnerable, to a tininess and insignificance in which the planet and the race are reduced to similar vulnerability. There is a certain satisfaction for the vulnerable and the insecure in being able to believe that vulnerability and insecurity are conditions of the universe, and that the world itself may be threatened as it threatens them....especially if the world can always be saved from even the ugliest of threats, perpetually snatched from the ultimate horrors of even the worst disaster.

Once having internalized the directive effect of discovering the science fiction perspective, however, the habit of reading becomes a maintenance strategy, and it is necessary to leave the wilder excesses of hyperbole to one side in order to ask the question of what kind of demand readers made (and still make) in order that the perspective might be maintained.

If we look at the expressions of disappointment which mark the reactions of particular readers to particular stories as recorded in the letter-columns of the pulp magazines, we find a remarkable consistency about them. There are continual complaints about stereotypy—the reuse of ideas already familiar—and there are continual complaints about the failure of plausibility. The following letter, written to *Amazing Stories* in 1929, singles out a story called "The Sixth Glacier" (by "Marius") as an antidote to a worrying trend which has already begun to threaten the reader's enjoyment:

> All stories of the scientific type must contain two elements: the "story" or "fiction" element and the "science" or "fact" element. Naturally, foresight and imagination are also requirements for the enjoyment of any story woven around a principle of science. But the author of such a work should at least offer some plausible excuse or reason for his theory which (but for a few exceptions like "The Sixth Glacier") the writers rarely attempt. In short, your average writer assumes that a scientific fact could be stretched—and then commences to stretch it beyond the limits of plausibility, and very often into the realms of sheer nonsense.
>
> "The Sixth Glacier" has, as I have mentioned above, happily combined both of the above values, the "fiction" element and the "fact" element, and the result is not a *pot pourri* of bewildering nonsense full of sound and fury, signifying nothing, but a neat work of sensible imagination, that savors of at least potentiality, which is the best taste with which to close the mouth of the gaping reader in stories of scientifiction. [8]

The editor commends this letter as being eminently sensible, taking it to be a wholehearted endorsement of *Amazing*'s prospectus. This, of course, it is—but it is also claiming that with few exceptions most of *Amazing*'s output was failing to live up to that prospectus. It is important to realize that there really is a disagreement here between editor and reader. Gernsback considered that it was the *educational* value of his stories that mattered—the nuggets of scientific information that they contained—and that the stories could be justified by these. Plausibility, in his view, was controlled entirely by fidelity to scientific possibility (though he was, admittedly, a very poor judge of such fidelity). But for the reader, plausibility is a much more impressionistic quality. If a story strikes him as plausible, then it is *good*, it is *useful*, and the extent to which it can be mined for nuggets of scientific information is really irrelevant. If, by contrast, the story is implausible—if it fails to convince him—then it becomes "a *pot-pourri* of bewildering nonsense full of sound and fury, signifying nothing." It fails to fulfill its function.

What is being demanded here is *not* fidelity to real science and real possibilities but a special kind of illusion. What the reader wants is to be assisted to believe that the story is in some special sense realistic, but what he asks for is the *savor* of potentiality. It must be remembered that science fiction writers and readers have always been willing to entertain and use notions which are impossible in the most literal sense—i.e., they involve us directly in logical paradoxes. Two such notions—faster-than-light travel and time travel into the past—are among the most common themes in modern science fiction. Instant-translation machines, once used almost universally for converse with alien beings, have fallen out of fashion, and appear to have lost a savor of potentiality which they one had, though their status in terms of scientific possibility has surely not altered at all.

When a science fiction reader such as the letter-writer quoted above calls on the one hand for the appearance of fidelity to known science, and on the other hand shows his willingness to accept certain absurdities, he is not being either hypocritical or foolish. If he is guilty of anything it is a careless expression of his demand, and it is at least arguable that he is not guilty of this either, and that it is our misrepresentation of his demand that leads to confusion. What the reader asks for is *the illusion of plausibility*, and he does not really care how this illusion is worked provided that it *does* work. He is not capable of analyzing exactly why it does not work when it does not, but he knows when he has been disappointed.

The necessity of this illusion is that it is only through the illusion, or at least only when it is present as a catalytic agent, that the reader can reach the essential perspective of science fiction—the world-view of "infinite horizons." The story-ideas themselves are not enough—unless they carry the illusion of plausibility they have no force.

The implication of this is that the reader characteristically asks more of science fiction than a series of imaginary worlds to which he can retreat in order to rest from the real world. He is asking that it supply him with an attitude *to* the real world which must be sustained by some pretence of realism. This is evident in the way that being a science fiction fan can (and for some people does) become a way of life. Science fiction, apparently—unlike other popular *genres*—extends its influence from its multiplicity of imaginary worlds to color the real one in the eyes of its devotees.

This point serves to highlight one of the main problems faced by science fiction writers and editors, and that is that standards of plausibility vary very widely indeed. There is no standard recipe for the creation of this illusion. The twelve-year-old is inevitably more vulnerable to it than anyone else, and the long-term science fiction fan is likely to become adept at inducing it in himself to some extent independently of work done by the author of the particular story he is reading. But the factors governing the probability that a particular reader will find a particular story plausible at the particular time of reading are, in fact, quite complex—and they are by no means all internal to the story. Unfortunately, the one strategy which seems safe—that of sticking to notions already established as conventional, and whose plausibility can be taken for granted—is almost certain to fail, because it runs up against the other personal source of disappointment experienced by the reader of science fiction—stereotypy of ideas.

Wonder Stories in 1934-35 ran a number of letters which contained some rather outspoken criticism of the material which it was publishing. Two of the most comprehensive catalogues of faults and insults came from prominent fans Milton Kaletsky and Donald Wollheim, who were beginning to find the fiction conspicuously lacking in inspiration. The change was in them as much as in the fiction. A third letter following up these earlier ones commented:

> Being an old reader of science-fiction....I believe I can diagnose the illness that seems contagious and is infecting the older class of reader (N.B., Messrs. Kaletsky and Wollheim) that you have surely of late noticed....In simple words, it is this: the earlier stories were more or less skimpy plots surrounded by a mass of scientific detail then practically unknown to the layman reader. Authors in that era could indulge in fanciful flights of world destruction by mad doctors, monstrous prehistoric beasties, or malignant whatnots from other and sundry planets. Today this kind of thriller will still hold all its charm for the beginning reader, but the veteran has heard the thunder of the Big Berthas and is blase; he demands a change. New science is not being discovered in enough quantity to supply the basic new plots; therefore the stf. story must undergo a house cleaning or you must interest enough new customers to make the old plot financially possible. [9]

It was in this year that *Astounding* and *Wonder*, having apparently made a similar diagnosis, began to emphasize "thought-variants" and "new plots." The simple fact was that without *some* kind of innovation in the stories they slowly lost their utility to the regular reader because of their apparent over-familiarity. An idea met before in virtually identical form in a similar context had no power to recapitulate the impression of infinite possibility and vast scale. Only innovation could reinforce the sense of illimitability so crucial to the world-view of science fiction.

It was this demand which really made science fiction different from other pulp *genres*. Innovation in other *genres* was rare, and tended to follow the pattern of deVriesian mutation, with new backgrounds and new styles appearing virtually fully clad (as, for instance, with the emergence of the "hard-boiled" school of detective fiction, largely through the work of two writers—Hammett and Chandler—working in a single magazine—*Black Mask*). Science fiction, by contrast, could only thrive through constant mutation of a rather less spectacular kind—more like the kind of mutation which actually does affect genetic systems. (Campbell, in fact, was at one time in the habit of calling innovative stories "mutants.")

The most eloquent testament to this preoccupation of the long-term science fiction reader with innovation is the historical and critical work of Sam Moskowitz, a man devoted to tracking down every last work of fiction whose content allows it to be called science fiction. He is scrupulous in his research, but his commentary on individual stories is obsessed with the matter of ideative priority. He is always concerned to track down the very first appearance of every single notion ever used in science fiction, and every work which is not the first to use its central hypothesis is in his eyes devalued, irrespective of its other merits. In Moskowitz's view innovation is the primary justification of every endeavor—an attitude which has infuriated some writers who felt themselves unjustly treated when their best stories were pushed to one side because they happened to have been anticipated by other stories which they had never read.

This demand for innovation is just as difficult for editors to contend with as the demand for plausibility—largely because it comes from the most vocal minority of their readers, the fans who already have several years of reading science fiction behind them. The new reader, especially today, is unlikely to find the problem of constantly encountering new ideas particularly difficult. There is fifty years of science fiction writing behind him, and writers have been struggling to find new notions and new ways to develop those notions all the time. Long-term readers, however, inevitably find this creeping *ennui* ever more difficult to contend with. Wherever older fans meet there is a constant complaint that science fiction has lost its essential *vitality* and that it no longer has the power to open up imaginative vistas—only memory, recapitulating the experiences of distant youth, can do that now.

It is easy to see that the two basic demands which are reflected in the characteristic complaints of the disappointed science fiction reader are to some extent in conflict. It is not easy to meet both demands simultaneously. To be genuinely innovative is to risk losing the illusion of plausibility, which is often a rather delicate illusion. For this reason the innovations which readers are always demanding are often met with hostility by a considerable fraction of the readership. This, too, is a source of much dispute between members of the science fiction community. To be truly successful, innovations must be small, but must give the impression of being large. They must make a greater impact on the imagination of the reader than their own imaginative content really justifies. The demand for innovation, like its partner, is very largely a demand for an illusion. In both cases, the illusion satisfies the demand far better than the reality. *Real* fidelity to known science involves too much technical discourse and is too limiting. *Real* innovation presents too difficult a challenge to an imagination which needs to find its fiction comfortable enough to be acceptable as "realistic."

If we were to assume that reading science fiction was a habit adopted to serve a *constantly* directive function, then this situation would be paradoxical, because the attitude required of the reader would be rather more ambitious and constructive than it characteristically is. In fact, the science fiction reading habit seems usually to serve the maintenance function, seeking to *preserve* a special attitude to the world and all it contains. Science fiction is an anomalous *genre* largely because what is required to maintain its basic perspective is not simply the repetition *ad infinitum* of a series of individual exemplars, but a constant supply of exemplars which perpetually and gradually change their form so as always to appear new while never becoming truly strange. It is not an easy requirement to meet.

There have been many attempts to define "science fiction," and the problem of how best to do it remains a constant source of discussion within the science fiction community. As virtually everyone concedes that some of what is habitually published under the label is not "really" science fiction at all, the main aim of these definitions is prescriptive: they attempt to say something about what "real" science fiction or "good" science fiction ought to be and do.

Although it was Gernsback who initiated the chain of events which eventually brought the term into common usage, his was not the first attempt to define a literary species of this nature. The first such prospectus was, in fact, issued as early as 1851 in a small book of criticism by a minor British poet, William Wilson. It passed, of course, completely unnoticed, but it is worth looking at Wilson's reasons for promoting the *genre* at least two decades before there was any significant amount of it being written. (Poe had died soon before, but he is not mentioned in the essay—the only work Wilson refers to is *The Poor Artist* by Richard Henry Horne.)

Wilson actually uses the term "Science-Fiction," and he characterizes it as fiction "in which the revealed truths of science may be given, interwoven with a pleasing story which may itself be poetical and *true*—thus circulating a knowledge of the Poetry of Science, clothed in a garb of the Poetry of Life. [10] This is remarkably reminiscent of Gernsback's prospectus, which was quoted in the last chapter, save that it puts a little more emphasis on the literary quality of the fictional matrix. However, when we investigate what Wilson actually means by the Poetry of Science we discover that he is not talking about the kind of straightforward, "vulgar" didacticism which was Gernsback's aim in promoting science fiction, but the teaching of a whole way of seeing.

He writes:

> Those Sciences which appear to us to be most attractive to the imagination, and to present the widest and best revealed fields of investigation, and to contain —even to a surface-inspection of their wonders, their beauties and their combinations—the most Poetry, are the studies of Philosophical Naturalist, the Botanist, the Geologist, the Astronomer, and the Chemist. The Study and extraction of Poetry from these sciences is like reading mighty books of Life, Beauty and Divinity. But we can only obtain in the end, even if we spend a life in abstract Scientific studies "a cloud-reflection of the vast Unseen."
>
> With what an advance of interest over that of ordinary men must the Man of Science wander in the Fields and the Woods, and traverse over mountains, seas and deserts. The Trees and the Flowers have tongues for him, and the Rivers and Streams have a History. He knows that the smallest insect, as well as the mightiest animal, has a direct parentage. He knows where the Zoophytes merge into one another; he knows not only the form and color of a Flower but the combinations that produce its symmetry and lovely hue; and he knows the laws by which the white sunbeam is thrown back from its surface in colored rays. He knows, O wondrous fact! "that the dew-drop which glistens on the Flower, that the tear which trembles on the eyelid, holds *locked in its transparent cells* an amount of electric fire equal to that which is discharged during a storm from a thunder-cloud." Here is Poetry! He knows that *minute insects* have built whole islands of coral reefs up into light from the low deep bed of the vast ocean. Here is Poetry! He knows that neither Matter nor Mind ever die; and that if the fixed laws of Attraction and Repulsion were for one instant disturbed, the whole physical Creation would fall back that moment into Chaos, and that the ponderous Globe itself would then and there vanish. [11]

The quotation within the quotation is from a book called *The Poetry of Science*, whose author Wilson identifies only by his surname, Hunt. This was apparently an early work in the popularization of science, and it seems that it had an effect on Wilson's mature mind as profound as the effect which *Amazing Stories* had on the minds of its juvenile readers. Wilson is a man who has undergone a revelation, which has shown him the world in a new light—a shift in perspective very like that claimed by the early members of the science fiction community.

The second manifesto for a literary species like science fiction was issued by an American writer named Edgar Fawcett in the "proem" to his cosmic voyage story, *The Ghost of Guy Thyrle* (1895). He lamented that with the advance of nineteenth century rationalism great territories of imaginative space had been rendered derelict, so that it had become difficult for the writer to be a visionary, reaching out for the sense of mystery and awe which once had attended myths and ancient legends. He proposed, therefore, to incarnate a new species of literature which he called "realistic romance," in order to recover this potential.

He writes:

> Perhaps I am only a poor pioneer....in the direction of trying to write the modern wonder-tale. It seems to me that this will never die till what we once called the Supernatural and now (so many of us!) call the Unknowable, dies as well. Mankind loves the marvellous; but his intelligence now rejects, in great measure, the marvellous unallied with sanity of presentment. We may grant that final causes are still dark as of old, but we will not accept more myth and fable clad in the guise of truth. Romance, pushed back from the grooves of exploitation in which it once so easily moved, seeks new paths, and persists in finding them. It must find them, if at all, among those dim regions which the torch of science has not yet bathed in full beams of discovery. Its visions and spectres and mysteries must there or nowhere abide....
>
> To make our romances acceptable with the world of modern readers, we must clothe them in rationalistic raiment....I should name them "realistic romances"— stories where the astonishing and the peculiar are blent with the possible and accountable. They may be as wonderful as you will, but they must not touch on the mere flimsiness of miracle. They can be excessively improbable, but their improbability must be based upon scientific fact, and not upon fantastic, emotional, and purely imaginative groundwork. [12]

Here we find the emphasis on plausibility—but plausibility very much as a means to an end. Fawcett sees the need that the imagination should not be offended as the servant of a more basic and more important need—the need to go beyond the parochial concerns of the everyday world into a greater context. In the novel, that is what Guy Thyrle accomplishes—with the aid of a drug he sets his consciousness free of the limitations of his body and embarks upon a cosmic voyage which takes him to the moon, then to the worlds of many stars, and finally to the edge of the universe where, in search of God, he encounters an enigmatic voice which stands as a barrier between the character (and thus the reader) and the ultimate mysteries which must, necessarily, be left undefined.

Fawcett was, of course, carefully and consciously planning a strategy to recover something which he considered lost (or at least endangered). His prospectus, like Wilson's, passed entirely unnoticed, largely because there were very few readers who shared his sense of loss. Thirty years later, however, there was a generation of teenagers—or a fraction of a generation—who not only were able to discover the kind of perspective Fawcett wished to preserve but were able to experience in that discovery a positive shock of surprise because what they discovered was so completely unexpected.

Most of the definitions which were put forward by members of the science fiction community in its early days were, like Gernsback's, fairly straightforward, their principle emphasis being on the criterion of induced plausibility. Donald Wollheim, for instance, coined the following definition in 1935:

Science fiction is that branch of fantasy which, while not true of present-day knowledge, is rendered plausible by the reader's recognition of the scientific possibilities of its being possible at some future date or at some uncertain period in the past. [13]

Sam Moskowitz had a similar definition:

Science fiction is a branch of fantasy identifiable by the fact that it eases the "willing suspension of disbelief" on the part of its readers by utilizing an atmosphere of scientific credibility for its imaginative speculations in physical science, space, time, social science and philosophy. [14]

Wollheim's cautious reference to "*the reader's recognition* of the scientific possibilities" and Moskowitz's even more cautious reference to "an atmosphere of scientific credibility" testify to their acceptance—or at least their awareness—of the fact that plausibility is usually secured by an illusion.

A definition which incorporates some rather more ambitious specifications was coined by Reginald Bretnor in his book *Modern Science Fiction* (1953), and was subsequently quoted with approval by Robert Heinlein. This claims that science fiction is fiction "in which the author shows awareness of the nature and importance of the human activity known as the scientific method, shows equal awareness of the great body of human knowledge already collected through activity, and takes into account in his stories the effects and possible future effects on human beings of scientific method and scientific fact." [15]

This prescription incorporates a rather tight fitting straightjacket which would exclude much of what goes under the name of science fiction. As laid out it contains no notion of the *purpose* of the activity, but Heinlein builds from it a case for science fiction as a medium of thought-experiments (which is, of course, entirely in line with Campbell's prospectus as outlined in the last chapter):

> Through science fiction the human race can try experiments in imagination too critically dangerous to try in fact. Through such speculative experiments science fiction can warn against dangerous solutions, urge toward better solutions. Science fiction joyously tackles the real and pressing problems of our race, wrestles with them, never ignores them—problems which other forms of fiction cannot challenge. For this reason I assert that science fiction is the most realistic, the most serious, the most significant, the most sane and healthy and human fiction being published today. [16]

This represents a complete change of scene from the ideas expressed by Wilson and Fawcett, with the only connecting thread being the criterion of fidelity to scientific possibility: a criterion which Bretnor and Heinlein want to apply much more rigidly.

Both Wilson and Fawcett were looking forward to a *genre* that did not yet exist. They were offering reasons why they felt the need for it. What was primarily important was what they *felt*—in Wilson's case a recently-discovered sense of awe at the wonders of nature, in Fawcett's case a sense of loss regarding opportunities for indulging a sense of wonder. Bretnor and Heinlein, by contrast, are writing about a *genre* already established, whose hold on the imagination of its habitual readers is secure. They are asking a different question—not "Why do we want it?," but "What can we do with it now we have it?"

There have been many claims for science fiction made on the same kind of basis that Heinlein uses here. J. O. Bailey, in *Pilgrims Through Time and Space* (1947)—the first major historical study of speculative fiction—ends with a hope that we may become wiser by experiencing, through the medium of science fiction, the horrors of atomic holocaust. The same point is made by Donald Wollheim in *The Universe Makers*. I think it is necessary to separate these claims regarding the potential social utility of science fiction from our investigation of the reasons which people characteristically have for reading it. This is not in any way to diminish those claims, but simply to point out that they cannot and do not explain the existence of science fiction. The same may be said of such studies of science fiction as Kingsley Amis' *New Maps of Hell* (1961), which claims that the most important potential utility of science fiction is its capacity for social satire.

Perhaps the boldest of all the definitions of science fiction is that given by Brian Aldiss in *Billion Year Spree* (1973).

He claims that:

> Science fiction is the search for a definition of man
> and his status in the universe which will stand in our
> advanced but confused state of knowledge (science), and
> is characteristically cast in the Gothic or post-Gothic
> mode. [17]

This, too, is largely a statement of potential utility, but
it may also be read as making a claim regarding the nature of the
perspective-shift which is characteristic of reading science
fiction. It may well be a valid one, for implied by my statements
concerning "a new way of looking at the world" is the notion of a
new way of conceiving of man's status in the world. [18]

When we move on to consider writers who are more concerned
with trying to analyze the effects of science fiction upon its
readership than with laying down specifications for recognizing
and writing it, then we find other notions appearing regularly—
particularly the emphasis on imaginative adventurousness—and we
also find more thoughtful analyses of the perspective-shift.

Science fiction did not find apologists outside the *genre*
until the late Fifties and early Sixties, when several British
literary figures confessed to liking it and went into print in
order to justify their liking. The most prominent names in this
party were Kingsley Amis, Robert Conquest, and C. S. Lewis.
Apologists in America were slower to emerge from hiding, but when
science fiction became suddenly fashionable in the Seventies
there was certainly no shortage of them, prominent among them the
mercurial Leslie A. Fiedler, whose two "explanations" of the rise
of science fiction (in *Love and Death in the American Novel* and
Waiting for the End) I have taken the liberty of ignoring because
they clearly contradict one another. (In the first passage
science fiction is said to be a characteristically Anglo-Saxon
form of "horror-pornography," while in the latter book it is an
expression of pseudo-Messianic expectations and is said to be
"typically Jewish.") [19]

Robert Conquest, in "Science Fiction as Literature" (1963),
notes that science fiction has two distinct "moods":

> If we divide science fiction into two moods, one might
> be said to lay out its imaginary world cooly and calmly
> and gain its effects by a cumulative objectivity; and
> the other which hustles the reader into acceptance by
> sheer high pace and obsessiveness....Similarly, a divi-
> sion might be made between stories of the extreme and
> fantastic future and work fairly rigorously covering
> changes which can be more or less definitely foreseen
> from present knowledge—going into the next fifty to a
> hundred years, perhaps, at the most. [20]

What Conquest is observing here is, of course, the tension

between the two basic reader demands—for the illusion of plausibility on the one hand and for imaginative adventurousness on the other—and the consequent "fictional spectrum" which they create. He goes on to make the following comments concerning the timeliness of the new *genre*:

> Whatever its satirical or other virtues, fiction is a dead loss if it does not present an imaginary world which is deeply believable, acceptable. Only thus, in some as yet unexplained way, are our own feelings given sustenance, our own imagination given exercise. Science-fiction is simply a neglected, and wrongly neglected, way of doing this. The particular type of excitement to be found in science-fiction is not, perhaps, entirely new: there is something of the same feeling in Elizabethan writing, when our culture's imagination was strongly directed to the possibilities of unknown lands, to Dr. Dee's projects for discovering the philosopher's stone, and so on, and when Utopias set in a quite imaginary Virginia entered into the creative literature....
>
> Anthropologists have held that a great literature, a cultural expansion, often goes with a physical expansion—that the ages of Greek and Elizabethan exploration were not accidently those of great literature. And that is only taking it at its crudest, the mere act of landing on Sicily or America—or Mars. In a culture like our own, the frontiers of knowledge have all sorts of other direction, and if a writer is being truly what I call modern, he is at least aware of them. [21]

Conquest is, of course, not claiming that the science fiction already written is great literature, but merely that in its attitude there are elements which are likely to play their part in the great literature of our own age when we find a Shakespeare to write it for us. (Joanna Russ, the leading feminist science fiction writer, once commented that science fiction today is in the situation of the Elizabethan drama after Marlowe but before Shakespeare—an interesting coincidence of metaphors.)

C. S. Lewis, in his essay "On Science Fiction" (1966), attempts a much more detailed breakdown of the various subspecies of the *genre*, largely because he wishes to attempt to justify only some of them. He rejects as examples of bad practice science fiction stories which are simply formularistic pulp adventure plots which have donned the apparatus of science fiction simply as a form of fancy dress. He also passes over (though he considers it to be a "legitimate" literary endeavor) what he calls "the fiction of Engineers," which is primarily interested in gadgets or undiscovered techniques as actual possibilities in the real world. He distinguishes from this as slightly more interesting the closely related subspecies which speculates on the nature of otherworldly environments:

When we learn from the sciences the probable nature of places or conditions which no human being has experienced, there is, in normal men, an impulse to attempt to imagine them. Is any man such a dull clod that he can look at the moon through a good telescope without asking himself what it would be like to walk among those mountains under that black, crowded sky? The scientists themselves, the moment they go beyond purely mathematical statements, can hardly avoid describing the facts in terms of their probable effect on the senses of a human observer. Prolong this, and give, along with that observer's sense experience, his probable emotions and thoughts, and you at once have a rudimentary science fiction. [22]

In Lewis' view, therefore, this subspecies of science fiction may justify itself simply as a reaction to natural curiosity. He comments that he cannot understand why anyone should think this illegitimate or contemptible as an aim of fiction. It is, however, worth noting that there is actually very little science fiction which fits into this category. Arthur C. Clarke and Isaac Asimov perform this kind of operation frequently, and very competently, but it rarely forms the principal focus of even those works in which it is most prominent. There is, however, some notable "science fiction artwork" which takes as its sole purpose the creation of the landscapes of other worlds with the utmost fidelity to known science—Chesley Bonestell and David Hardy have both made their reputations in this area. Lewis comments, sensibly, that although this kind of science fiction is "capable of great virtues," it is "not a kind which can endure copious production."

The next subspecies which he considers is one which he finds more interesting, and which he calls "eschatological." It is a rather narrow field, consisting solely of speculations about the ultimate destiny of the species *Homo sapiens*, but he comments:

Work of this kind gives expressions to thoughts and emotions which I think it good that we should sometimes entertain. It is sobering and cathartic to remember, now and then, our collective smallness, our apparent isolation, the apparent indifference of nature, the slow, biological, geological, and astronomical processes which may, in the long run, make many of our hopes (possibly some of our fears) ridiculous. [23]

Here we meet the perspective-shift of science fiction in a guise which tends to offer us a sense of humility rather than inspiring us with a special excitement. It is, however, the other aspect of the perspective-shift which Lewis is especially interested in, and to which he turns as the characteristic component of his last sub-species:

The last sub-species of science fiction represent simply an imaginative impulse as old as the human race working under the special conditions of our own time. It is not difficult to see why those who wish to visit strange regions in search of such beauty, awe, or terror as the actual world does not supply have increasingly been driven to other planets or other stars. It is the result of increasing geographical knowledge....

The defence and analysis of this kind are....no different from those of fantastic or mythopoeic literature in general....

If good novels are comments on life, good stories of this sort (which are very much rarer) are actual additions to life; they give, like certain rare dreams, sensations we never had before, and enlarge our conception of the range of possible experience. [24]

There is an echo here of Fawcett, but what is perhaps more important is that there is none at all of Wilson. Lewis has effectively split the notion of an *enlargement* of one's consciousness of the world from the notion of an *expansion* of consciousness to adopt the perspective that experience of the world is only part of the experience available to us—*if we care to make use of our imaginative faculties.* (He comments that this is a notion which many people cannot or will not accept.) It would be wrong, I think, to claim—as Lewis tends to do—that these two notions are distinct, serving to sort particular works within the spectrum of science fiction into two groups. They often—indeed, most frequently—occur in intimate relation within works although they represent different communicative functions.

The aspects of works which enlarge our consciousness of the world are consumed in service of the maintenance function, for they maintain a particular attitude to the world. But Lewis' final category, and his justification of it, is surely nothing else but the elevation of the restorative function of literature to high Art—which is why he finds so very little fiction satisfying in this regard. Lewis is, in fact, rather an anomalous figure in literary circles: a connoisseur (in Escarpit's sense as well as the ordinary one) of restorative fantasies, a man capable of reading the literature of imaginary worlds directively. (It seems that his friend and colleague J. R. R. Tolkien belonged to the same class. It is perhaps not surprising that both were brilliant fantasists who were to a large extent out of touch with, and had little taste for, the real world.)

The third apologist for science fiction I wish to consider here is the American Robert Scholes, who may be seen as taking up the thread of Lewis' argument concerning the nature, functions, and justification of the kind of literature that science fiction aspires to be (or ought to be).

Scholes rejects the label "science fiction" with its attendant problems of classification in favor of describing a literary species which he calls "structural fabulation," thus creating a new referent for the initials by which science fiction is commonly and conventionally known.

He writes:

> Fabulation....is fiction that offers us a world clearly and radically discontinuous from the one we know, yet returns to confront that known world in some cognitive way. Traditionally, it has been a favorite vehicle for religious thinkers, precisely because religions have insisted that there is more to the world than meets the eye, that the common-sense view of reality—"realism"—is incomplete and therefore false. Science, of course, has been telling us much the same thing for several hundred years. The world we see and hear and feel—"reality" itself—is a fiction of our senses, and dependent on their focal ability, as the simplest microscope will easily demonstrate. Thus it is not surprising that what we call "science" fiction should employ the same narrative vehicle as the religious fictions of our past. In a sense, they are fellow travellers. But there are also great differences between these kinds of fiction which must be investigated. [25]

He goes on to distinguish between "dogmatic" fabulation and "speculative" fabulation, the first taking as its basic assumption that we *know*, by some special revelation of power of the mind, what the metaphysical world that lies beyond our senses is like and what its implications are; the second taking the opposite hypothesis. (There is, of course, an area of overlap and compromise where it is held that we know some things but can only speculate about others.) Scholes maintains that over the last several hundred years there has been a dramatic change in the balance between these two kinds of fabulation—not merely a shift toward the dominance of speculative fabulation over dogmatic, but also a shift in the kind of things which, if we claim to know anything, we now claim to know about the world beyond experience. He ties this to a fundamental change in man's concept of himself and his universe brought about by science, particularly by Darwin's theory of evolution and Einstein's theory of relativity.

As a result of these historical changes, he claims that:

> We are now so aware of the way that our lives are part of a patterned universe that we are free to speculate as never before. Where anything may be true—sometime, someplace—there can be no heresy. And where the patterns of the cosmos itself guide our thoughts so powerfully, so beautifully, we have nothing to fear but our own lack of courage. There are fields of force around us that even our finest instruments of thought and perception are only beginning to detect. The job of fiction is to play in these fields. And in the past

few decades fiction has begun to do just this, to dream new dreams, confident that there is no gate of ivory, only a gate of horn, and that all dreams are true....

We require a fiction which satisfies our cognitive and sublimative needs together, just as we want food which tastes good and provides some nourishment. We need suspense with intellectual consequences, in which our minds are expanded even while focused on the complications of a fictional plot.

These may be described as our general requirements —needs which have existed as long as man has been sufficiently civilized to respond to a form that combines sublimation and cognition. But we also have to consider here the special requirements of our own age— our need for fictions which provide a sublimation relevant to the specific conditions of being in which we find ourselves. The most satisfying fictional response to these needs takes the form of what may be called structural fabulation. In works of structural fabulation the tradition of speculative fiction is modified by an awareness of the nature of the universe as a system of systems, a structure of structures, and the insights of the past century of science are accepted as fictional points of departure. Yet structural fabulation is neither scientific in its methods nor a substitute for actual science. It is a fictional exploration of human situations made perceptible by the implications of recent science. Its favorite themes involve the impact of developments or revelations derived from the human or the physical sciences upon the people who must live with these revelations or developments. [26]

Scholes recombines what Lewis was so careful to separate: the exploration of the imaginary and its recoil upon reality. He insists, in fact, on the combination of "sublimation" and "cognition," both in the general and the particular case. His emphasis, unlike that of the Campbellian school, is not on the exploration of situations made *possible* by the implictions of recent science, but on the exploration of situations thus made *perceptible* to the imagination. I think that this is a vital difference, and that it is in not recognizing this difference that the Campbellian school—represented primarily by Heinlein's essay cited earlier—fails to supply a complete rationale for the existence and function of science fiction. Other writers—even Wollheim and Moskowitz—come closer to understanding simply because they are prepared to blur the distinction. The readers quoted earlier do not even risk making the mistake, because they are entirely bound up by their own perceptions and are fully aware that what is necessary is that belief should be compelled rather than justified by recourse to some rigid logic of extrapolation.

If I might attempt to summarize all these views—to point to what I consider to be the common ground that underlies them all, it seems that in the opinion of all these people (all of whom know science fiction first-hand, as enthusiasts) science fiction *works* because it allows us to perceive and explore new possibilities (imaginative, not actual) for human existence. It operates within a framework of techniques which allows us to consider these situations as if they were real. It sees these situations as essentially relevant to the present personal and historical circumstances of the reader. It constantly expands the consciousness of the reader—and reinforces his faith in the possibility of such constant expansion—by continually extending the range of possibilities and situations which it explores.

Readers, for the most part, will only claim that science fiction is exciting and pleasurable. Writers are primarily interested in how its effects can be accomplished. Apologists—who may, of course, also be writers and are most certainly readers —make the further claim that this activity is valuable. They may claim that it is valuable on a personal level (as Lewis does) or even that it is socially adaptive (as Scholes does). These last claims will be examined again in the conclusion of this thesis, but cannot be properly considered until we have looked much more closely at the way the content of the fiction reacts to historical change. This will be the concern of the next chapter. In the remainder of this chapter I want to consider the question of why science fiction commonly appeals to the kind of people it seems to appeal to, and not to others, for this is a question which attacks the foundations of the claim that science fiction might be in some way adaptive. If, as Scholes contends, in today's world we *need* structural fabulation, why does it seem that so many of us not only seem not to need it but positively to hate it?

Virtually all science fiction writers "graduate" from being science fiction fans. Their autobiographical comments provide a record of their enthusiasm for science fiction and their dedication to it as readers as well as writers. There is one book of autobiographies of science fiction writers—*Hell's Cartographers* (1975)—and one book of biographies—Sam Moskowitz's *Seekers of Tomorrow* (1967)—but there are also numerous interviews in various professional and amateur magazines, in which authors are sometimes encouraged to talk about their early life. [27] From an inspection of all this material there arises a very strong impression of the isolation and alienation of many recruits to habitual science fiction reading. It is, of course, not universal, but it is a pattern which recurs constantly: stories of children who are precocious, imaginative, and virtually friendless but who seem to be able to find a special relationship with science fiction.

The following comment is by Robert Silverberg:

> I have no very fond recollection of my childhood. I was puny, sickly, plagued with allergies and freckles, and (I thought) quite ugly. I was too clever by at

least half, which made for troubles with my playmates. My parents were remote figures....It was a painful time, lonely and embittering; I did make friends but, growing up in isolation and learning none of the social graces, I usually managed to alienate them quickly, striking at them with my sharp tongue if not my feeble fists. On the other hand, there were compensations: intelligence is prized in Jewish households, and my parents saw to it that mine was permitted to develop freely. I was taken to museums, given all the books I wanted, and allowed money for my hobbies. I took refuge from loneliness in these things; I collected stamps and coins, harpooned hapless butterflies and grasshoppers, raided the neighbors' gardens for specimens of leaves and flowers, stayed up late secretly reading, hammered out crude stories on an ancient typewriter, all with my father's strong encouragement and frequent enthusiastic participation, and it mattered less and less that I was a troubled misfit in the classroom if I could come home to my large private room in the afternoon and, quickly zipping through the too-easy homework, get down to the serious business of the current obsessional hobby.

Children who find the world about them distasteful turn readily to the distant and the alien. The lure of the exotic seized me early. [28]

It seems that so far as its most dedicated readers are concerned—though we must remember that these constitute a tiny and probably unrepresentative sample of the whole readership— science fiction appeals particularly not just to young people but to people who think of themselves as being different (and hence think of themselves as being *special*).

This opinon is endorsed by Donald Wollheim—a man who has far more experience of science fiction fandom than most. In *The Universe Makers* he observes that:

The usual science-fiction devotee tends to be solitary and introverted in his youth. This is not an exact thing, of course, but in a general form it holds true for most of those I have met. They do not run with the pack—they are at home with their noses buried in the pages of speculation. Even if they are of a sociable nature, what they want to talk about is the wealth of wonders they have absorbed through their reading....

Such is my own history, for I was definitely that kind of solitary reader, devouring everything the magazines published, every book I could buy or borrow, and eventually writing to other fans and trying to write stories myself. The problems of daily life, getting through school, worrying about college, thinking about making a living, were never as real as the problem of how the moon flight was to be organized, what we would find on Mars, and whether atomic power would be released in our time. This was what counted. [29]

It is hardly surprising that the people most interested in a futuristic species of fiction should be young. The teenager's entire adult life is in his future, whereas a man in middle age or beyond often has enough of an investment (in every sense of the word) in the present and in the past to direct his attention to the status quo and its preservation (not necessarily in the historical sense, but in terms of his own psyche). This observation, however, goes only a small way to explaining the appeal of science fiction. Only a small fraction of the stories published in Wollheim's youth dealt with the span of time which we might designate as that lying within the "personal temporal horizon." It is true that the specific events he mentions above have now come to pass, but he has selected them with the aid of hindsight —these references constitute an attempt at justification rather than explanation.

From a superficial examination of Silverberg's autobiographical statement it would seem that Lewis' account of the merits of imaginative fiction have more truth in them than Scholes' more ambitious *apologia*. The alienated, who find the real world an uncomfortable place to live, have more investment in their imaginary worlds—places to retire to, where the life that really matters is lived. But an inspection of Silverberg's own science fiction hardly supports this view. He does not deal in comfortable lands of Cokaygne. There are no Edenic environments comparable to Lewis Malacandra and Perelandra, and there is certainly no Heaven comparable to the bright new world in *The Great Divorce*. Silverberg's later work, in fact, can be seen as an extensive series of metaphors illustrating and dramatizing the condition of alienation. [30] It has, in fact, attracted some bitter criticism from members of the science fiction community who find it uncomfortable and rather downbeat. If one were to read Silverberg's novels for their allegorical content—and many of them, especially *Nightwings*, *Son of Man*, and *Downward to the Earth*, are overtly allegorical—one would be driven to the conclusion that they do not represent attempts to escape alienation but attempts to heal it.

Science fiction certainly contains a great many Cokaygne fantasies. *The Lord of The Rings* was taken up more enthusiastically within the science fiction community than anywhere else, and the booming market in imitations thereof is aimed mainly at the overlapping fantasy/science fiction audience. Edgar Rice Burroughs has always been popular within the science fiction community, and there is a thriving market in imitations of his work. But there is also much science fiction which is insistently anti-Cokaygnian, imagining other worlds of a radically different kind.

It seems to me that young people who are lonely and who find themselves out of harmony with their immediate social environment find more than straightforward escape in science fiction, though they certainly *do* find escape. The perspective-shift which is one of the things science fiction "sells"—and one of the things its readers find most exciting about it—is not something which amuses the intellect in a whimsical way. It seems to have more than ordinary novelty-value to these readers. It offers, I think, something of a new sense of identity—a new way for the alienated individual to relate to the world in which he finds himself which compensates in some measure for a failure to relate in a more commonplace fashion. It gives a new significance to a life which is threatened with insignificance by its maladjustment to the ordinary criteria of social accomplishment.

In extreme cases this, I think, governs the inordinate devotion of the science fiction "addict." This is the essential "payoff" of the perspective-shift. It need not be an "either/or" phenomenon—individuals who relate perfectly well to their contemporaries and who feel perfectly well at home in the social world may find the different way of relating an interesting addition to their imaginative accomplishments, and to their enjoyment of reading in general. But in many cases I think that it does become a substitute rather than a supplement; and when science fiction enthusiasts eventually learn to relate better to the social world—as the great majority of them do—it is *this* relationship which is secondary and supplementary.

In brief, the extreme science fiction enthusiast tends to obtain his sense of identity from his notion of how he relates to a concept of the universe at large (viewed, as Scholes says, as "a system of systems, a structure of structures") instead of from his notion of how he relates to other human beings.

If this is true, then we may, indeed, be entitled to say that science fiction is "adaptive." But we cannot make that a universal statement, and we must also resist the tendency shown by Lewis and many ardent science fiction fans to argue that this adaptation is limited to people who are particularly intelligent or imaginatively superior. We can say only that science fiction is particularly attractive to people beset with a sense of alienation, and that it offers one possible answer to their need for a sense of their own identity and importance. This will apply equally to out-and-out connoisseur readers and out-and-out consumers, though they will, of course, have very different reading preferences within the *genre*. This observation should not be taken as an attempt to place all science fiction readers into a category which distinguishes them from non-science fiction readers. A spectrum extends from the most fanatical enthusiast to the reader who enjoys science fiction occasionally, but finds that a little of it goes a long way. Within that spectrum everything is a matter of degree.

It is worth noting that the fact that this explanation is phrased in terms of *sensation* rather than of *cognition*, with feelings rather than descriptions, helps to explain why attempts to describe the nature and value of the perspective-shift which reading science fiction involves are so helpless and so vague. The sense of one's own relationship with the enigmatic universe that seems so frequently to be attendant upon the reading of science fiction not only cannot be conveyed in words but is likely to be dissipated by them. This point is made particularly eloquently by Robert Sheckley in a paper called "The Search for the Marvellous," which was part of a series of lectures delivered at the Institute of Contemporary Arts in 1975:

> I believe that many people read science fiction for a sense of participation in the wonders to come. The quest for non-ordinary reality is something more than curiosity and wishful thinking. We are too crowded in our everyday lives by replicas of ourselves and by the repetitious artifacts of our days and nights. But we do not quite believe in this prosaic world. Continually we are reminded of the strangeness of birth and death, the vastness of time and space, the unknowability of ourselves. One would like to live differently, more significantly. One would like to participate in events more meaningful than our daily round, feel sensations more exquisite than is our usual lot. One reads science fiction in order momentarily to transcend the dull quality of everyday life.
>   There is a reason behind this search for the ineffable. The death of God is argued by the theologians; but for most of us it is a fact of everyday life. "God" is a word with unfortunate connotations for many. By it I mean the fundamental mystery forever untouched by our rationality. Even to call this mystery a mystery is somehow to limit it, somehow to fix it in our minds as a "thing" of properties presently unknown but eventually to be learned precisely. This definition seems rational, but is in fact a contradiction of the very idea of the marvellous. The thing we lack is to be glimpsed but not captured. It is not to be defined, contained, or truly known. [31]

Perhaps this makes the truth sound less banal and less ordinary than in fact it is, but it does, I think, provide an account which is consonant with the bulk of the data presented and summarized in this chapter.

V
THEMES AND TRENDS IN SCIENCE FICTION

1. MACHINES

One of the first significant literary encounters between man and machine was Don Quixote's duel with the windmill. At the time the would-be hero was considered rather foolish in his belief that this giant representative of technology was a dangerous enemy. Today, we are not so sure. Miguel de Unamuno writes:

> The knight was right; fear, and fear alone, made Sancho and makes all of us poor mortals see windmills in the monstrous giants that sow evil through the world ....Fear...alone inspires the cult and worship of steam and electricity, makes us fall on our knees and cry mercy before the monstrous giants of mechanics and chemistry. And at last, at the base of some colossal factory of elixir of long life, the human race, exhausted by weariness and surfeit, will give up the ghost. But the battered Don Quixote will live, because he sought health within himself, and dared to charge at windmills. [1]

Today the marriage of man and machine has, after a long courtship, been consummated. The honeymoon is over, and we begin to doubt whether we have done the right thing. Science fiction tells the story of our passage from infatuation to the brink of disillusionment with remarkable clarity.

The first major literary works which looked forward to a technological future were Francis Bacon's *New Atlantis* (1627) and John Wilkins' *Mathematicall Magick* (1648). Both were speculative essays rather than fictional works, though the former was cast as an imaginary voyage. Each provides an enthusiastic catalogue of mechanical wonders: flying machines, submarines, engines of war, etc. Both are remarkable for their foresight. Both take the view that bigger and better machines can bring nothing but good into the world—Bacon's work is a prescription for Utopia and for the Enlightenment of mankind.

When the Enlightenment actually came people grew more cynical, and the eighteenth century produced no prolific futuristic fiction. As the industrial revolution got under way, however, and began to produce many of the machines which Bacon and Wilkins had anticipated, the whole area of speculation was re-opened to the literary imagination. In the Vernean literature of the late nineteenth century submarines and flying machines abound, offering the freedom of the earth and the freedom to go beyond it. In 1895 H. G. Wells invented a machine that gave access to the distant future, creating a literary convention which made the realms of time as accessible to the imagination as the realms of space. These were machines that could work miracles, and they played the hero's part in the stories which were written about them.

There was, however, another side to the fascination with mechanical contrivance. There is a series of bizarre stories, often with heavy allegorical overtones, which runs from E. T. A. Hoffmann's "Automata" (1814) and "The Sandman" (1816) through Nathaniel Hawthorne's "The Celestial Railroad" (1843) and Herman Melville's "The Bell-Tower" (1855), in which machines play a quasi-diabolic role. The machines in these stories are sinister, and betray the humans who make or deal with them. A particularly telling scene is found in "The Sandman," where mechanician Coppelius reveals to the hero that he has fallen in love with a mechanical doll by plucking out her eyes. Verne, in his early days, was sufficiently influenced by Hoffmann to write a story in which a machine plays a diabolical role, "Master Zacharius" or "The Watch's Soul" (1853); and the same feeling for the sinister aspects of machine-power is present in Wells' "Lord of the Dynamos" (1894).

The possibility that machines might relieve man of much drudgery was celebrated by Edward Bellamy's Utopian best-seller, *Looking Backward* (1888), but William Morris, replying to that work in *News from Nowhere* (1891), was not at all sure that abandoning productive work to machines was a good idea. He felt that man robbed of the opportunity to be productive might be man robbed of the opportunity to be creative, and that this might lead to a feeling of uselessness that would destroy the quality of life. This notion that machines might make man feel redundant was put much more strongly by Samuel Butler in *Erewhon* (1880), where he developed from some early articles the notion that machines might "evolve" by Darwinian natural selection to become a fitter species than their human creators, and threaten then to replace them. The notion is developed satirically, but it exaggerated a real anxiety which was derived from the awe which people felt in the presence of vast and powerful engines.

The early science fiction magazines, under the influence of Hugo Gernsback, were wholeheartedly enthusiastic about mechanical technology—this was the very essence of what Gernsback wanted to teach his readers. It was, indeed, the very purpose of "scientifiction." In his own romance, *Ralph 124C41+* (1911), Gernsback produced a catalogue of wonders which echoed Bacon's. Just as Bacon had placed his catalogue in an imaginary voyage for communicative convenience, Gernsback placed his in pulp romance.

The miraculous potential of the machine was quickly pushed to its limit. There were machines to make gold, machines to heal all disease, machines to carry men into the farthest regions of the universe, through time and into the "world" of the atom. In John W. Campbell Jr.'s "The Last Evolution" (1932), machines inherit the universe and carry on the evolutionary story when the human race finally becomes extinct.

It was not long, however, before the other mode of thought began to creep in. E. M. Forster, in "The Machine Stops" (1909), had objected to Wellsian optimism regarding the prospect of a technological Utopia on two counts—first that an enforced life of pointless idleness would destroy man's initiative, and secondly that responsibility for the maintenance of society would pass so completely to the machines that there would be no way to cope with a major malfunction. Both these notions appeared quickly enough in science fiction, most strikingly in Miles J. Breuer's *Paradise and Iron* (1930).

Under the pseudonym of Don A. Stuart, Campbell wrote a new story about the machines inheriting the world called "Twilight" (1934), in which a time-traveller finds the men of the far future in decline, having lost their initiative, their ability to cope with change, and their will to achieve anything at all. Both their bodies and their minds are slowly atrophying. It was a theme that Campbell, as Stuart, returned to several times. In a sequel, "Night" (1935), a second time-traveller finds man extinct and the machines dutifully persisting in their maintenance of all conceivable services, despite the fact that there is no one to use them. In "The Machine" (1935), an alien machine which has taken over the world and which has supplied all mankind's needs renounces its paternalistic role and leaves Earth so that men can recover their humanity in fighting for survival. "Forgetfulness" (1937) features an evolved human race who seem to invaders to be technologically primitive, but who have merely given up machines because they have developed mental powers that make them unnecessary.

When Campbell took over *Astounding*, he asked for stories which would investigate much more closely and realistically the effects of technological innovation upon society. One of the earliest ones, and one which proved to be one of the most enduring, was Robert Heinlein's "The Roads Must Roll" (1940), which deals with the effects of a strike by the engineers who tend the moving roadways on which all transport in its society of the future is dependent. Campbell always had a fondness for stories which attempt to analyze the unintended consequences of technological innovations, and this type of story accounts for many of the humorous stories which the magazine carried during the thirty-four years he was involved with it. Interesting examples include George O. Smith's "Pandora's Millions" (1945), in which the invention of a matter-duplicator precipitates economic collapse; Murray Leinster's "A Logic Named Joe" (1946), in which a household information unit promotes anti-social behavior by its willingness to answer *all* questions put to it; and Christopher Anvil's "Gadget v. Trend" (1962), about the perils of trying to make overexpensive technology economically viable *via* insurance schemes. Anxiety concerning the power of machines and the danger of their getting out of control was also reflected in the magazine, notably in Lester del Rey's story about an accident in a nuclear power plant, "Nerves" (1942), and in Theodore Sturgeon's horror story about a bulldozer infused with life, "Killdozer!" (1944).

In prewar *Astounding* the prevailing mood was pragmatically optimistic. Faith in human ingenuity was virtually limitless. Unexpected difficulties and dangers, though always imminent, could always be mastered by common sense and intelligence. The mood of "Twilight" was never entirely lost (the story is still frequently reprinted and consistently appears on lists of the best science fiction stories ever written), but it was acknowledged that the far future was not something to worry about unduly. The immediate problem and all those which were likely to arise in the short term could be coped with.

That attitude, however, was severely threatened by the events of August 1945. After that date, suddenly there was a new upsurge in the suspicion that perhaps we could *not* cope with our technological innovations—that perhaps, after all, they might destroy us, not after a long decline when our evolutionary day was done, but imminently. There was, of course, a rash of atomic holocaust stories, many of which refused to hold out the traditional note of hope and confidence in the finale. Two significant examples from within the *genre* are Wilson Tucker's *The Long Loud Silence* (1952) and Judith Merril's *Shadow on the Hearth* (1950), but there were many others, most written by writers from outside the *genre*. [2]

A particularly good example of the post-war consciousness is provided by another "classic" story, T. L. Sherred's "E for Effort" (1947). In this story two men invent a machine which can see through time. They realize immediately the implications of such an invention, and set about trying to make enough money to build several duplicates in the hope of offering them to the world in order to banish all deceit and penetrate everything hitherto secret. They fail, and the mad scramble of power-groups to obtain control and monopoly of the machine precipitates all-out war. This, in the ruthless logic of the story, is inevitable, and no amount of ingenuity or goodwill on the part of the idealistic heroes could have prevented it.

In 1924, replying to an essay in which J. B. S. Haldane predicted that with the aid of science man could and would make a better world, Bertrand Russell made the following observation:

> Science has not given man more self-control, more kindliness, or more power of discounting their passions in deciding upon a course of action. It has given communities more power to indulge their collective passions, but, by making society more organic, it has diminished the part played by private passions. Men's collective passions are mainly evil; far the strongest of them are hatred and rivalry directed towards other groups.

Therefore at present all that gives men power to indulge their collective passions is bad. That is why science threatens to cause the destruction of our civilization. [3]

Until 1945 this kind of attitude was quite invisible in science fiction. Outside the magazines there was much more suspicion of technology, but few stories actually took this line. The most famous example of an anti-technological work, Aldous Huxley's *Brave New World* (1932), is primarily an emotional reaction against the kind of Utopia that technology might permit. Interestingly, this novel, like Russell's essay, is a direct response to the ideas of J. B. S. Haldane as expressed in *Daedalus* (1923), but the grounds of objection are quite different. It is the benevolence of the technocratic humanitarians that Huxley fears, not the by-products of the struggle for power. Until the war, Huxley's anxiety was dominant, but after Hiroshima, Russell's fears were the ones that seized the world. Orwell's *Nineteen Eighty-Four* (1949), though often paired with *Brave New World*, really manifests a very different species of hysteria.

Russell, after the war, turned his own hand to science fiction writing, and among his stories is the despairingly cynical "Doctor Southport Vulpes' Nightmare" (1954), in which scientists on opposite sides construct legions of war-machines which go forth to destroy the world in their conflict. This is an image which cropped up occasionally in the science fiction magazines too, most notably in Philip K. Dick's "Second Variety" (1953), about a lone man in a war-torn landscape who encounters a number of apparently helpless and harmless people, all of whom turn out in the end to be imitations created by machines which are still designing ever-more sophisticated devices to delude and kill enemy personnel.

This fear of machines continued to be reflected in science fiction throughout the Fifties. In Clifford Simak's "Bathe Your Bearings in Blood," also known as "Skirmish" (1950), the machines revolt and begin attacking and killing people. In "We, the Machine" (1951) by Gerald Vance, a mechanical Utopia disintegrates as its machines first begin to fail and then become arbitrarily homicidal. In Fredric Brown's brief allegory "The Weapon" (1951), a nuclear scientist receives an enigmatic visitor who disappears after giving the scientist's mentally retarded child a loaded gun to play with. In L. Sprague de Camp's "Judgement Day" (1955), another nuclear scientist looks back on his miserable childhood and his continued failure to like or be liked by his fellow men, as he hands his government plans for the ultimate weapon, certain that they will use it.

These new stories came into an environment in which the opposite attitude had previously been dominant, and there was, of course, some resistance put up by numerous writers who retained their essential faith in technology despite the intellectual climate of the day. The desperation of their defense, however, often testifies eloquently to their awareness of the opposition.

Their promises for a better future were no longer carelessly distributed, but had to be hammered home with insistent and persuasive arguments. A good example of this is provided by the Hugo-award-winning *They'd Rather Be Right* (1954) (also known as *The Forever Machine*), by Mark Clifton and Frank Riley, which includes a miraculous machine which can do almost anything, and which will even make men immortal if they still have the capacity for growth and change, rather than the strong resistance to change which manifests itself as bigotry and fear of technology. The characters who build the machine refer to it as "she," and name it Bossy. They love her, and want everyone else to love her, but they fear that they cannot prevail. The book ends with a dramatic appeal to society to accept the gifts which Bossy brings:

> There is still a challenge facing man....That challenge is Bossy. She will not command you or cajole you. She does not care whether you are made immortal or whether you would prefer clinging to your thin and single-valued ideas and prejudices—and die....She is a tool who will heat your homes, or bring you entertainment, or cook your food, or bathe the baby, or walk the dog, or figure your income tax. She will do all things as she is commanded, and not care whether they are big or small. Because Bossy is only a tool.
> She can also give you a tremendous comprehension in time, the nature of which we do not even dream. She can give you immortality. But you must rise to her requirements. You cannot make use of the tool unless you comprehend something of the laws of the universe governing life. [4]

The inventor's polemic ends the book. We do not get to hear the reply. The implication in the title is that the world is not really ready for the fruits of the machine.

Inevitably, this anxiety ebbed slowly away. If people did not, like Dr. Strangelove, learn to love the bomb, they did at least become accustomed to it. The realization grew that the products of technology, no matter how much anxiety they might cause, were not going to disappear. They could not simply be rejected out of hand: technology had its own impetus. The problem which became central to science fiction in the Sixties, insofar as it dealt with machines, was the problem of co-existence and adaptation.

The post-war era has been—and still is—the era of the computer, and it was the computer that eventually displaced the atom bomb as the principal symbol of mechanical technology in science fiction.

Anxiety has always been a very important aspect of stories about computers and the awesome powers that they might one day control. The evils of the computer-run society are the concern of a whole series of novels extending from Francis G. Rayer's

Tomorrow Sometimes Comes (1951) through Philip K. Dick's *Vulcan's Hammer* (1960) to Ira Levin's *This Perfect Day* (1970). [5] The notion of the liberation of mankind through the smashing of computers is present in all these novels, though they vary in their opinions of its practicality or desirability. The *New York Times* commissioned Isaac Asimov's exploration of the question, "The Life and Times of MULTIVAC" (1976), in which the hero is cast out by the revolutionary movement, wins the trust of the omnipotent computer, and ultimately manages to pull the plug out. He then faces the dissidents, who are already suffering the discomforts of being thrown back unexpectedly on their own resources. When they seem less than overjoyed he says: "But this is what you wanted—isn't it." The story ends before he hears the reply.

It was Asimov who was more committed to the notion of the goodness of technology than any other influential writer, and his post-war story "The Evitable Conflict" (1950), was quite exceptional in its enthusiasm for the prospect of a computer-run society. Here, though, the people do not know, or, at least, do not fully realize, the extent to which the computers have taken over. It was Asimov who wrote the ultimate computer story, "The Last Question" (1956) in which a great computer, still evolving though man has long since disappeared and entropy is winding down the universe, produces the magic formula "Let There Be Light!" and starts the whole affair all over again. A rather less enthusiastic version of the same idea is Fredric Brown's vignette "Answer" (1954), in which a new computer is asked the question whether there is a God, and replies: "Yes, *now* there is a God!," striking dead the man who tries desperately to reach the switch that will turn it off. The ability of computers to develop pseudohuman personalities and superhuman mental abilities rapidly became a cliché, and in many cases this proceeded to its logical limit as the computers involved nursed godlike ambitions. Novels built on this hypothesis include *Larger than Life* (1962) by Dino Buzzati, *Destination: Void* (1966) by Frank Herbert, *Colossus* (1967) by D. F. Jones, *The God Machine* (1968) by Martin Caidin, and a remarkable novel written by the Nobel prize-winning astronomer Hannes Alfven under the pseudonym Olof Johanneson, *the Great Computer* (1966).

There was a time in the Fifties when it was generally considered that computers were stupid as well as clever, and that they could be persuaded to have nervous breakdowns by being asked to ponder paradoxes—a good example is Gordon Dickson's story "Monkey Wrench" (1951)—but this particular cliché seems to have died. Its fallibility provided a neat ending for the film *Dark Star* (1973), and there are much more sophisticated examples of machine existentialism in such stories as Robert Silverberg's "Going Down Smooth" (1968), and R. A. Lafferty's *Arrive at Easterwine* (1973).

Another symbol which became prominent in the Sixties and Seventies—and one which is perhaps more telling in its implications—is the cyborg: the man/machine hybrid. In his book *As Man Becomes Machine* (1971), David Rorvik discusses technological developments in medical cyborgization, and looks forward to "the new era of participant evolution," in which man will become as intimately involved with the machine as is humanly and mechanically possible. Medical cyborgization, under the term "bionics," has become a popular cliché thanks to the TV series *The Six-Million Dollar Man* and other spinoffs from Martin Caidin's novel, *Cyborg* (1972).

Functional cyborgs—men modified mechanically for particular tasks—have been most prominent in science fiction in connection with space travel. Cordwainer Smith's story "Scanners Live in Vain" (1950), about the problems of men modified for handling starships who are faced with redundancy by the development of a new space-drive, failed to find a paying market when it was written and was given away to an amateur magazine, but has since been hailed as a classic as its relevance was realized. Other stories on the same theme are Thomas N. Scortia's "Sea Change" (1956) and Anne McCaffrey's series of stories begun with "The Ship who Sang" (1961). Samuel R. Delany's *Nova* (1968) features a society revolutionized by such cyborgization, which allows men to "plug in" to whole factory complexes in order to control and direct them. Frederik Pohl won two major awards with *Man Plus* (1976), about the mechanical modification of a man for life on Mars, while Arthur Clarke also won an award for his story "A Meeting with Medusa" (1971), about a man mechanically rebuilt after an accident, who thus becomes uniquely fitted for an expedition into the atmosphere of Jupiter.

The problem of identity which might face a cyborg is presented in Algis Budrys' novel *Who?* (1958), in which a scientist is rescued from the other side of the border. When he is sent back, much of his body replaced by metal, his superiors cannot tell whether or not he is the same man, and fear that he may be a spy. He, too, becomes uncertain of his own identity and humanity. The same question is attacked in a rather surreal manner in David Bunch's *Moderan*, an assembly of shorter pieces published between 1959 and 1971. In *Moderan* all men are willingly turning themselves into machines, discarding their "fleshstrips" and retiring into mechanized "strongholds" to plot the destruction of one another and their weaker fleshly brethren. The book is a compendium of extremely striking images.

Many science fiction fans find Bunch's black comedy distasteful, and he remains an esoteric writer, but his is merely the most exaggerated version of an anxiety which runs through a good deal of modern science fiction and which seems obviously to be tied to anxieties in society itself. When computers become gods, and men become machines, we are dealing with a species of nightmare (or black comedy) which is little more than a caricature of feelings common in society regarding our everyday relationship with machines.

There is one more illustration of this whole pattern of development which seems to me particularly clear and particularly expressive, and this is the history of the robot in science fiction. The robot—by definition an anthropomorphous machine—

has undergone some very striking changes in the roles character-istically allotted to it, and these serve to emphasize the histo-rical pattern which we can see in the evolution of attitudes in science fiction to machines in general.

The word *robot* first appeared in Karel Capek's play *R.U.R.* (1921), and is derived from the Czech *robota* (statute labor). Capek's artificial men were, however, organic rather than mecha-nical, and in the terminology which ultimately became convention-al in science fiction, would now be called androids. (Android, of course, simply means man-like, and in early science fiction it was reasonable to refer to "android robots," meaning manlike machines rather than manipulative machines which were not man-like. This was perhaps more sensible, as the real robots which now exist are not at all manlike, but the convention nevertheless grew up in American science fiction that robots were by defini-tion manlike. The word android was used by Jack Williamson in the early Thirties specifically to apply to men of artificial flesh and blood, but the usage became standard largely through the example set by Edmond Hamilton in his Captain Future stories —Future's back-up team included artificial men of both types, and the labels thus came to be used to distinguish between them. The convention is still violated occasionally—Philip K. Dick used the term android to apply to artificial men who are externally indis-tinguishable from humans but are nevertheless mechanical.)

Machines which mimic human form date back, in fiction and reality, to the early nineteenth century. The real automata were clockwork dummies or puppets, but their counterparts in fiction—notably the doll Olimpia in "The Sandman"—were much more sinis-ter. The notion of machines in human form was seen by many as a blasphemy. They appear very rarely before the founding of the science fiction magazines, though William Wallace Cook's *Round Trip to the Year 2000* (1903), does feature giant humanoid mecha-nical servants as one of the benefits of future life.

Early science fiction stories show an ambivalent attitude toward robots. "The Psychophonic Nurse" (1928) by David H. Keller portrays a robot as a good servant, though no substitute for a mother's love. Abner J. Gelula's "Automaton" (1931), in contrast, has lecherous designs on its creator's daughter, and has to be destroyed. Harl Vincent's "Rex" (1934) takes over the world and proposes to remake men in the image of the robot, and he too becomes a menace to be defeated. Eando Binder's "The Robot Aliens" (1935), on the other hand, are gentle creatures with no such purpose in mind, though they are misunderstood and mistreated by fearful humans.

The most obvious way to write a story about the creation of artificial man is to recapitulate *Frankenstein*, and, indeed, some writers did. But there was also a considerable reaction against the assumptions implicit in the plot of *Frankenstein*, which led to the frequent presentation of the robot as a misunderstood innocent wrongly suspected. Isaac Asimov claims to have invented his "three laws of robotics" as a reaction against such a "Frank-enstein syndrome," but he was by no means alone in this—in fact

104

he was part of the dominant movement.

In "Helen O'Loy" (1938) by Lester del Rey, a man becomes infatuated with a beautiful female robot and eventually marries her. The marriage is happy and she makes a perfect wife, having her features regularly changed so that she can age along with him, and allowing herself to be dismantled after his death. Despite this rather heavy sentimentality, which strikes some readers as a little absurd, this remains one of the most popular stories of the period, fondly remembered by many. Another ultra-sentimental story is "Robots Return" (1938) by Robert Moore Williams, in which explorers from a robot civilization rediscover Earth and learn the secret of their origin. Though their faces are metal masks one "sighs softly," one has a glint in his eye which holds "a touch of awe," and the third gasps in surprise when he finds the statue which reveals to him the secret. At first the robots are disgusted, but they overcome their natural reaction to find a suitable reverence for their long-gone crea-tors:

> Eight saw the statue lying on the ground and vague thoughts stirred within his mind. "They may have eaten grass," he said. "They may have eaten the flesh of other animals; they may have been weaklings; they may have risen out of slime, but somehow I think there was something fine about them. For they dreamed, and even if they died...." [6]

This so inspired del Rey, the author of "Helen O'Loy," that he wrote an accompanying piece, "Though Dreamers Die" (1944), explaining how the human race died out, leaving its heritage to the robots.

"I, Robot" (1939) by Eando Binder is an anti-Frankensteinian parable in which a robot is unjustly accused of having turned on its creator. The robot, Adam Link, is eventually exonerated, and went on to have further adventures in a series of sequels, along with his specially-created mate, Eve Link. In "True Confession" (1939) by F. Orlin Tremaine and "Almost Human" (1941) by Ray Cummings, robots display superhuman altruism in order to save their creators from difficulties; and in "Jay Score" (1941) by Eric Frank Russell, the intrepid hero of an otherworldly adven-ture turns out to be a robot.

In the midst of this welter of pro-robot propaganda Isaac Asimov began to publish the robot stories which eventually gave rise to the formulation of the "three laws of robotics." "Strange Playfellow," also known as "Robbie" (1940), was a straightforward story of robotic altruism; but the story which made a deep impression was "Reason" (1941), in which a robot on a space station slowly comes to realize that the things his human master tells him are not logically coherent, and who therefore formulates his own cosmology and quasi-religious system in oppo-sition to the myth of Earth and its corollary legends. Implicit in the behavior of the robots in this story was the system of programmed ethics which Asimov was later to use as a prolific source of plot-twists. The first law states that a robot may not injure a human being, or, through inaction, allow a human being to come to harm; the second that a robot must obey the orders of human beings except where they conflict with the first law; and the third that a robot must protect its own existence as long as this involves no conflict with the first and second laws. Most of Asimov's robot stories involve robots behaving in peculiar ways because of some subtle interpretation of one of these laws, and many feature the "robopsychologist" Susan Calvin, whose job it is to disentangle these puzzles. Because of their rigid and altruistic ethics Asimov's robots are *nicer* people than real human beings. The first set of robot stories culminated with "Evidence" (1946), in which Susan Calvin has to decide whether a prominent politician is really a robot. In the end, the robot convinces the world of his humanity by a cunning ploy, and proceeds to be a far better politician than any mere, corrupt human could ever be.

Throughout the period from 1938 to the mid-Forties the dominant attitude to the robot in science fiction was that a manlike machine could be just as human as a man, and perhaps more so. In another of the "classic" stories of the period, C. L. Moore's "No Woman Born" (1944), a dancer is killed in a theater fire but has her consciousness resurrected into a robot body. The man responsible has doubts about what he has done, feeling that ordinary people will hate and fear her, but the dancer herself has none. She finds the robot condition very little different from the human condition, and even slightly superior. The principal stories which deliberately opposed this view in this period were "Q.U.R." and "Robinc" (both 1943) by Anthony Boucher, which were very much pro-machine but championed "usuform" robots against manlike ones. It is probably significant that Boucher was a Catholic, and found the idea of making machines in the image of man somewhat distasteful for religious reasons.

The events of 1945, however, brought about a striking change in the balance of opinion. Asimov's "Evidence," though published late in 1946, did not reflect any change, and Asimov remained very much the champion of the robot throughout, but in 1947 he published his first sinister robot story, "Little Lost Robot," in which a robot with a modified first law takes an impetuous order to "Get lost!" literally. The most famous robot story of 1947 was Jack Williamson's "With Folded Hands," which showed a new side to robot altruism. The humanoid robots of the story are created "to serve man, to obey, and to guard man from harm." They take this mission very seriously, guarding men against their own weaknesses, eliminating all bad habits (smoking, drinking, eating harmful foods, etc.), and finally setting out to eliminate unhappiness, if necessary by the use of drugs and prefrontal lobotomy.

It must be stressed that for the most part the science fiction writers still wanted to be the champions of technology, but that they discovered a whole host of new anxieties and arrived at a new estimate of the resistance that would have to be overcome in order to promote the benefits of the machine. In the sequel to "With Folded Hands," ...*And Searching Mind* (1949), also known as *The Humanoids*, men go to war against the humanoids, and ultimately lose; but the novel ends on a curious note of hope when the hero's assumptions about the inimicality of the robots is challenged, their apologist putting the view that in doing what they did they really *were* serving man, protecting him from his self-abuse—and that if man could transcend his tendencies to self-abuse and measure up to the standard set by the machines he would be much better off. (It is, incidentally, probable that this twist at the end was suggested to Williamson by Campbell.)

The anxiety characteristic of the Fifties is reflected straightforwardly in a whole series of stories. Robots kill or attempt to kill humans in "Lost Memory" (1952) by Peter Phillips, "Short in the Chest" (1954) by "Idris Seabright" (Margaret St. Clair), "First to Serve" (1954) by Algis Budrys, and "Mark XI" (1957) by Cordwainer Smith. Even Asimov used robots to commit murder in *The Naked Sun* (1956). The mistaken identity story—a common comic theme—takes on sinister or ironically tragic characteristics in Asimov's "Satisfaction Guaranteed" (1951), Philip K. Dick's "Imposter" (1953), Walter M. Miller's "The Darfsteller" (1955), and Robert Bloch's "Comfort Me, My Robot" (1955). There is an interesting group of stories in which robots are earnestly defended against a variety of charges in open court. These include Clifford Simak's "How-2" (1954), Asimov's "Galley Slave" (1957), and Lester del Rey's "Robots Should Be Seen" (1957). Other pro-robot stories which dramatize the context of conflict include a number of man vs. robot boxing matches: "Title Fight" (1956) by William Campbell Gault, "Steel" (1956) by Richard Matheson, and "The Champ" (1958) by Robert Presslie.

Even though many writers still looked favorably upon the robot during the post-war decade the sentimentality was completely gone. The robot was thoroughly reified, its distinctness from man clearly recognized. It was the *mechanical* nature of the robot and its logical faculties (and fallibilities) which were emphasized very strongly in this period. (It is interesting to note that the Catholic writer Boucher now felt sufficiently comfortable with the idea of humanoid robots to write "The Quest for St. Aquin" [1951], in which a perfectly logical robot deduces the reality of God and becomes a preacher.) Asimov, in the first of his robot novels, *The Caves of Steel* (1953), took some considerable trouble to analzye and examine his human hero's anti-robot prejudices, which are only gradually and with difficulty overcome. Asimov, like the machine-apologist in *The Humanoids*, was determined to put across the point that the weakness giving rise to the anxiety was in man, and that the stigmatization of the machine was unjustified; but he was fully aware that this was now a difficult point to make, whereas in the early Forties it had seemed so easy and so straightforward.

By the end of the Fifties the anxiety had begun to ebb away, and this is clearly shown by a number of stories in which the robot-menace theme is presented as a comic notion, notably the stories collected in Harry Harrison's *War With the Robots* (1958-62), Brian W. Aldiss's "Who Can Replace a Man?" (1958), Fritz Leiber's *The Silver Eggheads* (1959), and "The Critique of Impure Reason" (1962) by Poul Anderson. Sentimentality returned to the robot story in full force in Clifford D. Simak's "All the Traps of Earth" (1960), in which a robot butler who has given generations of faithful service comes into his inheritance despite the law which says he must be destroyed. The new wave of sentimentality climbed to a sickly peak in Ray Bradbury's story about marvellous electric grandparents, "I Sing the Body Electric" (1968).

The "re-humanization" of the robot in the Sixties and Seventies was not simply a return to the attitude of the mid-Forties. The writers went far beyond the point that had been reached then. A dramatic change is evident in the work of Philip K. Dick, whose early robot stories include the horror stories "Second Variety" and "Imposter," and who also wrote such sinister machine stories as "Autofac" (1955) and "The Preserving Machine" (1953). Over the years he became increasingly more interested in "androids" and "simulacra," and many of his later novels are based on the interchangeability of man and humanoid machines. He persistently represents certain forms of mental illness as reductions of human beings to "androidal" status, and often credits machines—even robot taxis—with a sympathy that would be unusual in a human being. Notable examples include *Do Androids Dream of Electric Sheep?* (1968). Here the people of an Earth partly destroyed by war keep mechanical pets to assuage the sense of guilt they feel regarding the virtual extinction of all animal life, while the hero faces the difficult job of trying to track down and identify as non-human illegal immigrant androids from colonies on other worlds. In "The Electric Ant" (1969), a man has difficulty in adjusting to the fact that he is an electronic simulation of a human identity. In *We Can Build You* (1972), the hero is in love with a schizophrenic girl who builds simulacra of human beings—both wholly artificial personalities and re-creations of historical figures—and eventually suffers an identity crisis and a schizophrenic breakdown himself. [7] In an essay entitled "The Android and the Human," Dick wrote:

> Someday a human being may shoot a robot which has come out of a General Electronics factory, and to his surprise see it weep and bleed. And the dying robot may shoot back and, to its surprise, see a wisp of gray smoke arise from the electric pump that it supposed was the human's beating heart. It would be rather a great moment of truth for both of them. [8]

In another essay he wrote:

> A human being without the proper empathy or feeling

is the same as an android built so as to lack it, either by design or mistake. We mean, basically, someone who does not care about the fate which his fellow living creatures fall victim to; he stands detached, a spectator, acting out by his indifference John Donne's theorem that "No man is an island," but giving the theorem a twist: that which is a mental and moral island *is not a man*.

The greatest change growing across our world these days is probably the momentum of the living towards reification, and at the same time a reciprocal entry into animation by the mechanical....if a mechanical construct halts in its customary operation to lend you assistance, then you will posit to it, gratefully, a humanity which no analysis of its transistors and relay-systems can elucidate. [9]

Dick is perhaps the most self-conscious of the writers who are dealing with this convergence of identity, but he is by no means alone. Clifford D. Simak, always one of the most ardent champions of the robot, has established in his more recent work a standardized landscape and theater of operations in which robots, partly or wholly estranged from man, are wise and gentle and are often tied up in their own spiritual quest for a sense of cosmic purpose. The most notable examples are *A Choice of Gods* (1972) and *A Heritage of Stars* (1977). Other stories which deal with robotic religion are Roger Zelazny's "For a Breath I Tarry" (1966) and Gordon Eklund's "The Shrine of Sebastian" (1973); in 1971 Robert Silverberg won an award for his wryly humorous story about the election of the first robot pope, "Good News from the Vatican." Barrington J. Bayley's novel, *The Soul of the Robot* (1974), concerns the adventures of a robot who wants to know whether or not he has a soul, and by what means he might settle the question one way or the other. He eventually comes to the conclusion that his very uncertainty is a truly human feature. The climactic stories in Asimov's long sequence of robot stories are *"That Thou Art Mindful of Him"* (1975), in which robots given time to meditate on the precise meaning of the three laws ask what it means to be human, and finally come up with the conclusion that they can find no way of differentiating between man and robot; and "The Bicentennial Men" (1976), in which a robot fights for the right to be recognized as human, and finally for the right to a gradual surgical metamorphosis that will give him flesh and blood.

This merging of categories is surely highly significant, especially when one remembers the growing importance of the cyborg role in science fiction during the same period. It is difficult to argue that this is a straightforward reflection of attitudes to machines in society at large, even with the aid of the logic of "symbolism."

It is clear from an inspection of this historical pattern in the roles characteristically attributed to machines in science fiction that the fiction is sensitive to changes in general social attitudes. It seems overwhelmingly probable that the dramatic change in the attitudes manifested in science fiction after 1945 was occasioned by the revelation of the atom bomb. The fear of technology and its products which flared up after that revelation in the everyday world is clearly echoed in science fiction. But what we see there is *not* simply a reflection of that fear but a reaction to it.

It would be wrong to say that science fiction writers *en masse* reacted to the increase in anxiety in exactly the same way. The field had then (and retains today) a considerable degree of heterogeneity concerning attitudes on technology. But one can, I think, identify ideas which are more-or-less commonly held regarding the implications of what is happening in society as a result of technological progress. There are some extremely striking images to be found in the work of a considerable number of writers which show, effectively, men become "mechanized" while machines become "humanized," or even "superhuman." This is neither a symbolic statement about the way the world of today is, nor a prediction about things that will happen in the future; but an expression of an attitude: a way of looking at man in the context of his machines. These stories offer a perspective-shift which allows us to see ourselves in a new way—not the way we "really are," but a way we can be seen.

To a large extent, at least, the stories discussed in this chapter act *against* what their authors consider to be the prevailing public mood. The science fiction of the Fifties clearly gave voice to public anxiety about technological "progress" and its products, but the dominant opinion within the *genre*—often actively didactic—held that this anxiety was unjustified, and that the fear was misdirected. The real danger, according to the science fiction stories of the day, was not the machines themselves, but our moral and intellectual inability to deal with them. This opinion remained dominant from then until the present day, when the machines have been rehabilitated but we have not.

This was the kind of question which pre-war science fiction never asked. To doubt the moral or intellectual fitness of humankind was unthinkable. In the Fifties, this human chauvinism took something of a beating, and the beating was all the harder because science fiction writers, by and large, refused the easy answer of stigmatizing the machines themselves as evil. Even the computers which become deities in the various stories quoted earlier are never charged with malevolence or implicit evil—on the contrary, they are often charged with an infallible benevolence (the one major exception is Harlan Ellison's story, "I Have No Mouth and I Must Scream" [1967]). It is largely as a consequence of the fact that science fiction writers retained their commitment to technology that they became afflicted with a loss of faith in man. The extent to which post-war science fiction manifests this loss of faith, often in open hostility, is astonishing when one recalls that it is a popular *genre* geared primar-

110

ily to the service of the restorative and maintenance functions. (Though one must also recall that it appeals particularly strongly to people who tend to be somewhat alienated from their fellow men.)

2. ALIENS

Cosmic voyagers of the seventeenth and eighteenth centuries met no genuinely alien beings, though they met some rather curious creatures. They *could not* meet alien beings because there was no such imaginative category available. The only categories available were those of man and animal, which were quite distinct. Men were sentient, moral beings with souls. Animals, by definition, had none of these advantages. Many satirical writers envisaged "men" in animal forms, and Swift went so far as to imagine beasts in human form, but all characterizations were limited by the crucial category distinction.

In the nineteenth century, however, the situation changed with the rise of evolutionary philosophy and the notion that the category-distinction might not be absolute. Lamarck, in France, suggested that living creatures evolved by adaptation to their environment, and that sentience and intelligence represented nothing more than the "highest" adaptations to a particular way of life.

The idea of alien intelligences was first popularized by Camille Flammarion in *Real and Imaginary Worlds* (1865)—a speculative essay in which he imagined the dominant life-forms of other worlds adapted in their physical forms to environments very different from those of Earth. In *Récits de L'Infini*, a series of fictitious dialogues first published the same year and revised several times subsequently (the final version was published in English as *Lumen* in 1887), he imagined the souls of men set free after death to roam the universe at will, experiencing serial reincarnations on other worlds under very different conditions. Aliens also appeared frequently in the work of another French writer of scientific romances, J. H. Rosny *aîné*—notably in "Les Xipéhuz" (1887, translated as *The Xipehuz*), "La Mort de la Terre" (1910), and *Les Navigateurs de l'Infini* (1925). Both writers saw man and alien existing as parts of a great cosmic plan, and their attitudes to alien life-forms were quite positive—Rosny, in the last work, found no incongruity in a love affair between a human and a six-eyed, tripedal Martian.

In Britain, however, evolutionary philosophy owed little to Lamarck and Bergson and much to Darwin and Thomas Henry Huxley. H. G. Wells was taught by Huxley, who made a great impression on him, and Wells went on to write about alien beings as Darwinian competitors in a struggle for existence which permitted no quarter. When Wells' Martians came to Earth in *The War of the World* (1898), they came to destroy mankind and steal the Earth's resources. The role which Wells gave to the alien in this story

111

became one of the most prominent clichés in early science fiction, and his representation of alien beings as loathsome monsters became standard.

Pulp romance thrived on lurid confrontations between men and alien monsters—battles on a colossal scale with the fate of worlds hanging in the balance. Writers found it easy to produce prolific wordage dealing with such conflicts, and artists were able to let their imagination run riot. The exceptionally ugly creatures who decorated the more garish illustrations quickly became known as "bug-eyed monsters," and it became a cliché that this was what other worlds contained. The variations on the theme were, in the early days, rather few. Occasionally human explorers would find other races locked in combat with one another, and would throw in with one side or the other in order to tip the balance. There was never any difficulty in deciding which was the "right" side. Often the battle was between humanoids and monsters, in which case there could be no possibility of a mistake. Where both races were non-humanoid the preference was for creatures with avian or mammalian characteristics, whose enemies were compounded out of reptilian, arthropodan, and molluscan characteristics. This biological chauvinism was for a long time taken to be an infallible guide to moral and intellectual kinship.

Occasionally, science fiction writers were willing to turn the Darwinian perspective around, making the human race the invaders and aliens (humanoid or small, furry and mammalian) the victims. Notable early examples are Edmond Hamilton's "The Conquest of Two Worlds" (1932), and P. Schuyler Miller's "The Forgotten Man of Space" (1933). The first really significant stories which broke the pattern were, however, published in 1934. The first, still remembered as a classic story of the period, was "A Martian Odyssey" by Stanley G. Weinbaum. Weinbaum imagined a Mars populated by all manner of bizarre beings engaged in the business of going about their everyday lives. He was the first writer to make any real impact with the notion that aliens were primarily *strange*, and that hostility was neither here nor there. He was also the first to try and plan alien life-systems so as to show some kind of ecological balance. He went on to design a whole series of other-worldly biospheres, and provided in "The Lotus Eaters" (1935) an interesting picture of the fatalistic psychology of an intelligent plant. His stories hardly seem realistic by today's standards, but at the time they represented a whole new approach to the matter of life on other worlds. The second important story of 1934 was Raymond Z. Gallun's "Old Faithful"—also an oft-reprinted and fondly remembered story. This is a story set on a Mars very like that of Wells' *War of the Worlds*—a dying world whose resources are almost at an end. A scientist, who has been exchanging signals with Earth by means of a flashing light, is condemned to death as a non-productive drain on the water-supply. Instead of surrendering for execution he decides to attempt a hazardous space-journey to bring his notebooks to Earth. The journey kills him and the scientists of

Earth find him dying in his capsule. They are first horrified by his repulsive appearance, but they see that he is in pain and they realize why he has made the trip, and the sense of intellectual kinship overcomes the horror. The communication between them has been highly inefficient, consisting of little more than acknowledgement of one another's signals, but the author is insistent of the value of this communication and its transcendence of the logic of vulgar Darwinism. Gallun went on to write two sequels. This new emphasis on the necessity for communication and amity between alien beings became slowly more apparent in the science fiction of the Thirties and Forties, its spirit encapsulated by the marvelous last line of Ralph Milne Farley's "Liquid Life" (1935): "For he had kept his word, even to a filterable virus." Biological chauvinism was slowly being eroded.

It was during the war years that the problems of communication—linguistic and political—between man and alien came into sharper focus and were explored with somewhat greater intensity. In "Co-operate or Else!" (1942) by A. E. van Vogt, a man and an alien are cast away together in a harsh alien environment during an interstellar war, and must combine their efforts to survive. The protocol of human/alien contact is the subject of two stories by Murray Leinster published in 1945, the first of which was subsequently elevated to the status of a "classic." This was "First Contact," in which two spaceships meet in the void. Each crew wants very much to make friends, but each is desperately suspicious of the other, fearful of giving away any information which might give the other race an advantage that might be exploited. Their triumphant solution to the deadlock is to exchange ships, thus managing a precisely equal exchange of information and demonstrating mutual good will. The second story, "The Ethical Equations," concerns a man faced with a difficult decision when he discovers an alien warship drifting in the solar system, with its crew in suspended animation, unable to revive because of a malfunction. In the end, he sets its controls to take it back to its homestar, because he feels that this is the correct thing to do, although it may well result in his being court-martialled.

It was in the Forties that science fiction writers first began serious attempts to construct credible alien beings adapted to environments radically unlike that of Earth—Hal Clement rapidly built himself a reputation in this area with such stories as "Attitude" (1943) and "Cold Front" (1946), preparing the way for later novels like *Mission of Gravity* (1953), about life on a planet whose gravity varies tremendously from equator to pole because of its rapid spin; and *Cycle of Fire* (1957), about life on a planet whose eccentric orbit results in extreme seasonal changes of climate. All these stories involve the problems of human/alien communication and co-operation.

These stories, though among the most notable of their day, still represented a quantitative minority—the dramatic potential of human/alien confrontation was far too great for it to suffer any marked decline, at least while the pulp magazines were the primary vehicle of science fiction. Leinster, whose stories for *Astounding* were thoughtful and by no means superficial, turned out a considerable number of invasion stories for the other pulps, and continued to use the alien menace story as his most frequent plot when he went on to write paperback novels in the Fifties and Sixties. There was, however, a noticeable trend during the Fifties to use alien beings and alien races more and more as a standard of comparison against which human beings and human nature might be judged and found wanting. There was a steadily-growing tendency to attack the biological chauvinism of earlier years and human intolerance and xenophobia in general. This trend was, however, restricted in one important respect, and that is that it was allowed only limited expression in *Astounding*. Campbell had no objection to stories in which humans learned (preferably the hard way) to communicate and make friends with aliens, but he was convinced that it was the destiny of the human race to inherit the universe and that human beings were implicitly and necessarily superior to all alien races. Thus, Campbell was willing to publish a story like L. Ron Hubbard's *To the Stars*, also known as *Return to Tomorrow* (1950), which ends with its human heroes committing genocide and preparing to wipe the whole galaxy clean of alien races who might one day compete with man, but he was not willing to publish Robert Silverberg's *Collision Course* (1959), which questioned the ethics of such an outlook.

Silverberg commented:

> I believe then, and believe now, that it's a good idea to examine your motives, to ask *why* actions are appropriate. My characters tend to be introspective, tend constantly to question themselves, tend sometimes to decide that their values need revision. Campbell didn't exactly disagree with these notions, but John was an outrageous *Homo sapiens*-chauvinist....For John, a story about Earthmen who have doubts, who admit the possibility that grabbing half the galaxy on behalf of imperialistic Earth might not be a good idea, and who ultimately run into superior opponents, was not a story he was going to publish because it advocated points of view that were just downright *wrong*. I didn't realize this. I knew it in an intellectual way, because I had been reading his magazine for a long time and was aware that the Earthmen always won, but I hadn't quite digested the fact that he was unwilling to consider alternate possibilities. [10]

Nevertheless, the vanity of human imperialism was attacked, and even mocked, in such stories as Clifford D. Simak's "You'll Never Go Home Again" (1951), and "The Waitabits" (1955) by Eric Frank Russell. The latter was published in *Astounding*, but this was a special case in that the aliens, though unconquerable, are quite harmless. It is notable that in several other strongly anti-militaristic stories written by Russell for *Astounding*, either there are no aliens or the aliens are the dupes outwitted by humans.

Racialism was strongly attacked in such stories as John Wyndham's "Dumb Martian" (1952) and Leigh Brackett's "All the Colors of the Rainbow" (1957), the victims in each case being aliens. The politics of colonialism were subject to careful scrutiny in Poul Anderson's "The Helping Hand" (1951), and attacked bitterly in Robert Silverberg's "We, the Marauders" (1958), which was expanded to novel-length as *Invaders from Earth*.

One *Astounding* story which did allow the bubble of human vanity to be pricked was "Immigrant" (1954) by Clifford Simak, in which human beings find out that they are as children compared to alien races. Poul Anderson's "The Martyr" (1960), however, which builds up to the revelation that the story's aliens have immortal souls but have been trying to protect humans from the knowledge that we do not, appeared elsewhere. Human sexual prejudices were fiercely attacked in a story by Theodore Sturgeon, "The World Well Lost" (1953), about homosexual aliens, but this, too, would not have been permitted in *Astounding*.

The decay of editorial taboos permitted more ambitious speculations linking aliens to religious mythology, and allowing their use in the exploration of sexual and psychological themes. The question of the plurality of worlds which had troubled theologians in the distant past now began to trouble science fiction writers, and all variants of the theme were explored. Missionaries undergo significant experiences in contact with alien beings in Ray Bradbury's "The Fire Balloons," also known as "In this Sign" (1951), Katherine Maclean's "Unhuman Sacrifice" (1958), and Philip José Farmer's "Prometheus" (1961). The last story is part of a series, an earlier story being "Father" (1955), in which a godlike alien offers a bishop an opportunity to take over his responsibilities. More ambitious stories in this vein include James Blish's "A Case of Conscience" (1953), in which a Jesuit concludes that an alien world whose inhabitants are apparently without sin must be a snare set by the devil to destroy faith in Christian redemption from original sin; and Lester del Rey's "For I Am a Jealous People" (1954), in which alien invaders of Earth turn out to be in possession of the ark of the Covenant, God having forsaken man in their favor.

In the Sixties, man's inhumanity to the alien continued to be a dominant theme. Savage satires on human vanity and prejudice were produced in Brian Aldiss' *The Dark Light-Years* (1964) and Thomas M. Disch's *White Fang Goes Dingo*, also known as *Mankind Under the Leash* (1966). Serious treatments include Robert Silverberg's *Downward to the Earth* (1969), in which a man returns to a former colony to expiate the sins he committed in cruelly exploiting its alien inhabitants, and Ursula K. Le Guin's "The Word for World is Forest" (1972), involving the rape of a forest world and the hopeless rebellion of its natives. There were also a great many stories dealing soberly and delicately with problems arising out of cultural and biological differences between man and alien. [11]

As with stories featuring robots, the stories which adopt a positive attitude to alien beings, stressing the value of communication, cooperation, and friendship, generally assume resistance on the part of the mass of mankind. The heroes who have to meet and establish friendly relations with aliens are usually faced with a task made more difficult by the hostility of at least some of their own kind. These anti-xenophobic stories do not underestimate the strength of xenophobic tendency in men. They are, to a large extent, stories deliberately promoting an ideology.

It is interesting to note that the most famous story by the writer responsible for a minor science fiction boom in the U.S.S.R., "Cor Sepentis" or "The Heart of the Serpent" (ca. 1957) by Ivan Yefremov, is actually framed as an ideological reply to Leinster's "First Contact." Yefremov argues that by the time man is sufficiently advanced to build his starships his society will have "matured" to the point where the suspicious and militaristic attitudes of Leinster's starship crews would be out of the question. In his story two spaceships meet in the void, and despite extreme biological dissimilarity they exchange friendly greetings, and the humans attempt to render assistance to the aliens. In all the East European science fiction that has so far been translated into English [12], there is no trace of the alien menace story—all fiction about first contacts is optimistic and positive in attitude, although *Solaris* (1961), by the Polish writer Stanislaw Lem, features an alien so utterly different and incomprehensible that attempts to understand it come to nothing, and its reaction to its human visitors proves profoundly disturbing. It seems that the Russian authorities take the ideological slant of science fiction very seriously—rumor reached the West some years ago that the most notable of contemporary Russian science fiction writers, the brothers Arkady and Boris Strugatsky, could no longer get their work published; and a letter from two science fiction writers reached both the British Science Fiction Association and the Science Fiction Writers of America early in 1978 complaining about suppression of their own work and the posthumous suppression of several of Yefremov's novels.

America, too, has seen calculated ideological replies. One of the most famous alien menace stories of the post-war period was Robert Heinlein's *The Puppet Masters* (1951), in which parasitic lumps of protoplasm invade Earth, assuming total command of human minds and bodies. Ted White's *By Furies Possessed* (1970) is a deliberate reaction to this—the lumps of protoplasm here are regarded with horror by the people of Earth, but are really symbiotes rather than parasites, turning their hosts into better people rather than puppets. Heinlein also wrote a space-war novel, *Starship Troopers* (1959), in which man is locked in a genocidal war whose battles range across vast interstellar territories; and though it is not an overt ideological reply, *The Forever War* (1975) by Joe Haldeman, presents a strongly-reminiscent scenario. At the end of the latter book it turns out that the war was a big mistake. In Heinlein's novel it is assumed that an alien species with a hive-mind is so biologically different from man that no hope exists for meaningful communication or for co-existence, but Haldeman's novel suggests that the human race might derive great benefits, not merely from peace but also from imitation. (Haldeman is a veteran of the Vietnam war. Heinlein graduated from the U.S. Naval Academy in 1929 and served on aircraft carriers until 1934, but was invalided out of the service without ever experiencing combat.)

What is perhaps most remarkable in the attitude to aliens in contemporary science fiction is the quasi-mystical significance often attached to the matters of communication and social intercourse. Several science fiction stories which deal with the erection and use of devices to receive and beam radio signals across interstellar distances are heavily impregnated with mystical awe, notably James Gunn's *The Listeners* (1972), in which the team of scientists seem embarked upon a spiritual quest, and in which the final victory over popular prejudice is sealed when a charismatic religious leader interprets a computer-decoded picture of one of the aliens as the image of an angel. Other examples are Robert Silverberg's *Tower of Glass* (1970), in which the communication device is compared to the Tower of Babel and its builder is unknowingly worshipped by his android workforce, and Arthur Clarke's *Imperial Earth* (1975). Mystical awe is also evident in such stories as Roger Zelazny's "A Rose for Ecclesiastes" (1963), in which a poet reignites the spiritual curiosity of the decadent Martians and saves them from extinction; Robert Silverberg's *Downward to the Earth*, in which the hero ultimately participates in alien religious experience and undergoes a spiritual and metamorphic rebirth; and George R. R. Martin's "A Song for Lya" (1974), another story about alien "parasites," this time offering a kind of immortality because they absorb the consciousness of their "victims" as well as their bodies, delivering the "soul" into a Nirvanic afterlife. Philip K. Dick also makes elaborate use of religious and mystical imagery in *Galactic Pot-Healer* (1969) and *Our Friends from Frolix-8* (1970).

Today the alien menace story is virtually extinct. The stories quoted above are the most exaggerated versions of a new attitude which is not only dominant but enjoys a virtual monopoly. When there are wars between men and aliens in contemporary science fiction they are matters of political dispute, not matters of biological inevitability. Their ends are not genocidal but settlement and the restoration of harmony. This is true even at the very bottom of the market, where the crudest hack fiction is produced. It is notable that even in the cinema, which thrived for many years on the alien menace plot, the mystical awe of first contact has enjoyed a significant breakthrough in the very popular *Close Encounters of the Third Kind* (1978) (which itself reflects the fact that on the lunatic fringe flying saucer mythology has been gradually infused with an optimistic mysticism which threatens to displace the traditional paranoia). Even in

117

the successful melodrama *Star Wars* (1977), there is a marked lack of biological chauvinism—the enemy is human and one of the heroes is a giant anthropoid ape.

This pattern of development in the role of the alien—which was not interrupted in the way that the pattern of development of machine roles was—has not been simply a matter of an older generation of writers being replaced by a new. No writer featured more genocides in his fiction than Edmond Hamilton, yet in 1962 he wrote "The Stars My Brothers," in which Earthmen visit a planet where humans are enslaved by reptilian masters, but who discover that the humans are non-sentient domestic animals, and then recognize that their true kinship is with the reptilian species, who have human minds if not human form. A less ambitious inversion was subsequently popularized by Pierre Boulle's *Monkey Planet* (1963) and its various film and TV spinoffs. Also in 1962 Hamilton wrote "Sunfire," in which an encounter with an alien being that lives in the sun's corona has all the force of a religious revelation in its effect upon a human astronaut. Other writers adjusted to the change in intellectual climate too, although as in the case of the robot, there were a few who had always endeavored to promote a more positive attitude, or had at least been willing to entertain one.

A good argument could be made for this change in attitude being reflective of changes in attitude in society at large. There has, in the real world, been a considerable advance in the cause of tolerance. Laws prohibiting racial discrimination have been passed both in America and in Britain, and the movements which seek to obliterate racial hatred are now dominant, whereas in the Twenties and Thirties their voices fell largely on deaf ears. As in the case of attitudes to machines, however, it seems that the attitude to aliens dominant in contemporary science fiction is somewhat ahead of this trend. It is not simply a matter of dramatization or symbolization: science fiction appears, by and large, to place a value on communication and cooperation that goes far beyond tolerance and racial harmony, seeming to affirm something much more ambitious.

It would, I think, be a mistake to construe the alien in science fiction simply as an exaggerated version of a man of another race. In many instances, the alien represents not merely someone who is different, but something unknown and unfathomable. In many cases we can draw a direct analogy between man/alien encounters in science fiction and real encounters between men of different colors or men of different political persuasions; but that analogy breaks down well before we can interpret most of the examples cited in this section. In many of the most impressive science fiction stories—and those which made the deepest and most lasting impression on their readers, if frequency of reprinting and award-winning are reliable guides to this—the man/alien encounter represents man's encounter with the unknown and the unknowable. It is the example *par excellence* of what Sheckley referred to in the essay in Chapter Two as "the search for the ineffable." Seen in this light, the heavy mysticism and prolific use of religious symbology in connection with man/alien encounters becomes much easier to understand. But if this interpretation is accepted then it becomes much harder to see the striking change in the role of the alien over the last fifty years as a straightforward reflection of attitudes in society.

In the science fiction of the Twenties and Thirties there was nothing implicitly mysterious about alien beings. They were simply organisms, attractive or repulsive, and sometimes tolerable in spite of their repulsiveness. Even in the Forties, when more serious attempts to imagine the sort of organisms that might develop in alien environments were made, the business of interaction with aliens was seen as a set of fairly straightforward biological and political problems.

As the situation changed in the Fifties, however, the problem of what might come out of the human/alien intercourse (now that the priority was very much on tolerance and communication) began to seem much more complex. One new aspect of the problem, hitherto unconsidered except at the most superficial level of swapping scientific information and technological expertise, was the question of what we might *learn* from contact with alien beings, about the universe at large or about ourselves. As noted in the last section, before the war the image of man had seemed perfectly secure. Faith in human ingenuity and intelligence was more or less unlimited. After the war, however, this faith was threatened and partially eroded, and this loss seems to have had a good deal to do with the new attitude to human/alien contacts and interactions. The attack on our habitual racial prejudices was only part (albeit a particularly prominent part) of a general assault on all assumptions about the way of the world. The new fascination for metaphysical themes and the many investigations of alien religion is, it seems to me, partly a response to the feeling of vulnerability which followed the explosion of the first atom bomb. The alien became much more important than mere biological speculation could ever have made him, as a result of this new uncertainty, because of his potential as a standard of comparison, and, in some cases, as a mentor.

Science fiction writers have never been particularly fascinated by alien societies as Utopian designs (though they have used them satirically on occasion), but from the early Fifties until the present day there has been an ever-increasing preoccupation with alien philosophies and ways of thinking. It is the alien *mind* which has interested writers in the last two decades, much more than his body or his social organization. It is now very common for aliens to be regarded as superior to man (despite the fact that Campbell, the most influential individual in the *genre*, was bitterly opposed to such a representation); and that superiority is almost invariably represented as consisting in a superior *wisdom*, not in superior scientific knowledge and technology. Even primitive aliens who have been conquered, exploited and persecuted by men are seen in very many stories to have something very valuable that we lack—an empathy with one another and a sense of harmony with their environment. Often they are portrayed as being possessed, one way or another, with a direct line to the ultimate cosmic mystery, however that may be imagined or suggested. Anderson's short story "The Martyr" is perhaps particularly clear in this regard: we no longer believe in our own immortal souls (or our own salvation, or our God, or our Heaven) but we are still able—and, what is more important, willing—to imagine aliens who have all these things in a perfectly literal sense. Sometimes, as in Silverberg's *Downward to the Earth*, humans can find these kinds of salvation too, if they are able and willing to *become* alien, but often they cannot.

A particularly striking example of this loss of confidence can be seen in the work of one of the most prolific transformers of religious symbology into the vocabulary of science fiction, Clifford D. Simak. In "Desertion" (1944), men find Heaven on Jupiter, and the whole human race chooses to undergo biological metamorphosis in order to live there. In "Seven Came Back" (1950), a human dying in the Martian desert is welcomed into the Martian Heaven, which lies in another dimension, as a reward for helping the natives against his less generous fellows. In *Time and Again* (1951), every living entity has an alien symbiote which survives the death of its host—a substitute for the soul. In more recent work, however, particularly in *A Choice of Gods* (1972) and *A Heritage of Stars* (1977), the quasi-religious goal of fusion with a kind of Cosmic Mind has become very distant, remote from the human characters who can do no more than glimpse its significance, and perhaps more accessible even to robots.

Science fiction today, in comparing men against the aliens which men very often meet in its imaginary *milieux*, shows a very strong sense of human limitations, which is often fatalistic and sometimes despairing. Science fiction writers are willing to imagine aliens possessed of all the existential advantages that men once thought they had or might aspire to, but which we no longer believe that we have, or can hope for. There is still a current of optimism which holds that the situation might change, but very often the envisaged price of our winning back these advantages is that of radical evolutionary change.

If we see these changes in the role of the alien in science fiction as a radical shift in the image of human beings *relative to* aliens, then it becomes much easier to tie in the nature of the shift with historical changes. We can, in fact, see the change as a response to (though not a simple reflection of) changes in our general awareness of our existential situation: the steady erosion of religious faith, the post-war lack of confidence in our ability to use our technology sensibly and constructively, and the corollary lack of confidence in the ability of our society to survive the disasters which threaten it.

3. SOCIETIES

The most obvious, and perhaps the most remarkable, change which has overtaken speculative fiction about the future during the last hundred years has been the replacement of the Utopian image of the future by a pessimistic image which has been dubbed, inevitably, "dystopian." In his book, *Image of the Future* (1973), Fred Polak sees this change as something which sets our age apart from all others. Throughout human history, he argues, Utopian and eschatological images of the future have given men goals by which to orient themselves within the pattern of history, giving them in both the literal and colloquial sense "something to look forward to," a sense of hope and a sense of purpose. He is quite at a loss to account for what has happened in the twentieth century:

> Today all images of the future, utopian and eschatological alike, have been driven into a corner and out of time. They appear to be the victims of a common conspiracy, and yet they themselves set in motion the processes of their own dissolution. The denaturing process first began with both of these movements. Why this strikingly parallel development in both eschatology and utopia? Is there a hidden factor at work which drives both images to self-destruction?
> The most remarkable aspect of this entire development is the blindness of our generation in regard to it. How is it possible that this abrupt breach in our times, occurring midway through the century and already challenging the future historian to find a new label for this period, goes unnoticed?....
> The rejection and destruction of old images of the future is not the basic phenomenon with which we are concerned. This is a historical process which has always gone on. The unique aspect of our present situation is the existence of a vacuum where the images had once been. There is a literal aversion to images of the future as such, whether of a natural or supernatural order. [13]

In quantitative terms Polak's final statement is clearly wrong. Literary images of the future are being produced now more prolifically than ever before, and the number of works of futuristic fiction produced each year has increased steadily since the 1870s. The decline of Utopian and Christian eschatological images over that period has left not an empty void, but a rapidly proliferating dystopian literature based on the assumption that the future is to be feared, because the probability is that it will be worse, not better, than the present. That this change reflects a genuine and growing anxiety within society is surely indubitable.

Dystopian images first began to appear in the last decades of the nineteenth century. Their appearance was logically inevitable following the shift in the characteristic form of Utopian social modelling from imaginary contemporary locales to imaginary futures. Once Utopian models ceased to be simply standards for comparison and began to be offered as social prospects and goals, the parallel expression of fears about social prospects was bound to follow. Where any vision of a future Utopia incorporated a manifesto for political action or ideological commitment, opponents of the political scheme or the ideology inevitably attempted to show that the "real" consequences would be horrific. Thus, stories about the wonderful world of equality which might be reached under socialism soon called forth visions of the oppressive and anti-individualistic socialist state. [14]

There was, however, more to the emergence of the dystopian image of the future than simple political differences of opinion. These were concerned with the way that the world *ought* to go. A much more basic difference of opinion arose as to which way the world actually *was* going.

It was virtually taken for granted in early nineteenth century thought that things were getting better, that social progress was a reality. Many nineteenth century Utopias are not simply visions of a possible future, but visions of the predestined future. When *that* faith came under threat, then the way was clear for a very profound change in the images of the future owned by ordinary members of society. It is possible to track this development through futuristic literature, and also possible to identify the thinking behind it. The background to the change was provided by certain developments in scientific theory which had considerable implications for the image of man.

There was in the nineteenth century a very close imaginative kinship between the notion of social progress and the notion of biological evolution. Both notions began—or at least achieved their first significant expression—in France. Lamarck saw biological evolution as many French social theorists saw social evolution, as a matter of progress from "elementary forms" toward a kind of perfection, motivated by a continuous striving on the part of organisms to "better themselves." However, when Darwin discovered and revealed the actual principles governing the evolution of biological species, he found them to be very different. He saw evolution as a matter of the survival of the fittest in the struggle for existence, in which adaptation was a matter of accident rather than strategy, and in which the concept of an evolutionary goal became meaningless and redundant. Inevitably (though quite without any logical warrant), this new notion of evolutionary process reflected back on social theory. Darwin had borrowed some of his notions from economists like Malthus and Ricardo, and some economists—notably Spencer—were glad to welcome their ideas back again, now sanctified as "natural law." The idea of the market held by the classical economists, with its competition and "adaptation" of production to meet demand, was very similar to Darwin's idea of the natural world. Whereas early sociologists like Comte had constructed elaborate models for the evolution of society through a series of predetermined phases, Spencer employed a very different mode of thought, making elaborate use of analogies between social organizations and biological organisms, and sharing many metaphors with Darwin.

The Enlightenment image of man as a rational and morally perfectible being was severely endangered by Darwin. Vulgar Darwinian thought saw man as an animal who had become the lord of creation by being a more effective killer than all his rivals, and there seemed to be no prospect of a reconciliation between the prescriptions of "Social Darwinism" and those of traditional morality, whether advanced on Christian or on humanist grounds. [15] The work of Freud offered a further threat to the humanist view of human nature, and these seeds of doubt spread rapidly within the popular imagination.

The first significant literary expression of the new pessimism was one of the replies to Bellamy's *Looking Backward*. While most reactions offered alternative views of the way that the socialist Utopia ought to be organized, Ignatius Donnelly in *Caesar's Column* (1890) flatly contradicted Bellamy's assumptions that this was the way the thrust of history was taking American society. He looked forward to a future in which the rich get steadily richer and the poor steadily more wretched, until the situation explodes in violence so drastic that society cannot survive.

This anxiety is nowhere better documented than in the work of the man who was ultimately to be left as the last of the Utopians: H. G. Wells. Wells desperately wanted to believe in the possibility of Utopia, and was extremely conscientious in continually revising his designs for a perfect state. He took objections far more seriously than any other Utopian designer, working through a whole series of prototypes before coming up with his final and definitive prospectus in *The Work, Wealth and Happiness of Mankind* (1932), coupled with a historical map showing the way by which it might be attained in *The Shape of Things to Come* (1933). His plans, however, were perpetually haunted by the idea that his contemporaries might be neither willing nor able to live up to his expectations. [16] No one could say that he did not try hard to persuade them and enlist their support—he personally interviewed both Stalin and Roosevelt and spoke in universities in many different countries—but he was never able to convince himself that he had succeeded. His last work of all, *Mind at the End of its Tether* (1945), not only gives passionate voice to his despair, but also, and perhaps more importantly, makes it abundantly clear why he thought that the world could never reach Utopia. The work is an essay in mystical Darwinism, asserting the failure of man to take command of his own destiny, and proclaiming that the inevitable corollary of that failure is extinction:

> The writer finds very considerable reason for believing that, within a period to be estimated by weeks

and months rather than by aeons, there has been a fundamental change in the conditions under which life, not simply human life but all self-conscious existence, has been going on since its beginning. This is a very startling persuasion to find establishing itself in one's mind, and he puts forward his conclusions in the certainty that they will be entirely inacceptable to the ordinary rational man.

If his thinking has been sound, then this world is at the end of its tether. The end of everything we call life is close at hand and cannot be evaded....

The writer sees the world as a jaded world devoid of recuperative power. In the past he has liked to think that Man could pull out of his entanglements and start a new creative phase of human living. In the face of our universal inadequacy, that optimism has given place to a stoical cynicism. The old men behave for the most part meanly and disgustingly, and the young are spasmodic, foolish and all too easily misled. Man must go steeply up or down and the odds seem all in favor of his going down and out. If he goes up, then so great is the adaptation demanded of him that he must cease to be a man. Ordinary man is at the end of his tether. Only a small, highly adaptable minority of the species can possibly survive....

But my own temperament makes it unavoidable for me to doubt, as I have said, that there will not be that small minority which will succeed in seeing life out to its inevitable end. [17]

Wells was seventy-nine when he wrote that, and he died the following year, but his decline into pessimism was not simply a corollary of his decline into old age, for the imaginative literature of the twentieth century shows much the same pattern of gathering and deepening pessimism and an escalating sense of the imminence of destruction.

By the time that Gernsback first published *Amazing Stories*, the decline of the Utopian image had already set in, but it had not advanced far. Only one of the classic dystopian novels had so far been published—Zamyatin's *We* (1924)—and that had passed virtually unnoticed. Scientifiction, of course, as Gernsback envisaged it, was an implicitly Utopian literature. Its most fundamental proposition was the notion that the advancement of science would remake the world, irrespective of any political and moral questions, for the benefit of all mankind. However, as pointed out in the first section of this chapter, it was not long before a certain anxiety began to creep in. The assumption of such stories as Breuer's *Paradise and Iron* and Campbell's pseudonymous "Twilight" was that, if things became too easy for men, then society might "stagnate" and become "sterile" in the absence of any urge to further improvement. A particularly vivid expression of the notion is found in "City of the Living Dead" (1930) by Fletcher Pratt and Laurence Manning, in which machines that can simulate any possible experience lead men to live their lives completely in pleasant dreams, cocooned within mechanical life-support systems, deserting the struggle for existence forever. In most stories of this type, however (Campbell's "Night" is an exception), it was assumed that some clear-sighted individuals would see the danger and rebel, finding humanity new challenges to face, or at least restoring the old ones.

Dystopian images of the future, however, began to appear more frequently in science fiction of the Forties, many of them being static, sterile societies in which a ruling elite preserves itself in power by means of a religious ideology. Notable examples include *If This Goes On...* (1940) by Robert Heinlein, *Gather, Darkness!* (1943) by Fritz Leiber, and *Renaissance*, also known as *Man of Two Worlds* (1944), by Raymond F. Jones. Other variants included futures in which the U.S.A. has been conquered, or in which the dereliction of the world by war has led to tyranny and oppression. All these stories were stories of rebellion, often by means of rather odd strategies—in *Gather Darkness!* the religious orthodoxy is smashed by a group who deliberately adopt the trappings of Satanism. The tyrannies are overthrown and democracy is restored—and with it, at least by implication, progress. This formula was, of course, well-suited to pulp fiction and invited extensive use.

After the war there was a curious change in this pattern which led to some quite bizarre literary works. The early Fifties produced a veritable flood of novels offering images of the near future in which American society has been "taken over" by some particular social group which is running the world according to its own priorities. Religious groups, of course, still were featured occasionally, but virtually everybody got their chance. The archetype of this particular subspecies is *The Space Merchants* (1953) by Frederik Pohl and Cyril M. Kornbluth, in which the world is run by advertising executives who use every trick in order to keep the wheels of commerce turning smoothly. Insurance companies run the world in *Preferred Risk* (1955) by "Edson McCann" (Frederik Pohl and Lester del Rey). Supermarkets run the world in *Hell's Pavement*, also known as *Analogue Men* (1955) by Damon Knight. Organized gangsterism prevails in *The Syndic* (1953) by Cyril Kornbluth. The medical profession is supreme in *Caduceus Wild* (1959) by Ward Moore and Robert Bradford. A cult of hedonists takes over in *The Joy Makers* (1955) by James E. Gunn. All these novels are really gaudy fakes, which use dystopian images for melodramatic convenience, setting up cardboard targets for their revolutionaries to knock down. In the early Fifties, magazine science fiction produced only one genuine dystopian vision with any real imaginative power: Ray Bradbury's *Fahrenheit 451* (1954), about the career of a fireman whose job is burning books, in a society where ordinary citizens are discouraged from thinking and kept free from all stimuli to thought. This is remarkable when one recalls that outside the magazines dystopian fiction was flourishing as never before, producing some of the most intense nightmares ever envisioned: Orwell's *Nineteen Eighty-Four* (1949), Kurt Vonnegut's *Player Piano* (1953), David Karp's *One* (1953), and, in a slightly later period, L. P. Hartley's *Facial Justice* (1960) and Anthony Burgess's *A Clockwork Orange* (1962). There were, in addition, a number of scathing black comedies: Aldous Huxley's *Ape and Essence* (1949), Evelyn Waugh's *Love Among the Ruins* (1953), and Bernard Wolfe's *Limbo* (1953).

This fashion in science fiction novels was still very prominent in 1957, when a series of lectures by science fiction writers on the science fiction novel as social criticism was offered at the University of Chicago. The opinion of the four writers was that science fiction had very little to offer in the way of social criticism as such. One interesting commentary was that provided by Robert Bloch, who claimed that the failure of portwar science fiction in this regard was largely attributable to the over-reliance of writers on the role of the hero. (It is, of course, implicit in the formulae of pulp fiction that everything revolves around this central role.)

In his lecture, Bloch pointed out that the future society employed by the majority of recent science fiction novels was itself put together according to a standard recipe, observing that:

> In general, we can count on some—or all—of the following ingredients:
>
> 1. A TOTALITARIAN STATE. Maybe it's ruled by Big Business, or Advertising, or a new Religious Center. It can be controlled by Mass Psychologists or Super-Criminals, or even by Quiz-Masters. The ingenuity of our novelists and the logic of their extrapolations are often very intriguing. But almost inevitably, they think of the future in terms of a military dictatorship, complete with force and espionage.
>
> 2. Secondly....the UNDERGROUND....mainly the Underground is represented as a revolutionary movement, governed within its own ranks by a totalitarian order as strict—or stricter—than the one it opposes....
>
> 3. Thirdly, we find the dominance of FORCIBLE PSYCHOTHERAPEUTIC TECHNIQUES....Where would the science fiction novel of tomorrow be without "brain-washing"?....
>
> 4. Also standard is the assumption that SCIENCE WILL GO ALONG WITH THE GAG and obediently wash brains for Capital, Labor, the Military, the Clergy or

whatever group is posited as being in power. In fact, the whole fabric of all these novels hangs by a single thread—that scientists will always be willing to bend their backs over the washboard in a brain-laundry—that they will labor unthinkingly and unceasingly to produce new techniques, new technological advances and new weapons for the use of the group currently in power.

5.   This in turn seems to be based upon another standard assumption—that in the future ECONOMIC INCENTIVE will still reign supreme....

6.   A variation of PRESENT-DAY "ANGLO-SAXON" CULTURE will continue to rule the world....

7.   Furthermore, if the inhabitants of Earth ever reach other planets and discover life there, WE WILL COLONIZE AND RULE THE NATIVES....

8.   The ultimate assumption, actually the sum total of the rest, is simply that THE FUTURE HOLDS LITTLE BASIC CHANGE....

9.   It is almost unnecessary to add a minor point which runs through these considerations: INDIVIDUALISM IS DEAD. The hero rebels, yes—but not to superimpose his own notions upon society; merely to restore the "normal" culture and value-standards of the mass-minds of the twentieth century. [18]

With the exception of one important element, which I will discuss in due course, this is a reasonably accurate summary of the recipe for a magazine science fiction novel of the Fifties. Bloch's scorn did not prevent him from adding later in his speech that if he were ever to write a science fiction novel he would play safe and follow the formula—and, indeed, he did, in *Sneak Preview* (1959).

Although Bloch considered the whole recipe which he recounted so carefully to be quite banal, there are, in fact, two important elements in it which, though familiar in 1957, were virtually unknown in the pre-war period. These were points three and four. Point three is the assumption that people are basically manipulable, and can be made to think what people in authority want them to think (this is intimately bound up with the image of a host of alternative futures as many variants of a confidence game). Point four is the assumption that science will be used by already-dominant power groups to serve their own ends. Bloch seems to have considered the latter assumption unlikely, but in view of the historical circumstances of the time, this judgment is harsh. The world had seen the efforts of German science exploited by Hitler—and had seen, in the aftermath of the war, the German scientists shared out between two new masters and put immediately to work. America had seen nuclear scientists suffer pricks of conscience, and had noted that many of them carried on regardless, protected by a security blanket that came down after the leakage of atomic secrets to Russia.

These two assumptions, concealed to some extent by the ingeniously colorful apparatus of the future societies of Fifties science fiction, represented a considerable shift in the attitude to the future underlying science fiction. The change in attitude did not—as it did outside the magazines—result in an immediate decline into outright pessimism, but rather in a peculiar compromise with the dictates of pulp convention. Most science fiction stories were still success stories, but now the success had to be won against the threat of a sinister future, against the machinations of the scientists of the future, and against the odds. The Gernsbackian future of unlimited opportunity and technological benefits for all mankind was now a thing of the past.

There is, however, one inaccuracy in Bloch's summary which suggests that the compromise with pulp convention was more comfortable than it actually was. Bloch points out, correctly, that the goal of the hero in this kind of fiction was always to restore "normal" cultural values—the standard of normality being decided by the values of the time. What he does not point out is that the failure rate of the heroes to attain this end is, for a popular *genre*, astonishing. These novels are all stories of rebellion and usually of revolution, but in very few instances can the world actually be saved. What happens in most instances —and certainly in the most famous examples—is a piece of literary sleight-of-hand which sidesteps the manifest goal in favor of a different one which *is* achieved: not salvation, but *escape*.

A key symbol in many of these stories is the spaceship. Usually the reader knows nothing of this at the beginning of the book, but discovers toward the end (with a shock of revelation) that though the revolution is doomed there is still hope. The hero and other right-thinking people can blast off, leaving the whole sad and sorry mess behind, to begin a new life on a new world, where life may be very hard but culturally "normal."

This loophole came from the vocabulary of conventions built up by pre-war science fiction, and it is hardly surprising that the dystopian novels written outside the labelled *genre* made no use of it. It enabled the magazine writers, by and large, to get off the hook by allowing them to write stories that were pessimistic about the tide of history while retaining their uplifting and morale-boosting finales. *The Space Merchants* provides the perfect example of this sleight-of-hand. The importance of the spaceship as a quasi-supernatural symbol of hope in this period is demonstrated by several stories which celebrate in quasi-mystical fashion (and often in lyrical tones) the launching of the first rocket or starship: Cyril M. Kornbluth's *Takeoff* (1952), and Fredric Brown's *The Lights in the Sky are Stars*, also known as *Project Jupiter* (1953). Perhaps the clearest example of all is provided by Isaac Asimov's *The End of Eternity* (1955), in which a history-controlling superstate is subverted so that mankind can expand into space. The last lines of the novel read: "With that disappearance, he knew....came the end, the final end of Eternity—and the beginning of Infinity."

The decline and extinction of this compromise pattern at the end of the Fifties came about through a combination of circumstances. The real space program made the hopes and expectations of fictitious space programs a good deal less credible. The rapid decline of the magazines and the corresponding rise of paperback books as the principal medium of science fiction helped to set aside the restrictions of pulp convention in the "upper strata" of the market. Most important of all, however, was the fact that the public, like Bloch, grew accustomed to the new image of the future. It came to be taken for granted that the future would be difficult; science fiction writers found that it was no longer necessary to write about the problems of trying to change or escape from the society of the future, but that there was enough potential for a success story simply in writing about how to survive in it.

The science fiction of the Sixties and Seventies, insofar as it is concerned with the society of the future, was mainly concerned with estimating the nature of the disaster. In the late Fifties science fiction belatedly discovered Malthus, and for a while images of overpopulation displaced images of atomic holocaust as the major expressions of apprehension. In the late Sixties the pollution crisis added its own fears. In the early Seventies resource crises suddenly became fashionable as well. Once one accepted that the future would be worse than the present, there was no difficulty at all in finding reasons to support that belief.

Once released, the tendency of many science fiction writers towards anguished pessimism soon found lurid expression. Among the most impressive horror stories whose key theme is overpopulation are *Make Room! Make Room!* (1966) by Harry Harrison, *Stand on Zanzibar* (1968) by John Brunner, "The People Trap" (1968) by Robert Sheckley, and *The World Inside* (1971) by Robert Silverberg. [19] Pollution is the principal destructive force in "We All Die Naked" (1969) by James Blish, *The Sheep Look Up* (1972) by John Brunner, *The End of the Dream* by Philip Wylie, and "The Big Space Fuck" (1972) by Kurt Vonnegut [20] Few stories deal with resource crises alone; it has simply become an additional factor in the logic that sees the future human condition as one of acute deprivation. Another factor which has received special consideration is Alvin Toffler's notion of "future shock"—stress disease caused by an inability to cope with the pace of change—which is explored in *The Shockwave Rider* (1975) by John Brunner.

This fiction was, of course, fed—and the audience for it partly created—by a wave of futurological speculations. The population problem was first popularized by such writers as Paul Ehrlich, and the pollution scare by Rachel Carson's *Silent Spring* (1962). There is no doubt that to a large extent these stories are reflecting waves of anxiety which have passed through society as a whole, but they also represent a response to it. It is hardly surprising that the response fits in very well with the pattern we have already noted in connection with the role of the alien, reflecting a very considerable lack of faith in our ability to solve, or even cope, with these problems. There are numerous stories forecasting the end of the world which take a malicious delight in contemplation of these crises. Such tales as "The People Trap" and "The Big Space Fuck" are as black as black comedies can be. It is interesting to note that both "The Big Space Fuck" and "We All Die Naked" also take special pleasure in mocking the escape-into-space *motif* which had been, in an earlier period, so intimately associated with dystopian visions in science fiction.

It is worth pointing out that the rapid proliferation of dystopian novels in the literary "mainstream" during the Fifties was not sustained into the late Sixties and Seventies. Although science fictional disaster themes have been prominent in the mainstream of late, there have been very few dystopian images. Only Michael Frayn's *A Very Private Life* (1968), Adrian Mitchell's *The Bodyguard* (1970), and Ira Levin's *This Perfect Day* (1970) seem worthy of note, and none of these has had the imaginative force of the earlier post-war works. Because the dystopian image has become ordinary, writers in the mainstream can no longer wring from it the intensity of feeling that they once could. Science fiction writers have made the idea work for them primarily because their main interest is in the mechanics of the tragedy rather than the tragic quality itself.

Insofar as it still holds to pulp convention and functions as restorative fantasy, science fiction has been driven out of the imaginative space of the near future. Future Earth figured very prominently in the great majority of pre-war science fiction stories, but in a great many post-war stories it is hardly even mentioned, with the action confined to entirely imaginary settings. One of the longest-running exotic adventure stories in contemporary science fiction, E. C. Tubb's "Dumarest Saga," is built around its hero's search for an Earth forgotten by all mankind and mislaid by all mapmakers. In many other adventures set in an imaginary galactic civilization, Earth is a dead world, having been ruined in the remote past. The kind of galactic culture first shown to good advantage in Isaac Asimov's *Foundation Trilogy* (1942-49) has become a standard background in post-war science fiction; but this is not, as Donald Wollheim suggests in *The Universe Makers*, because this is the way the future is going to be, or even because it is the way that science fiction writers think the future is going to be, but simply because Earth is no longer a viable setting for romances of the future which require a gaudy, glittering, and pseudo-Utopian *milieu*.

Utopian thought during the last half-century has to a large extent dissociated itself from the mythology of progress, and has found expression primarily in terms of a technological retreat to a simpler way of life. This pattern is clear in virtually all the Utopian novels which came after *The Shape of Things to Come*: *Lost Horizon* (1933) by James Hilton, *Islandia* (1942) by Austin Tappan Wright, *Seven Days in New Crete*, also known as *Watch the Northwind Rise* (1949) by Robert Graves, *Island* (1962) by Aldous Huxley, and *In Watermelon Sugar* (1970) by Richard Brautigan. B. F. Skinner's *Walden Two* (1948) pins its hopes not on technology but on psychological training. In Herman Hesse's *Magister Ludi*, also known as *The Glass Bead Game* (1943), the hero eventually rejects the Utopian claims of his society, and even in Franz Werfel's *Star of the Unborn* (1946), there is a great deal of doubt, both practical and ethical, about the viability of the theologically sound Utopian state.

Attempts by *genre* science fiction writers to imagine ideal states have been similarly ambiguous. The Utopian state of Theodore Sturgeon's *Venus Plus X* (1960) is ultimately rejected by the story's protagonist. Ursula K. Le Guin's *The Dispossessed* (1974) carries the subtitle "An Ambiguous Utopia," and imagines its anarchist state surviving only in conditions of extreme deprivation. Samuel R. Delany's *Triton* (1976), in response, is subtitled "An Ambiguous Heterotopia," and presents a picture of a society which, in theory, caters for all possible ideals, but which is still ravaged by war and which still leaves the hero searching fruitlessly for some kind of fulfillment. Even the writers who have been most dogmatic in their insistence on the beneficence of technological progress, Isaac Asimov and Arthur C. Clarke, have managed to give no real Utopian expression to their hopes, with the exception of Clarke's self-conscious *Imperial Earth* (1975). A more powerful image from Clarke's earlier work is the city of Diaspar in *The City in the Stars* (1956), a technological miracle whose inhabitants have become listless and decadent. Asimov's most memorable images of future Earth are the dystopian society of *Pebble in the Sky* (1950) and the claustrophilic society of *The Caves of Steel* (1954). The one exception to this generalization is Mack Reynolds, whose work includes a whole series of tales set in a Utopian state of the year 2000, which are openly didactic. The first two volumes deliberately echo Edward Bellamy—*Looking Backward from the Year 2000* (1973) and *Equality in the Year 2000* (1977)—but later volumes in the series, especially *Perchance to Dream* (1978) and *After Utopia* (1978), show the gradual return of an insidious pessimism recalling that of Manning and Pratt's "City of the Living Dead." Even in Eastern Europe, where Utopianism is not only ideologically sound but to some extent ideologically favored, the lead given by Ivan Yefremov's *Andromeda* (1959) has not been followed up. Images of future Earth in the work of the brothers Strugatsky—e.g., *The Final Circle of Paradise* (1965)—show a dystopian anxiety comparable to that evident in western science fiction, while the work of Stanislaw Lem is either set elsewhere in the cosmos or deals in heavy-handed satire.

Nevertheless, there are in contemporary science fiction many images of society which give powerful expression to a yearning for some kind of ideal social organization. All these images are of alien society, or at least of human societies adapted to alien circumstances and fundamentally altered in nature. The archetypal example of this kind of exercise is *Out of the Silent Planet* (1938) by C. S. Lewis, which is from outside the science fiction community and from a different period; but it is in the last ten or fifteen years that science fiction writers have become especially preoccupied with alien societies and with the notion that alien societies might have something essential that human society lacks, and perhaps must always lack.

Two of the most popular science fiction novels of recent years have been Frank Herbert's *Dune* (1965), with its picture of life among the desert-dwelling Fremen of Arrakis, and Ursula K. Le Guin's *The Left Hand of Darkness* (1969), with its account of life on the planet Winter, whose inhabitants are hermaphrodite. Neither of these novels is Utopian, but each finds in the description of its imaginary society some key element which adds significantly to the quality of life within them. There are similar glimpses of the superior quality of alien ways of life in many other novels, including Robert Silverberg's *Downward to the Earth* (1970), Ursula K. Le Guin's *The Word for World is Forest* (1972), and George R. R. Martin's *Dying of the Light* (1977). It is perhaps most explicit in James Tiptree Jr.'s parable "The Milk of Paradise" (1972), in which a human child brought up by mud-wallowing bestial aliens finds a serenity and a feeling of belonging which he cannot find anywhere in human society.

There are several different suggestions as to the nature of the vital "missing ingredient," but they all boil down to some mysterious kind of *rapport* between individuals that human beings experience only rarely. It is not so much sympathy as empathy, and not so much love as trust. (In Heinlein's *Stranger in a Strange Land* the missing *rapport* is referred to as "grokking," and this word was, for a while, taken up by some members of the American "counter-culture.") In many stories this empathy is associated with the notion of telepathy.

A particularly significant change in attitude related to this point is that involving the notion of "hive-minds." The most obvious model available to us of a radically different mode of social organization is, of course, the ant-hive, and this was used by Wells for the first-ever study of alien society in *The First Men in the Moon* (1901). The notion then was repellent, and it continued to be so for many years. The notion of a human hive-society was employed as a nightmare in Joseph O'Neill's anti-Fascist dystopia, *Land Under England* (1935), and in John Beresford and Esmé Wynne-Tyson's dystopia *The Riddle of the Tower* (1944). An alien hive-society is featured in Robert A. Heinlein's *Starship Troopers* (1959) as an enemy with whom no reconciliation is possible. During the Sixties, however, the notion was to some extent rehabilitated. The insect hive-mind in Frank Herbert's *The Green Brain* (1966) is benevolent, protecting the world's ecology against the short-sighted policies of man; and Herbert went on to consider the possibility of human hive-society in a moderately open-minded fashion in *Hellstrom's Hive* (1973).

As previously noted, Joe Haldeman contradicted the basic assumption of *Starship Troopers* in *The Forever War* (1975). The powerful fascination of the hive-mind is also evident in Barrington J. Bayley's "The Bees of Knowledge" (1975). [21]

The preoccupation with the Utopian aspects of alien society is, of course, no more than the other side of the coin whose face is the preoccupation with the dystopian aspects and prospects of our own society. It is further testimony to the extent to which the role of the alien in science fiction reflects our dissatisfaction with ourselves. In many of these stories the protagonists can find a kind of "success" in "going native," but there is perhaps nothing quite as pessimistic as the ready acceptance of such a wholly illusory answer. In a great deal of contemporary science fiction it is presumed that the only way to escape the predicament of the near future will be to *become something different*. It is perhaps a good measure of our desperate need to find more hope than is readily available to us that there are so many science fiction stories which present the accomplishment of this hope. This can be very clearly seen in the historical development of the role of the evolved man—the superman.

4. SUPERMEN

In the same way that evolutionary theory provided the imaginative context for the development of the concept and role of the alien, so it governed the invention of and attitudes to the superman. The implications of Darwinism were very important in generating early attitudes to literary supermen, encouraging writers to think of the mutant superman as a threat to *Homo sapiens*, a competitor and a nemesis. Darwin's, however, was not the only evolutionary philosophy of the day, and it is possible in some works to see the influence of Bergson and, of course, of Nietzsche.

The superman, by definition, is the species which will ultimately replace mankind; and thus there are a number of early stories in which ordinary men fight a desperate rearguard action against lone supermen, hoping to buy themselves a few extra millennia of evolutionary lifetime. An example from outside the science fiction *genre* is Noëlle Roger's *The New Adam* (1926), while early stories from the magazines on this theme are John Russell Fearn's *The Intelligence Gigantic* (1933), and Stanley G. Weinbaum's "The Adaptive Ultimate" (1936). These stories, however, are isolated examples, for the dominant attitude to the superman was very different. The reason is that most of the writers who produced early superman stories were harshly critical of contemporary human society, and the superman provided a ready made mouthpiece for their criticisms. Thus we find both the Darwin-inspired Wells in *The Food of the Gods* (1903) and the Bergson-inspired J. D. Beresford in *The Hampdenshire Wonder* (1911) very much allied with their supermen, though unable to

133

identify with them. Olaf Stapledon, in *Odd John* (1936), took this pattern to its extreme, while Claude Houghton's *This Was Ivor Trent* (1935) reveals in its conclusion an almost hysterical bitterness.

The traits in human nature of which these authors and their supermen were critical were fairly conventional targets: prejudice, narrow-mindedness, and unjustified beliefs (particularly religious ones). The one point on which the authors consistently differed in attitude from their creations was in the matter of emotion. Virtually all these early supermen were passionless creatures whose minds were capable of great feats of objective analysis of scientific and social problems, but their creators remained uncertain as to whether this was really a desirable way to be.

Most writers took care to dispose of their supermen when the scathing criticism ran out. The Hampdenshire Wonder was drowned in infancy, while Odd John allowed himself and several of his kin to be destroyed as a gesture of his disgust for common humanity. One of the few writers who looked forward confidently to the triumph of the superman was George Bernard Shaw in *Back to Methuselah* (1921), but the key to this enthusiasm is to be found in the prologue, in which Shaw renounces Darwinism in favor of neo-Lamarckism. It is much easier to be a wholehearted advocate of the superman if you believe that by striving to be one you can eventually become one, and the idea had such powerful attractions that even the diehard Darwinian Wells toyed with it briefly in *Star-Begotten* (1937).

The early science fiction pulps had little time for social criticism, and thus we find straight superman-as-menace plots like *The Intelligence Gigantic* alongside a rather curious but oft-repeated *motif* which represented humanity's evolved successors as a decadent and far *less fit* species. This theme used an image of the evolved man derived according to the logic of Wells' essay, "The Man of the Year Million" (1893), portraying the man of the future as a being with a vast cranium and a wasted body. Many science fiction writers, blissfully unaware of the Darwinian illogic of their case, saw this development as a well-set evolutionary trend with no survival value. In such stories as Harry Bates' "Alas, All Thinking!" (1935), these "supermen" become extinct.

A more melodramatic superman story is John Taine's mutational romance *Seeds of Life* (1931), which presents its superman as a figure of menace, who tries to destroy the world and comes to a very nasty end, and yet retains a note of sympathy. There is also a note of sympathy in Weinbaum's "The Adaptive Ultimate" (1936). Weinbaum was already dead when that story appeared, and among the manuscripts he left behind was his *magnum opus*, a superman story called *The New Adam*, which was finally published in 1939. It was published as a book and was not reprinted in magazines until 1943, largely because it represented a significant break with pulp formula. The novel is not only sympathetic to the superman, but offers the superman as protagonist for reader-identification. It consists of a biography, an analytical account of a "superhuman" viewpoint which is not fueled by the desire to criticize contemporary society, but the desire to investigate hypothetically what a superhuman viewpoint might be like. Use is made of the analogy of feral children—the superman reared by humans grows up knowing that his rearing has in some sense crippled him, so that he cannot attain his full potential. In the end, he arranges his own death, but leaves behind a child with a mother of his own kind.

The New Adam had little impact despite Weinbaum's popularity in the science fiction community, but it was not long before two novels appeared in the pulps which broke the old pattern decisively. *Slan* (1940) by A. E. van Vogt and *Darker Than You Think* (1940) by Jack Williamson both offered heroic supermen as protagonists. In the former, the young hero is persecuted because of the stigmatizing mark which shows him to be a latent superman; he grows slowly into his super-powers in order to win, though the hand of every man is turned against him. In the latter, the hero sets out to fight a second species of the genus *Homo* which threatens *H. sapiens*, but discovers that he is one of the other race himself, and accepts the dictates of his genes. There is no compromise in these stories—the reader is expected to identify with the superman in each case, and there is no question of his final demise, because human society cannot accommodate him. Both stories became "classics" of the *genre*, and both writers found it profitable to repeat the formula. Williamson repeated it only once, in *Dragon's Island* (1951), but van Vogt has done so many times. At least a dozen of his novels and stories involve apparently-ordinary human beings who develop awesome super-powers in order to contend with threats to themselves or to the world. [22] It is significant that van Vogt abandoned writing for some years while he ran one of L. Ron Hubbard's Dianetics Foundations—Dianetics (later Scientology) transformed this fantasy into a pseudo-scientific theory, and then into a religion.

The hero superman—especially the superman whose powers developed in the course of the plot, or the superman whose powers had to be kept secret because of persecution—rapidly became established as a science fiction cliché. Two science fiction fans, Jerome Siegel and Joe Schuster, stripped the theme to its basics for development in the new comic-strip medium, and established with their character Superman a pattern which has dominated the American comic book ever since.

The basic psychological appeal of the fantasy is easy enough to appreciate. There is perhaps no fantasy more comforting or more pleasing than the notion that the weak and unprepossessing character one presents to the world hides a person of great dynamism and almost-infinite capability. It is especially attractive to children, who are implicitly weak and lacking in any real power. Whether Hubbard (who wrote what may well be the earliest example of the species in "The Tramp," published in *Astounding* in 1938) simply saw the potential of the notion or genuinely fell for it himself is uncertain; but he certainly found that telling people they could become supermen with a little help from him was an excellent way to make money. Another man who found massive popular support for his ideas was the parapsychologist J. B. Rhine, whose experiments to detect ESP at Duke University were first written up in *New Frontiers of the Mind* (1937). Rhine provided a new image of the superman—someone outwardly ordinary but possessed of one or more extra-sensory perceptions: telepathy or precognition. Later he began looking for evidence of psychokinetic ability, and lumped all these "talents" together under the heading of *psi* powers. According to Rhine, anyone might have these powers latent within him, waiting only to be brought to the surface by pressure of circumstance or training.

Stories of *psi*-powered supermen became very common in the science fiction of the late Forties, and Campbell became so fond of them that for a period in the early Fifties they virtually displaced all other types of fiction from *Astounding*. Notable examples of the species include Henry Kuttner and C. L. Moore's "Baldy" series (1945 as by Lewis Padgett), Wilmar H. Shiras' *Children of the Atom* (1948-50), Zenna Henderson's stories of "The People" (1952-66), Wilson Tucker's *Wild Talent* (1954), and a trilogy of novels by Randall Garrett and Laurence Janifer written under the name "Mark Phillips" (1959-61). All of these stories were wholeheartedly pro-supermen, although there were a number of stories in which good supermen had to fight and destroy evil supermen who wanted to take over the world. James Blish's *Jack of Eagles* (1951) and George O. Smith's *Highways in Hiding* (1956) belong to this class, as does Frank M. Robinson's *The Power* (1956). In the latter case the plot develops as a straightforward menace story, the hero's super-ness only developing at the last moment to provide a *deus ex machina*. The everyone-can-be-superman myth reached its height in *Brain Wave* (1954) by Poul Anderson, in which the Earth passes out of a warp in space which has damped human intelligence throughout history, and even idiots and dogs acquire genius practically overnight.

It was not long, however, before the role of the superman began to acquire overtones which went somewhat beyond the requirements of simple power-fantasy. The change is particularly noticeable in the work of two writers: Theodore Sturgeon and Charles L. Harness, both of whom have specialized to an inordinate extent in superman stories. Sturgeon's "Maturity" (1947) is a story about a gifted child crippled with acromegaly who is helped medically to develop his talents to the full. When he becomes "normal," however, he gives up much of his creative endeavor in favor of socializing—once his alienating condition is overcome there is no need for him to be a superman any longer. In "...And My Fear is Great" (1953), an old lady trains a youth to exploit his talent, but tries to isolate him from all human contact in the process. Eventually he rebels, and discovers that the alienation is not necessary. In the classic *More than Human* (1953), a group of social misfits, each with some odd talent that is of little use in isolation, combine to form a *gestalt* individual and grow slowly to mature command of their powers and a sense of social responsibility, whereupon they are greeted into a community of group minds. In "To Marry Medusa," expanded as *The Cosmic Rape* (1958), an alien entity equipped with a group mind attempts to unite the minds of the human race so that it can absorb them; but once united the human group-mind has such awesome power that it absorbs the invader. The plot of the story focuses on the way that a number of extremely alienated individuals have their painful lives made purposeful (if only through their dying) in the formation of the super-entity. Many more of Sturgeon's stories feature characters in states of extreme alienation who transcend their condition in acquiring the power to unite with their fellows. [23] In the earlier work the transcendence is metaphorical, but in the later work it becomes extremely literal.

The theme of transcendence is central to Charles L. Harness's first three novels, *Flight into Yesterday*, also known as *The Paradox Men* (1949), *The Rose* (1953), and *The Ring of Ritornel* (1968). All three feature climaxes in which the central characters achieve a kind of transcendental metamorphosis *via* death into some kind of superbeing. The most explicit is the highly stylized finale of *The Rose*, in which a ballerina is transformed into an angelic being. Although the story could not find a market in America at the time of its writing and was published in a minor British magazine, it has since acquired a considerable reputation.

The most dramatic single illustration of the pattern which emerged during the Fifties is Arthur C. Clarke's *Childhood's End* (1954), which is probably the best-known book ever to appear under the science fiction label. In this novel alien "overlords" assume command of Earth's destiny and bring about a Utopian period of calm. Their true mission, however, is to act as "midwives" to the human race, so that an entire generation of children may associate their minds into a single unit, which then leaves its material base to fuse with the "cosmic mind." The Overlords are making their second attempt to achieve this end, their first having gone wrong and resulted in various unpleasant myths and legends correlated with their physical form, which is that of the devil in Medieval art.

Clarke denies that there is any religious symbolism in this novel, and objects to the interpretation of the events of the story in terms of religious symbology. It is, however, difficult for the observer not to see in the Overmind of the story a secular version of God, and the climactic event certainly invites at least a metaphorical description as an apotheosis. The analogy has not been lost on certain theological scholars who have taken an interest in science fiction. Eric Hopkins, writing in the Journal of the Epiphany Philosophers, *Theoria to Theory*, discusses *More than Human* and *Childhood's End* in an essay entitled "New Maps of Heaven." Of the former novel he says:

The story *More than Human* can be regarded as a response

to the general feeling of insecurity felt by many today. The response is the fantasy of a man, or group of men, who is virtually invulnerable to disaster. And such fantasies spring from our anxiety, our sense of helplessness, incompetence, the unbridgeable gulf between our demands for survival and any source of effective action. As the starving dreams of banquets so we, in fantasy, are transformed into omnicompetent supermen. [24]

Childhood's End, he thinks, goes even further:

Clarke is taking the religious view that man and his institutions are intrinsically defective. Even if God gave man a utopia man's condition would remain unsatisfactory. In his symbolism utopias, however acceptable, are the gifts of the devils whose real function in the scheme of things is that of enabling intelligent beings to leave earthly things behind, to destroy their utopias. Clarke's "message" is that, though an earthly paradise is desirable, it is only a stage towards the final consummation, the end of childhood, which is union with God. [25]

This "message" is certainly *not* what Clarke intended to convey. His intention was simply to explore a hypothesis—and, for that matter, one which was not congenial. Clarke was an urgent propagandist for the space program, yet *Childhood's End* embodies the dictum that "the stars are not for man" (his destiny being a "higher" one). For this reason the novel carries an emphatic note saying: "The opinions expressed in this work are not those of the author." [26] *Childhood's End*, therefore, cannot be read as an allegory—yet the parallels with aspects of Christian mythology remain; and one is strongly tempted by the hypothesis that if what happens in the story is not intended to *represent* the ideas of Christian mythology, then it is in some sense an ideative substitute for them.

A particularly striking parallel can be seen between *Childhood's End* and the ideas developed in a book published the following year—*The Phenomenon of Man* by the French Jesuit, Pierre Teilhard de Chardin. Teilhard attempted to reconcile his scientific knowledge (he was a paleontologist) with his religious faith by developing a cosmic scheme of evolution in which the sentient minds of man form a "realm of thought" called the noösphere (by analogy with the biosphere). In Teilhard's scheme the noösphere becomes unified into an organized whole by a process of "megasynthesis." This can happen because of the influence of an organizing force or principle called Omega, and in the fullness of time all noöspheres become one with the principle at the Omega Point.

There is no doubt about Teilhard's intentions: what he wanted to do was to build a mythology that would confirm Christian teaching and render it viable in the context of modern scientific knowledge and natural philosophy. His ideas were never recognized as orthodox and were published only after his death. There is one science fiction novel based explicitly on Teilhard's cosmology—George Zebrowski's *The Omega Point* (1973)—and A. E. van Vogt has borrowed from Teilhard's terminology on occasion (notably in *Supermind* [1977]); but the direct influence of Teilhard on science fiction has been slight. Nevertheless, the notions contained within his work are persistently echoed in science fiction in the same way that they are echoed in *Childhood's End*. The idea of a cosmic mind or principle recurs throughout the recent work of Clifford D. Simak, and the notion is explicitly associated with the role of the ESP superman in *The Uncensored Man* (1964) by Arthur Sellings, *The Infinite Cage* (1972) by Keith Laumer, and *Tetrasomy Two* (1975) by Oscar Rossiter. The "moment of apotheosis" provides the climactic *motif* for both of the last-named novels. It is difficult to believe that there is nothing in this parallelism except, as Clarke has contended, "pure coincidence." [27]

The extension of the role of the superman in science fiction to contain these images of transcendence is also seen in the work of Alfred Bester, again in novels which are among the most popular works to bear this label. In *The Demolished Man* (1953), a psychopathic murderer subject to terrible visions is trapped by a telepathic police force and forced to undergo "demolition"—a process of psychic cleansing which frees him from his visions and their cause (a burden of guilt), and releases him, fully healed, to begin his life anew. In *The Stars My Destination*, also known as *Tiger! Tiger!* (1956), the central character is trapped in a burning building and moves back through time to appear to himself and to others as a fire-shrouded vision, being similarly "cleansed" in the process, and eventually finding a kind of peace in an interplanetary limbo. In Bester's third, less well-received novel, *The Computer Connection*, also known as *Extro* (1974), a group of supermen attempt to recruit others by the only means known to them—induced metamorphosis *via* violent death.

In the last ten years this tendency toward the science-fictionalization of ideas associated with Christian mythology has continued and become more obvious, usually, but not exclusively, in connection with the notion of the superman. Literal survival of the *persona* after death is featured in *Camp Concentration* (1969) by Thomas M. Disch, *Traitor to the Living* (1969) and the "Riverworld" series (begun 1965) by Philip José Farmer, and in two novels by Robert A. Heinlein: *I Will Fear No Evil* (1971) and *Time Enough for Love* (1973). The notion of superhumanity is coupled with the idea of rebirth in many works by Robert Silverberg, including *To Open the Sky* (1967), *Nightwing* (1970), *The Second Trip* (1971), *Son of Man* (1971), *The Book of Skulls* (1972), and "Born With the Dead" (1974). Silverberg has also written a novel which presents the rebirth *motif* in terms of the decline and loss of a superhuman power, *Dying Inside* (1972).

It is difficult, having identified the common theme which

unites so many of the post-war science fiction stories dealing with superhuman "evolution," to avoid the conclusion reached by Eric Hopkins, who claims that:

> What these SF writers are doing is using the language of modern technologies and disciplines—rocketry, cybernetics, sociology, psychology, parapsychology, mathematical logic—to express emotions, needs and interests which in earler times might have been formulated in orthodox Christian language. [28]

If this *is* true, then the statement must be carefully qualified. It is almost certain that none of the authors cited are doing this purposefully, although some—Silverberg, for one—are certainly conscious of the symbolism. *Son of Man* is probably the only work mentioned which has as its purpose the examination of the religious nature of man. Nevertheless, the works do express emotions and interests—and perhaps also needs—and it is true that in times past similar emotions and needs would have required the vocabulary of symbols of some religious system (not necessarily Christian) for their expression. To say this does not involve any claim regarding the philosophical depth or literary expertise of the works involved, but merely points out that they *are* expressive, and that the vocabulary of symbols which they use functions, to some extent, in the same way that religious vocabularies of symbols have functioned and can function in the expression of similar emotions and interests.

When one compares the use of superhumans in modern science fiction with the use of superhumans in comic books since the war, the most startling fact that attracts attention is how far they have diverged. In the Thirties the pulp supermen of science fiction had a great deal in common with the comic book supermen of the Forties and Fifties. Indeed, there was a certain amount of transmission from one *genre* to the other. But the superman stories of post-war science fiction, including the great majority of trivial *psi* stories, as well as the works mentioned individually above, have few ideative links with the straightforward power-fantasy whose archetype is Siegel and Schuster's *Superman*. Their main concern, even at the lowest levels of the market, is with social and psychic integration. The powers, whether they be extrasensory perceptions or psychokinetic abilities or simple physical attributes, are the means and not the ends. The actual ends envisaged by the stories may be ordinary—there are several neat telepathic love stories, notably "And Then She Found Him" (1957) by Algis Budrys—and they are very often mundane even when extraordinary; but they are also very often transcendental. In the latter case what the writers are attempting to do is to imagine an evolutionary potential for human beings which goes beyond the apparent restraints of the mundane world. They are not producing revelations, but fictions; and they are not armed, as Teilhard was, with an indestructible faith in a set of dogmas which only had to be transformed in order to manifest again its ineluctable truth. They are, for the most part, thoroughly agnostic visionaries who not only do not deal in belief, but often actively despise the commitment that belief, in its religious modes, involves. Nevertheless, it seems to me to be wholly reasonable to suggest that they are expressing similar emotions, and through the communicative medium of their work, serving similar needs.

5. SUMMARY

In this chapter I have attempted to isolate and illustrate the main trends visible in the development of the characteristic themes of science fiction. The trends which I have examined here are not the only ones that can be seen, but they are, I think, the ones which are most interesting and which offer specially significant information in service of the attempt to draw the connection which exists between the literary *genre* and its social context.

Because of the way I have presented these data, I run the risk of being suspected of selecting examples to suit my case. I have, indeed, paid particular attention to stories which best illustrate the account I have given, but this should not prejudice my claim to the effect that the trends which I have pointed out are real. I have made no attempt to quantify the data or to carry out a formal content analysis based on such quantified data, primarily because this kind of approach is singularly inappropriate to the exercise which I am trying to carry out. It seems to me to be logically necessary, given that I am considering the *genre* as a medium of communication, to pay close attention to the communicative efficacy of particular works of fiction. I have throughout this research given priority to those works which were not only widely-read but widely-remembered, and which made sufficient impact on their audience to be reprinted or given awards. It seems to me to be not only reasonable but vital for the sociologist of literature to identify as significant those works which the readers identify as significant (for whatever reasons). This claim is by no means similar to the one made by Goldmann in *The Hidden God*, whereby he sought justification for his sociology by its ability to single out as significant those works already deemed esthetically meritorious—in fact, it is the reverse of this claim, because it takes the acclaim of the audience as one of the most important data to be used in *identifying* a sociologically interesting text. In my view, the sociologist assumes far too much if he thinks he can tell the audience that they are "right" to acclaim a work (and, by implication, that he can also tell them when they are "wrong" to do so).

In isolating the trends which I have pointed out, I have, indeed, selected from the whole range of the data; but such selection is part and parcel of *any* process of observation. If my selection has been prejudiced, then any attempt to justify this prejudice must be made on the grounds that it is a prejudice which is at least similar to the average prejudices of the audience. I have, as far as possible, allowed their prejudices to guide my own, insofar as those prejudices are expressed in influence upon the market itself, though I have in certain instances referred to works that were not initially popular, citing them as exaggerated and extreme examples of the various trends.

Further objection might be made to the fact that the observations made in this chapter are inextricably entangled with an interpretative commentary. This is true, and the fact that all observation is to some extent interpretative cannot excuse the fact that I have made no strenuous attempt to minimize the intrusion of my interpretations into my account of the data. Once again, I must take refuge in the claim that the data do not warrant such an attempt. To be able to identify these trends is, to a large extent, to interpret them. It would be very difficult indeed to describe them without using language that interprets them. It would be possible, I suppose, to perform an elaborate series of feats of linguistic gymnastics in order to leave the impression that the data can be presented in flat, neutral terms, so that the interpretation of their significance can be superimposed upon them at a later stage; but I have not endeavored to do so, firstly because such presentation would misrepresent the actual intellectual processes involved in this research, in the course of which the processes of observation and interpretation *were* inextricably interlinked; and secondly because it would in the vast majority of cases be a distortion of the stories themselves to pretend that one can separate description of their ideative content from judgments as to what kind of response they are to what kind of stimuli. Many stories overtly and actively *invite* interpretation, because that is the kind of thing that many stories—even those in popular *genres*—are. To attempt rigorously to exclude interpretation from the observation of literature is mistaken, because it leaves out an important aspect of the phenomenon. Literature, unlike most things that most scientists observe, is created *in order to be* "observed" in a special way. It would be unscientific for the sociologist to ignore this fact for the sake of mimicking the procedures of scientists who do not have such things to contend with.

What the data of this chapter show us can conveniently be summarized in the observation that during the Forties—and especially following the end of the second world war—the content of science fiction underwent drastic changes. The attitudes to entities both real and imaginary contained within the *genre* were altered, in two cases—attitudes to technological artifacts, and attitudes to the society of the near future—suddenly and dramatically. In both these cases it seems that the principal agent effecting the sudden change of attitude was the spectacular introduction into the world of the achievement of atomic power. Few technological achievements have made their *entrée* into the public arena by killing a hundred thousand people, and it is not wholly surprising that this particular achievement made such an imaginative impact on a species of fiction so intimately interested in the effects of technology on society and upon man in society. It seems, however, that the wider significance of this "break" in history may better be perceived by looking at those trends which were not so dramatically interrupted: attitudes to aliens and superhumans. These trends may have been accelerated by the concluding event of the second world war, but not nearly so dramatically as the trend in presentation of future societies. By setting these trends alongside the others it is easy to see that *all four* are significant of a loss of faith in the capacity of modern man and modern society to cope with the conditions of contemporary life. Two of the trends show that the explosion of the first atom bomb was a key event in the erosion of that faith, but the other two suggest that the loss was in any case inevitable.

It is, I think, manifestly clear that the content of science fiction is responsible to the historical crises of our time, and primarily to one particular dimension of historical crisis: that which we face as a result of the pace of technological progress. This is a banal observation, but it needs to be made, because there are some commentators who would disagree with it. Establishing this point, however, is merely the prelude to the important question, which is: what *kind* of a response is it? Or, more likely: what *kinds* of responses can be seen within it? Corollary questions arise from different hypotheses: is science fiction simply *reflective* of common anxieties arising from our historical situation? Does it exist primarily to allow us to escape from these anxieties and to enjoy relief from them? Does it, conversely, feed and maintain these anxieties by sustaining the attitudes out of which they arise?

VI
CONCLUSION: THE COMMUNICATIVE
FUNCTIONS OF SCIENCE FICTION

1. DIRECTIVE FUNCTIONS

It has already been pointed out that it is not within the scope of this inquiry to analyze in depth the directive potentialities of particular works of science fiction. The analysis of reader demand summarized in Chapter Four has, however, indicated the possibility of a species of directive function served by science fiction as a *genre*, at least with respect to the first encounters with the *genre* experienced by some readers. It may be necessary to associate some of the preoccupations exposed in the analysis of themes and trends with this exceptional directive function.

The two principal promoters of magazine science fiction, Gernsback and Campbell, both thought of science fiction as a medium with didactic potential, though they differed very much in their notions of the kind of didacticism to which the medium might best be adapted. Nowhere in the analysis of reader demand is there anything to suggest that Gernsback's prospectus for science fiction as a carrier of scientific facts was ever justified to any measurable extent in practice, but there is some evidence for his rather vaguer hope that the medium might function inspirationally. If, at the most mundane level of meaning, it failed to inspire many people to become inventors, it certainly compensated by inspiring the kind of interest in the future and its possibilities for which Gernsback hoped. That interest was not rewarded by the same confident optimism which Gernsback himself embraced, but it was nonetheless real. Campbell's basic demand was that the interest in the future thus stimulated should not only be real but *realistic*, and though it is much harder to build up a conclusive case for this having been a real effect of science fiction, there is certainly some evidence for it. Had science fiction continued to serve only the maintenance and restorative functions, as did the other pulp *genres*, one would not have expected the kind of developments—especially with respect to the roles of machines and images of future society—that were very obvious in post-war science fiction.

If we are to look for measurable effects of science fiction upon the real history of science then we shall find none, with the possible exception of the fact that a number of rocket scientists appear to have been much involved at an early age with science fiction. [1] It is, of course, much more difficult to judge whether science fiction has had any measureable effect on the *attitudes* of people in general to technological innovation, but it seems that here a case can be made. That *some* people's attitudes have been profoundly affected there seems little doubt —it is difficult to believe that the image of the alien in contemporary science fiction played no contributory role in the events following Orson Welles' *Mercury Theatre* broadcast of 1938, which found a surprising readiness among the American people to accept the possibility of alien invasion. Similarly, the success of such quasi-religious groups as the Scientology movement and the Aetherius Society is partly dependent on the readiness of recruits to accept arguments whose strategy rests very much on the devices used in science fiction to create the illusion of plausibility on which the medium leans so heavily. The fact that people continually see "unidentified flying objects" is not particularly significant, but the fact that they show a strong bias in *interpreting* what they see (or think they see) in terms of extraterrestrial spacecraft seems to owe much to the mythology of science fiction.

These examples imply that science fiction is at least capable of having a directive effect upon the world-view of particular individuals. Whether we may legitimately generalize from what are, admittedly, bizarre examples must still remain dubious. There is, however, considerable evidence in both the naive reactions of young readers and in the claims made by some apologists, that science fiction does communicate new attitudes to the potentialities of the present, especially in terms of the way that science functions as a motor of historical change. Much science fiction—especially that written for Campbell's magazine—seems geared to this function; and the stories in which characters confront the products of technology directly show a definite trend toward consideration of the social effects of, and social reactions to, mechanical inventions. Whether science fiction overestimates the importance of science and technology as motors of historical change is, of course, irrelevant to the point at issue, which is whether science fiction does, in fact, influence attitudes in this respect.

We must be careful ourselves not to overestimate the role played by *genre* science fiction in terms of affecting general attitudes to change and the future. It is arguable that two individual novels, neither labelled science fiction, have had as much influence on the way we commonly think about the future as all others put together (I refer, of course, to *Brave New World* and *Nineteen Eighty-Four*). In the case of such technological innovations as the atomic bomb, there was little enough need for fiction to assist in creating attitudes of extreme anxiety. Nevertheless, it is for many people the fictional exploration of the possibilities attendant on such innovations which clarifies and dramatizes the issues involved. It would probably not be overambitious to suggest that general attitudes to computers have been quite heavily influenced by fictional representations of "mechanical brains."

Determination of whether, in fact, the habitual reading of science fiction commonly results in a measurable shift in attitude is, of course, a matter for empirical inquiry, and could probably be determined either by a longitudinal study of "new recruits" to the science fiction community over a period of some two to three years, or by a lateral comparison of hardened science fiction writers with a matched sample of non-readers. The present study can only offer tentative suggestions as to what *kind* of attitudinal change might be involved. The comments on the experiences and enthusiasms of readers first discovering science fiction suggests strongly that the change consists of some kind of perspective-shift, analogous to "gestalt switches," in the same way that, according to Thomas Kuhn [2], changes of allegiance to scientific paradigms are so analogous. What seems to be involved is a re-ordering of the context in which ideas relating to science and technology are held, emphasizing certain aspects very heavily: the image of man as a relatively insignificant creature in a vast and complex universe; gadgets as instances of ongoing technological effort leading toward the total human control of the environment. To some extent these emphases conflict with one another, and it is from this conflict that many of the basic preoccupations and themes of science fiction emerge.

The question of whether this kind of attitudinal change, if it does commonly happen, has any real utility, is a rather vexed one. Apologists, naturally, are willing to claim that it does, though they make their claims on a number of different bases. The question becomes fairly trivial if one takes C. S. Lewis' view that the utility of the attitudinal change is simply that it facilitates service of the restorative function; but it is by no means trivial if one takes the view put forward by Robert Scholes that the characteristic world-view of science fiction is one that is particularly well-suited to the times. A number of different cases could be made out in support of this general claim, the simplest being that science fiction reflects the world-view of modern science itself, and may thus help to make scientific knowledge less alien and more comprehensible. Alvin Toffler, [3] on the other hand, has suggested that the mental flexibility encouraged by science fiction might provide a useful foil against the potential stresses involved with the high rate of innovation (particularly technological innovation) in modern environments. A more specific variant of the same case, relating to the contemporary media environment, is put forward by Marshall McLuhan. [4] The basis of claims such as these is that science fiction, by presenting, collectively, an image of the future as an array of possibilities, each dependent upon hypothetical innovations, allows its readers to confront new developments—whatever they may be—with a sense of confidence. In this view science fiction readers are, in effect, already attuned to the processes of change, and are thus less likely to suffer alienation as the world develops from the one they already know to one which they do not.

146

There may well be something in the Toffler/McLuhan argument—which is certain plausible—but there are one or two reasons for treating it with suspicion. One is that the science fiction community seems to be so very conservative in its attitudes towards science fiction *itself*. There is no more common complaint to be heard from long-term readers than that science fiction has lost its "sense of wonder," and there is extreme and widespread suspicion of literary experimentation. If reading science fiction does not inculcate sufficient flexibility of mind to allow the majority of its adherents to accept change within science fiction as a *genre*, it seems a little optimistic to accept unquestioningly that it makes them better prepared for changes in the real world. The other reason is that, as was discussed at the end of Chapter Four, science fiction can actually be seen to pander to the sense of alienation commonly felt by the young; and there seems to be a certain contradiction in arguing that a literature which has such attractions to the alienated should have as a common function the property of protecting its readers *against* alienating forces. Certainly it seems to ameliorate the sense of alienation, but to a large extent to do this by *justifying* the sense of being different and apart rather than by remedying the situation. These two objections are, however, not entirely damning as far as the hypothesis is concerned, and the best conclusion one can reach with respect to this point is that the issue must remain undecided. Nor are these hypotheses such as to lend themselves to convenient testing, so that it is not easy to indicate how the matter might be settled, or how corroborative evidence for either point of view might best be obtained.

Even if we do conclude that science fiction is or can be associated with particular attitudinal changes in its readers—leaving aside any judgment as to the utility of such changes—there still remains the question of the extent to which we are dealing with a directive effect, and the extent to which we are concerned only with the maintenance function. It seems reasonably clear that science fiction can function directively when people encounter it for the first time, but it is not altogether certain that the *continued* reading of science fiction does anything more than maintain the perspective-shift already achieved, plus, of course, maintaining sentiments originating elsewhere and fulfilling the restorative function. If science fiction really did anticipate social problems, as its apologists sometimes claim, there would be no problem in claiming an ongoing directive function; but in fact its track record in this regard has been very poor. Overpopulation was invisible as a theme in science fiction until it became a subject of concern in the real world, and the same is true of such issues as environmental pollution and resource crises. Only in the case of atomic power, and to a lesser extent in the case of space technology, has science fiction any claim at all to prophetic aptitude. Nevertheless, a case might still be made for a continuing directive effect because of the way in which these issues were taken up when they *did* become matters of popular concern.

Science fiction writers have usually been quick to seize on such popular anxieties as overpopulation and environmental pollution. Response to these emergent concerns was rapid, and, more significantly, exaggerated. Science fiction writers have always been ready not simply to *reflect* anxieties of this kind, but also to *amplify* them. It seems to be not simply a matter of registering the existence of such anxieties and maintaining them, but of actively feeding them, emphasizing their importance. It is this readiness not only to jump on contemporary bandwagons, but also to give them an extra shove, which gives science fiction much of its affective power and much of its apparent timeliness. The strategies of exaggeration involved are particularly noticeable in trend analyses pertaining to societies of the future, and to machines.

As a didactic medium, science fiction has never been very powerful, but as an *affective* medium it has enjoyed considerable success. As a *genre*, its primary appeal has always been to the emotions, however paradoxical that may seem in the light of its title. Its use of ideas has always been, in the most literal sense of the word, *sensational*—its principal appeal is commonly said to be to the "sense of wonder," and it is expressive much more than it is descriptive. This in itself, of course, does not qualify it as a directive medium—most popular *genres* make their appeals affectively—but the striking difference between science fiction and other popular *genres* is its rapid and radical pattern of change compared with their emotional conservatism. Not only do the striking patterns of change evident in the treatment of ideas in science fiction have no parallel in other popular *genres*, but the very possibility of such patterns of change is precluded by the basic assumptions on which other *genres* characteristically proceed.

The directive potential of science fiction, so far as the long-term reader rather than the initiate is concerned, is to a large extent dependent upon its affective aggression—its ability to call attention urgently to new concerns, and to force some kind of emotional response thereto. (It is, of course, also true that the imaginative works produced outside the *genre* which have had considerable impact upon the popular imagination have done so by means of affective aggression—*Brave New World* and *Nineteen Eighty-Four* again provide the cardinal examples.) Some apologists for science fiction—notably Kingsley Amis—have construed this affective aggression as a kind of satire; but this is a misrepresentation, in that the pertinence of science fiction's hypothetical worlds to the real social situation of the reader is usually too tenuous to permit any real satirical impact. The warnings and social criticisms that emerge from science fiction's affective appeals are rather more general and less immediate than those contained in satire—though satire, of course, also employs the strategy of exaggeration which leads to fantasization.

In conclusion, therefore, it is probably reasonable to assert that the manner in which science fiction absorbed into its

148

images of future society such anxieties as those pertaining to overpopulation and pollution does suggest that there is some degree of directive communication involved.

2. MAINTENANCE FUNCTIONS

When we come to study characteristic patterns of resolution in the science fiction story, what strikes us most forcibly is the apparent instability of the patterns. The characteristic resolutions which are common today often bear little resemblance to those which were prominent forty, or even twenty, years ago. Much pulp science fiction, of course, relied heavily on types of resolution common to all *genres*—most pulp stories were stories in which villains were vanquished and the hero got the girl. The factors unique to science fiction in the pre-war period were mainly consequent upon its extended *répertoire* of villains, and —more importantly—the strategies by which they were vanquished. In post-war science fiction, however, there has been a strong tendency, at least in the upper strata of the market, to abandon villains altogether in favor of problem-solving situations of a more complex kind. The means by which resolutions are characteristically brought about have changed in consequence.

Most early pulp science fiction featured contests of super-science. There was a high priority on inventiveness and hardware. The problem most commonly faced by heroes was the invention of a device which could nullify or overcome the devices used by the enemy (whether human or alien). Characteristically, it was by means of new technology that conflicts were resolved. The notion promoted by this type of story is simply that existential and social problems can be met and adequately answered by technological innovation. This was certainly what Gernsback believed and was trying to persuade his readers to believe, and Campbell thought along much the same lines.

It is easy to imagine a situation where there might never have been any more to science fiction than this. It is a reassuring "message" with a certain plausibility, and is particularly well-adapted to pulp fiction-writing, in that it is a formula producing an infinite series of plots which work, essentially, on a principle of *deus ex machina*. In fact, however, it is an outlook which has become much less fashionable with the passing of time, and even somewhat despised.

The decline of faith in this kind of resolution—and the ideas encouraging that decline—are very clear in the analysis of attitudes to machines in science fiction. The first mechanophobic stories appeared in science fiction as early as the Thirties, expressing the fear that overdependence on technology might lead to decadence; and it was this fear that gradually became the basic tenet in science fiction's rejection of the Utopian image of the future. In early science fiction there was no real conflict between the affirmation of the power and the virtue of technology on the one hand, and the suspicion that the supply of human needs might become all-too-easy on the other. The notions were kept separate because they were assumed to pertain to very different periods of history—the former to the near future, the latter to the very far future. Before 1945 the notion of unlimited power for the fulfillment of human needs seemed very distant and Utopian to most writers and virtually all readers. The achievement of atomic power, though it made relatively little difference to the actual historical situation, brought the possibility of high-technology society imaginatively much closer. This was when the ideas came into conflict, and in the immediate post-war period we can see in stories dealing with societies of the future the first conventional resolution of the conflict in the emphasis on the role of the spaceship as an "escape mechanism" allowing the sterility of a finite Utopia to be sidestepped. The "escape into space" *motif* became common in the Fifties, and remained so for ten years or more before it began to lose its fashionability.

The reasons for the decline of the post-war spaceship mythology have already been pointed out in Chapter Five. Firstly, the real space program put the *naïveté* of the idea into better perspective; and secondly, the shift away from pseudo-Utopian images of the future went far enough to generate such pessimism with respect to the near future that the priority shifted to a more urgent and more pragmatic kind of fiction. It is not immediately obvious how the "escape into space" stereotype should be interpreted. Certainly, it is only marginally concerned with maintaining attitudes to the real space program, though there are several works whose main purpose *is* to reemphasize the virtue of the program. What it is rather more concerned with maintaining, it seems, is a particular attitude toward the social forces tending to favor the Utopia of comfort. It is an emphasis on the need for novelty and the need for *challenge*. Spaceship literature's rapid waning and virtual disappearance from the scene is connected with the rise of the view that the probable state of near-future society itself promises a challenge, not only to the would-be rebel, but even to the would-be survivor.

In large measure, science fiction of the Sixties lost what consensus it had had concerning appropriate resolutions. Its main stereotypes had lost their currency, and there was no new one waiting in the wings to take over. Stories began to appear whose principal concluding assertion was that there no longer *are* any formularistic solutions, and whose plots were resolved only by the hero's acceptance of the difficulties of his situation and the realization that he would have to live with them.

It was this process—the loss of conventional, formularistic, and ritual resolutions—which resulted in science fiction's becoming, in the Sixties, something more than another in a series of popular *genres*. It was out of this uncertainty that the affective aggression of much contemporary science fiction arose, offering much more scope than had been previously available, for the use of the *genre* as a directive medium of communication.

The decline of those characteristic resolutions so far discussed seems to be very much in tune with attitudes currently in the social matrix, though they represent, of course, a narrow selection from it. The suspicion of technology that has become widespread since the second world war, and the increasing tendency to blame "runaway technological advance" for contemporary social problems (after the fashion of Bertrand Russell in *Icarus*), posed something of a challenge to science fiction writers, most of whom had been hitherto committed to an incompatible viewpoint, actively maintaining sentiments which had now lost their credibility.

The consequences of this challenge have been various. For one thing, there is now and has been since the early Sixties a considerable degree of tension within the science fiction community, with those favoring the retention and reinforcement of the old commitments against the tide of popular opinion facing the uneasy opposition of a new *avant garde*, who preach the total redundancy of such an attitude and the necessity for science fiction to undergo a metamorphosis of some kind, finding new concerns and (possibly) new methods adapted thereto. The bulk of recent science fiction, however, steers a course along a *via media* somewhere between pro- and anti-technological viewpoints, often featuring resolutions which reaffirm the notion that, even if the marriage of man and machine is not so harmonious as could be desired, the prospects of a divorce are even worse. This is the emergent stereotype so far as the resolution of stories specifically concerned with man/machine encounters are concerned. It is a resolution of reconciliation, by which man and machine somehow find a viable mode of productive coexistence, whether comfortable or not.

Another consequence of the challenge presented by the drift of popular opinion to the attitudes once habitually maintained by science fiction has been the tendency to place much more emphasis on *communication* and the achievement of social and/or spiritual "harmony," in such a way as to sidestep entirely the likely problems of society in the near future. The whole preoccupation with metaphysical themes and religious symbology can be seen in terms of an "escape" from the awkward situation into which science fiction was delivered by the course of history and changes in the intellectual climate. It is the dramatic change in the role of the alien in science fiction which poses one of the greatest challenges to the historian of the *genre*, for the extremeness of the change renders it unlikely that it is simply symptomatic of the advance of liberal attitudes; and the impulse of the evolutionary sequence seems to have been rather powerful when one recalls that the single most influential voice in the science fiction community—Campbell's—was deeply entrenched on the side of human chauvinism.

This change reflects, at least in part, rather more than the influx of new political attitudes into science fiction. The other main factor to be taken into consideration is the transfer of allegiance from one vocabulary of characteristic resolutions—

those concerned with technological "answers" to hypothetical predicaments—to a new vocabulary, mainly concerned with social, psychological, and transcendental "answers." The moment of first contact with aliens, which was used most commonly in pre-war science fiction as a prelude to conflict, became in the post-war period a common *conclusion* for stories—a triumphal cry of "We are not alone!" More often, of course, it is not the moment of encounter that is important, but the moment which symbolizes the first significant *understanding* of one species by the other. This *motif* has come to dominate contemporary science fiction. As has already been observed, the situation finds a less frequent but more exaggerated parallel in stories dealing with "human aliens"—usually, though not always, superhumans.

One notable feature of *these* resolutions is that they seem to have very little connection with real possibility. Gernsback's insistence on the virtue and potential power of technology may have been naive, but he really was dealing with potentialities which existed in the real world: atomic power, television, computers, spacerockets. The world in which Gernsbackian science fiction came into being really *was* a period of rapid technological advance, and people really *did* find technological solutions to many of their problems. By contrast, while we cannot rule out *a priori* the possibility of contact with alien beings or the evolution of superhuman faculties, we must concede that the probability of either of these things actually happening comes very close to negligibility. It hardly seems possible, therefore, to argue that these new kinds of resolution represent in any direct way attitudes that are in any sense viable in the real world. People who spend their real lives trying to make contact with alien beings or trying to become supermen are a good deal more common than the more sceptical of us consider to be reasonable; but the whole world has not yet fallen prey to flying saucer mania, Scientology, or transcendental meditation, and neither has the science fiction community. We must, therefore, look much more closely at the question of what, precisely, might be being maintained here—if, indeed we are dealing with the maintenance function at all.

If it is to be taken literally, the kind of resolution which represents solutions to social or existential problems in terms of some kind of personal transcendence has very little utility. (Perhaps the best example of the attempt to take it literally is to be found in the works of Colin Wilson, beginning with *The Outsider*, and continuing through his various studies of occultism and murder. Wilson himself, however, does not seem to be much of an advertisement for his prospectus.) Nevertheless, this kind of resolution does constitute an affirmation of faith in a certain *kind* of solution. It represents what Frank Manuel [5] has called a "eupsychian" mode of thought—the conviction that the ideal state of being is to be sought not in terms of a better place (eutopia) or a better time (euchronia), but in terms of a "better adjusted" or "healthier" state of mind.

If the new predominant resolutions of science fiction are to be interpreted symbolically rather than literally, then we find that they are not so very different from the tradition of twentieth century mainstream fiction referred to in Chapter Two, whose stereotyped resolution involves the hero's coming to terms with and/or triumphing over his own state of alienation by intellectual effort or by the acquisition of a new perspective. This contact between the aims and concerns of much recent science fiction and those of a particularly strong and prestigious vein of mainstream fiction, is a major factor permitting and encouraging the interest taken in science fiction by American universities during the last ten years. To the extent that these patterns of resolution *can* be said to serve the maintenance function, therefore, they are not particularly unusual and are new only within the *genre*.

However, it would probably be mistaken to interpret these trends in science fiction *only* by reference to their symbolic significance in the service of the maintenance function. Undoubtedly, the new predominance of eupsychian thinking in science fiction is *partly* explicable in terms of the maintenance function; but only partly, for the actual symbology involved is much more extreme than would be required if eupsychian symbolism were the only thing at stake. If this were all there was to it, its extremism would actually threaten its utility. It is one thing to be continually confronted by stories in which heroes end up with extended mental faculties and a sense of psychic well-being, but it is quite another to be frequently confronted with heroes who become one with God or who obtain direct access to the mysteries of creation. This might be explicable by reference to the policy of affective aggression noted earlier in this chapter, but we must beware of co-opting that argument without due consideration of the alternative hypothesis, and without investigating the probable involvement of the restorative function.

3. RESTORATIVE FUNCTIONS

In Chapter Two I stressed the point that the maintenance function and the restorative function tend to operate in conjunction, the former commonly determining the characteristic pattern of resolutions to be found in a *genre*, while the latter determines the environment of the story so as to reinforce the appropriateness of the resolutions. Put briefly, the argument is to the effect that we choose as worlds to "escape" into those imaginative *milieux* which permit and encourage the formularistic affirmation of the things we want to believe in, and the things we already do believe in.

If we look at the early science fiction which is geared primarily to the service of the restorative function—the escapist fantasies of Burroughs and Merritt are the cardinal examples—we find ideal settings for wish-fulfillment fantasy: new versions of the classical "parallel-world," the Land of Faërie. The emphasis is on gaudiness, with a touch of decadence, where flying can be combined with swordplay, and courage will always prevail against the ever-present threat of the strange and the supernatural. Similarly, the technological landscapes of early "hard" science fiction provide a perfect *milieu* for fantasies of dispensing awesome power and journeying as far as the imagination can take a naive mind. These landscapes are designed to facilitate the typical resolutions connected with the maintenance functions of science fiction: they are *milieux* in which triumph by technological innovation becomes both possible and "valid." It is worth reemphasizing here that readers habitually choose as "escape-worlds" *not* worlds in which the kinds of problem-situations which they perceive as relevant to their own lives do not and cannot arise; but worlds in which those kinds of problem-situations (often exaggerated) *can be met and dealt with.* Much early science fiction is straightforward power-fantasy, called forth by the feeling of vulnerability that is characteristic of early adolescence and of various modes of social alienation; and obtains its identity and coherency as a *genre* by featuring one particular "strategy" for overcoming vulnerability: technological invention and the attainment of intellectual security *via* scientific knowledge. The worlds of science fiction, broadly speaking, are worlds where knowledge and inventiveness *pay off* in conquering threats and achieving success.

Burroughsian fantasy still exists in *genre* science fiction, relying on the conventions of science fiction to support its tentative appeal to plausibility. There is still a spectrum by which such imaginary worlds as these shade gradually into the alien worlds designed according to more rational criteria. Many members of the science fiction community, however, consider—as a substantial fraction of the readership always has—that this kind of fantasy is not "real" science fiction. In the Twenties and Thirties "real"—i.e., archetypal—science fiction was represented by the superscientific romances of Edward E. Smith and John W. Campbell and the high-technology societies of near-future Earth; but the situation has since changed, and if we *now* want to contrast archetypal science fictional environments with those of Burroughsian fantasy, we cannot do so simply by reference to the prevalence of technology and the preoccupation with scientific apparatus. Many alien worlds in post-war science fiction must be contrasted not only with the exotic environments geared for straightforward power fantasy that are represented by imitators of Burroughs, but also with the environments geared to technological power fantasy that were typical of pre-war science fiction.

The first consequence of the decline of the imaginative *milieux* facilitating the stereotyped resolutions of the pre-war period was that alien worlds became much more enigmatic and considerably less hospitable. This is very obvious in stories of the Fifties which deal with the theme of colonizing alien worlds. [6] The threatening qualities of alien environments became central to such stories as it came to be accepted that the problems of environmental control were by no means so simple as had once

154

been taken for granted. This essential inhospitability had somehow to be met in a new way.

The imaginary worlds that emerged to become characteristic of the science fiction of the Sixties had to be worlds which facilitated the new kind of stereotyped resolutions. They had to be worlds which, by their very nature, permitted and validated eupsychian perspectives and psychic adaptations. This requirement is seen to be answered most straightforwardly in the trend toward "ecological mysticism" which is very prominent in Sixties science fiction. [7]

The role played by alien beings in this kind of scenario is, of course, crucial. It is necessary that aliens should very often be seen to be integrated into their environment more completely and more harmoniously than humans are, and should sometimes be capable of guiding humans to similar mystical states of harmony, perhaps even supervising them in a kind of spiritual rebirth. This kind of alien role does, of course, feature very prominently in the science fiction of the last twenty years, particularly in the last decade; and the mysticism which has invaded science fiction during that period is at least partly explicable in these terms: it exists, in part, to provide the kind of existential context that facilitates eupsychian resolutions, and thus becomes a predominant feature of preferred fantasy-worlds. The frequent appearance of alien religious systems which turn out to be literally true is, of course, a corollary to this.

There is no great difficulty in designing alien environments to suit this particular scheme. However, it is not only alien environments that science fiction writers deal in. When we are concerned with imaginary Earths (present or future), rather different problems arise in connection with designing contexts for the kind of psychic transcendence customarily associated with contemporary patterns of resolution. The designing of a context for the evolution of man into superman is not difficult—as has already been observed—for a devout Lamarckian such as George Bernard Shaw; but from the viewpoint of a more orthodox evolutionary philosophy the situation is more problematic. For some years after the close of the war the logic of mutations (often associated with nuclear radiation) producing humans with Rhinian *psi*-powers was much exploited, but the recourse waned in popularity quite markedly in the Sixties, and was largely replaced by more mystical notions of transcendence. It is not immediately obvious why this should have happened, in that Rhine's strenuous attempts to apply scientific method to the study of ESP and psychokinesis certainly succeeded in giving these notions a scientific gloss that assured their plausibility within the ideative conventions of science fiction. Rhine's work undoubtedly declined in fashionability as it failed, eventually, to deliver the goods; but it has never been thoroughly discredited and still commands respect in many quarters. There seem to be no grounds within the history of popular opinion relating to *psi* research by which we might seek to explain why science fiction writers have, to such a great extent, abandoned it in favor of a much more exotic doctrine of transcendent superhumanity which resembles the kind of evolutionary *schema* invented by Teilhard de Chardin.

This particular tendency is unaccountable simply in terms of the restorative function. There is, however, something of a link between this recent preoccupation with metaphysical and theological issues, and the kind of directive function which science fiction seems to fulfill for some "new recruits" to the science fiction community. It reaches out to the most ambitious ideas of all, providing—or at least offering—a context for existence which is universal, preserving something of "the search for the ineffable." It is, for many readers, part of the function of science fiction that it conveys the sense that the universe as a whole is a unique kind of entity. Early science fiction accomplished this by extending a rather naive Newtonian view of the universe that was already out of date in theoretical physics—early space operas clearly take place in a stable clockwork universe which is an infinite extrapolation of an Earthly playground. Even in its more sophisticated pre-war and early post-war versions this kind of fiction conveyed an idea of the universe as, in Scholes' words, "a system of systems," essentially comprehensible if rather peculiar. The recent tendency, however, is to give the impression of an essentially alien universe, whose nature and totality is quite beyond human imaginability. This is, perhaps, the ultimate in affective aggression, but it can hardly be directive in the same sense that "awful warning" stories about overpopulation and pollution are. It seems, in fact, that it can be interpreted only as a rather extreme expression of existential insecurity, crediting the insecurity not merely to the social or psychological situation of the protagonist, but to the whole universe which surrounds him. If such is to be the case, of course, then the only conceivable solutions have to be of the sweeping transcendental nature of Teilhardian mythology or some analogue thereof.

The function of this particular kind of material must remain rather dubious, but it seems to me that it cannot be fully explained by reference to the maintenance or restorative functions, despite its obvious thematic links to material clearly geared to serving those functions. It seems most likely that it functions directively in the sense that it actively calls attention to and aggravates a sense of insecurity that is unlikely to be promoted in such an extreme form by any other communicative source, though it does provide its own ritual exorcisms of that sense of insecurity in its vaguely triumphant images of apotheosis. These resolutions, however, are not invariable, and even if they were, it would be very difficult to argue that stories of this kind can possibly be maintaining convictions which have any kind of social utility. It remains to be seen how this particular trend will develop; but if one were to venture a prediction on the basis of what has already been observed about the kind of communication that seems to be taking place *via* science fiction, I would argue that if these exercises in phantasmagorical metaphysics *do* function directively in stimulating a sense of existential insecurity, then the rituals of exorcism will not only have to become more prominent, but more mundane, reaffirming confidence in the effectiveness of ordinary human action rather than in mysterious processes of transcendental metamorphosis.

NOTES AND REFERENCES

CHAPTER ONE

1. L. Lowenthal. *Literature and the Image of Man*, p. x.

2. S. Freud. *Introductory Lectures in Psychoanalysis* (1917).

3. *cf.* A. Swingewood & D. Laurenson. *The Sociology of Literature*, pp. 29-30.

4. L. Goldmann. *The Hidden God*, pp. 14, 15, 17.

5. L. Goldmann. *Towards a Sociology of the Novel.*

6. I. A. Richards. *Principles of Literary Criticism*, pp. 18-19.

7. *ibid.*, pp. 22-23.

8. *ibid.*, p. 47.

9. *ibid.*, p. 159.

10. F. R. Leavis. *Mass Civilization and Minority Culture*, p. 2

11. R. Williams. *The Long Revolution*, p. 42.

12. *ibid.*, p. 51.

13. *ibid.*, p. 55.

14. R. Williams. *Culture and Society, 1780-1950*, p. 294-295.

15. *ibid.*, p. 297.

16. In addition to works specifically cited, *cf.* T. Cauter & J. S. Downham, *The Communication of Ideas*; J. T. Klapper, *The Effects of Mass Communication*; and W. A. Belson, *The Impact of Television.*

17. The perspectives contained in this book derive very largely from the work of Kenneth Burke, but this tripartite classification appears to be Duncan's own, at least in this formulation.

18. H. D. Duncan. *Language and Literature in Society*, p. 5.

19. *ibid.*, pp. 20-21.

20. *ibid.*, pp. 42-43; 47.

21. I have adopted the term "communiqué" rather than the simpler word "message" because of the ambiguity introduced into the latter by the common habit of referring to a book's moral or philosophical commentary as its "message."

22. G. D. Wiebe. "The Social Effects of Broadcasting" in *Mass Culture Revisited*, ed. B. Rosenberg & D. White, p. 161.

23. C. S. Lewis. *An Experiment in Criticism*, pp., 1-3.

24. *ibid.*, pp. 139-140.

25. R. Escarpit. *The Sociology of Literature*, p. 88.

26. H. Herzog. "Motivation and Gratification of Daily Serial Listeners," in *The Processes and Effects of Mass Communication*, ed. W. Schramm, pp. 50-51; abridged from "What Do We Really Know About Day-Time Serial Listeners?" in *Radio Research 1942-3*, ed. P. Lazarsfeld & F. Stanton.

27. P. Mann. *The Romantic Novel: A Survey of Reading Habits* (1969).

CHAPTER TWO

1. V. Kavolis. *Artistic Expression: A Sociological Analysis*, p. 5.

2. A. Rand. *The Romantic Manifesto*, p. 40.

3. T. S. Kuhn. *The Structure of Scientific Revolutions* (2nd ed., 1970), pp. 46-47.

4. J. Dewey. *Art as Experience*, pp. 16-17.

5. D. Knight. "Knight Piece" in *Hell's Cartographers*. ed. B. W. Aldiss & H. Harrison, p. 122.

6. G. Greer. *The Female Eunuch* (1970), p. 188.

CHAPTER THREE

1. *cf.* B. M. Stableford. "Proto-Science Fiction," in *The Encyclopedia of Science Fiction*, ed. P. Nichols.

2. *cf.* B. M. Stableford. "The Marriage of Science and Fiction," in *The Octopus Encyclopedia of Science Fiction* ed., R. Holdstock.

3. H. Gernsback editorial in *Amazing Stories*, April 1926.

4. H. Bates "Editorial Number One" in *A Requiem for* Astounding, by Alva Rogers, p. x.

5. Some information on the economics of science fiction writing during the Thirties has recently been provided by the commentary material in a number of collections of early pulp SF published in the U.S.A. by Doubleday—*cf.* especially, *The Early Williamson* (1977) and *The Early Pohl* (1976).

6. H. Bates, *op. cit.*, pp. xiii-xiv.

7. These circulation figures are given in Jacques Sadoul's *2,000 A. D.*, p. 11, and in various other secondhand accounts. Information about the circulation of *Amazing Stories* probably originated with Ray Palmer, whose contentions were first reproduced in *All Our Yesterdays* by Harry Warner, p. 77. All the evidence is hearsay, and perhaps not entirely to be trusted.

8. F. O. Tremaine. "Editorial Number Two," in *A Requiem for* Astounding, by Alva Rogers, p. xvii.

9. See no. 7 above.

10. *cf. The Early Pohl* (1976).

11. J. W. Campbell, Jr. "Introduction" to *Venus Equilateral* by George O. Smith (1947), pp. 12-13.

12. J. W. Campbell, Jr. "Concerning Science Fiction," in *The Best of Science Fiction* (1946), ed. G. Conklin, p. ix.

13. Accurate figures are available after 1960, when American magazines were required to publish their circulation data once a year. The lowest average circulation figures recorded by *Analog* was 74,400 for 1960 (the year of the title change), the highest was 116,500 for the year 1973. Figures for the other major magazines show that *Amazing*, which sold about 50,000 monthly in the early '60s, gradually lost its popularity, and is now selling about 25,000 four times a

year; *Galaxy*, selling more than 90,000 bimonthly in 1961-62, slipped to about 50,000 in the early '70s, but picked up dramatically in 1977, averaging 81,000 over six issues; *The Magazine of Fantasy & Science Fiction* has maintained a monthly circulation in the region of 50,000 throughout the period.

14. G. Conklin. "Introduction" to *The Best of Science Fiction*, p. v.

15. J. W. Campbell, Jr. "Concerning Science Fiction," in *ibid.*, p. viii.

16. See no. 13 above.

17. *Galaxy* reportedly reached a circulation of 180,000 in the early Fifties, but this is hearsay.

18. The earlier figures are hearsay based on statements by writers. The more recent figures are based on my own royalty returns and on consultation with other writers. Data on the number of science fiction titles produced each year depends to some extent on the criteria used to include or exclude titles, but a rough indication is given by censuses taken by various fans and bibliographers. The fanzine *Destiny* published a "Fantasy Index" in 1954, which reveals that in 1953 in the U.S.A. there were 81 new SF titles appearing in hardback, plus 3 reprints, while 8 titles appeared for the first time in paperback, with 28 paperback reprints. The SF newspaper *Locus* now takes a regular census, and reveals that between 1972 and 1976 the number of new SF titles appearing in hardback in the U.S.A. increased from 85 to 186, while the number of reprint hardbacks increased from 28 to 160. The number of new paperback titles increased from 140 to 284, and the number of paperback reprints from 95 to 324.

19. *Locus*, Vol. 10, No. 6 (203), August 1977. A Survey of SF readers was carried out at a convention in Toronto by sociologist Albert I. Berger in 1973, but only 282 responses were obtained from 3,400 attendees. The results of Berger's survey and a summary of data derived from various magazine surveys is given in "SF Fans in Socioeconomic Perspective: Factors in the Social Consciousness of a Genre," *Science Fiction Studies*, Vol. 4, Part 3 (13), November, 1977.

CHAPTER FOUR

1. D. Suvin quoted in *Alternate Worlds* by James Gunn, p. 226.

2. T. Whalen letter in *Amazing Stories*, September 1928, p. 563.

3. *cf.* P. Nicholls "Conceptual Breakthrough," in *The Encyclopedia of Science Fiction.*

4. D. Kyle in *Wonder Stories*, May 1935, p. 1517.

5. I. Asimov. "Science Fiction I Love You," in *Alternate Worlds*, by James Gunn, p. 9.

6. J. Gunn footnote to *ibid.*, p. 9.

7. D. A. Wollheim. *The Universe Makers*, p. 2.

8. J. Henderson letter in *Amazing Stories*, June 1929, p. 278.

9. E. R. Manthey letter in *Wonder Stories*, June 1935, p. 121.

10. W. Wilson. *A Little Earnest Book Upon a Great Old Subject*, quoted in "William Wilson's Prospectus for Science Fiction, 1851," by B. M. Stableford, *Foundation*, 10 June 1976, pp. 9-10.

11. *ibid.*, p. 7.

12. E. Fawcett proem to *The Ghost of Guy Thyrle*, quoted in "Edgar Fawcett," by B. M. Stableford, *Vector*, 79, November-December 1976, p. 13.

13. D. A. Wollheim, *op. cit.*, p. 10.

14. S. Moskowitz. *Explorers of the Infinite*, p. 11.

15. R. Bretnor paraphrased in "Science Fiction: its Nature, Faults and Virtues," by R. A. Heinlein in *The Science Fiction Novel: Imagination and Social Criticism*, ed. B. Davenport, p. 16.

16. R. A. Heinlein in *ibid.*, pp. 44-45.

17. B. W. Aldiss. *Billion Year Spree*, p. 8.

18. *cf.* B. M. Stableford. "Definitions," in *The Encyclopedia of Science Fiction.*

19. L. Fiedler. *Love and Death in the American Novel* (1960), p. 463; *Waiting for the End* (1964), p. 76.

20. R. Conquest. "Science Fiction as Literature," in *Science Fiction*, ed. M. Rose, p. 39.

21. *ibid.*, pp. 41-42.

22. C. S. Lewis. "On Science Fiction," in *ibid.*, p. 107.

23. *ibid.*, p. 109.

24. *ibid.*, p. 111-113.

25. R. Scholes. *Structural Fabulation*, pp. 29-30.

26. *ibid.*, p. 38-42.

27. *Foundation* has also run a series entitled "The Profession of Science Fiction," in which writers offer accounts of their relationships with the *genre*.

28. R. Silverberg. "Sounding Brass, Tinkling Cymbal," in *Hell's Cartographers*, ed. B. W. Aldiss & H. Harrison, pp. 10-11.

29. D. A. Wollheim. *op. cit.*, pp. 7-8.

30. *cf.* B. M. Stableford. "The Metamorphosis of Robert Silverberg," *SF Monthly*, Vol. 3, No. 3 (1976).

31. R. Sheckley. "The Search for the Marvellous," in *Science Fiction at Large*, ed. P. Nicholls, p. 192.

CHAPTER FIVE

1. M. de Unamuno quoted in "Quixote Mills: the Man-Machine Encounter in Science Fiction," by Robert Plank. *Science Fiction Studies*, Vol. 1, Part 2, Fall 1973, pp. 70-71.

2. Examples include *The Fairy Chessmen* (1946) and *Tomorrow and Tomorrow* (1947) by "Lewis Padgett" (Henry Kuttner and C. L. Moore); "Thunder and Roses" (1947) by Theodore Sturgeon; *The Murder of the U.S.A.* (1947) by Will F. Jenkins; *Ape and Essence* (1949) by Aldous Huxley; *Tomorrow Sometimes Comes* (1951) by Francis G. Rayer; *False Night* (1954; later expanded as *Some Will Not Die*) by Algis Budrys; *Extinction Bomber* (1956) by S. B. Hough; *On the Beach* (1957) by Nevil Shute; and *Level Seven* (1959) by Mordecai Roshwald.

3. B. Russell. *Icarus* (1924), pp. 62-63.

4. M. Clifton & F. Riley. *They'd Rather Be Right*, in *Astounding Science Fiction* (British Edition), April 1955, p. 108.

5. Further examples include: *The Programmed People* (1963) by Jack Sharkey; "Dial F for Frankenstein" (1964) by Arthur C. Clarke; *A Fistful of Digits* (1968) by Christopher Hodder-Williams; and *The Computer Conspiracy* (1968) by Mack Rey-

nolds.

6. R. M. Williams. "Robots Return," in *The Robot and the Man*, ed. M. Greenberg (Grayson 1954), p. 159.

7. *cf.* also Dick's novels: *The Game Players of Titan* (1963), *The Simulacra* (1964), and *Now Wait for Last Year* (1967).

8. P. K. Dick. "The Android and the Human," *Vector* 64, March-April 1973, pp. 7-8.

9. P. K. Dick. "Man, Android and Machine," in *Science Fiction at Large*, ed. P. Nicholls, pp. 202-203.

10. R. Silverberg in *SF Review* 23, November 1977, p. 12.

11. *cf.* B. M. Stableford. "Aliens," "Life on Other Worlds," "Living Worlds," "Biology," in *The Encyclopaedia of Science Fiction*.

12. Several anthologies were produced in the late Fifties and Sixties by the Foreign Languages Publishing House, plus collections by Yefremov and Konstantin Tsiolkovsky and a number of novels. In the Seventies several more titles were issued by Mir Publishers. Since 1973 numerous translations have appeared from American publishers, notably Seabury Press and Macmillan.

13. F. Polak. *The Image of the Future*, p. 183.

14. *cf.* B. M. Stableford. "Utopias" and "Dystopias," in *The Encyclopaedia of Science Fiction*.

15. *cf.* B. M. Stableford. "Social Darwinism in SF," in *The Encyclopaedia of Science Fiction*.

16. *cf.* B. M. Stableford. "H. G. Wells," in *The Encyclopaedia of Science Fiction*.

17. H. G. Wells. *Mind at the End of its Tether* (1945), pp. 1, 30, 34.

18. R. Bloch. "Imagination in Modern Social Criticism," in *The Science Fiction Novel: Imagination and Social Criticism*, ed. B. Davenport, pp. 107-109.

19. *cf.* B. M. Stableford. "Overpopulation," in *The Encyclopaedia of Science Fiction*.

20. *cf.* B. M. Stableford. "Pollution," in *The Encyclopaedia of Science Fiction*.

21. A further example is my own novel, *The City of the Sun*, but this was written with the pattern in mind.

22. Examples include "Recruiting Station" (1942, also known as *Masters of Time* and *Earth's Last Fortress*); "The Chronicler" (1946); "The Reflected Man" (1971); and the three novelettes combined in *Supermind* (1977).

23. Examples include *The Dreaming Jewels* (1950); "The Touch of Your Hand" (1953); "The (Widget), the (Wadget) and Boff" (1955); "Need" (1961); and "Case and the Dreamer" (1972).

24. E. Hopkins. "New Maps of Heaven," *Theoria to Theory*, October 1966, p. 100.

25. *ibid.*, p. 101.

26. Clarke has confirmed that this was the reason in private conversation, and also reiterated his rejection of the interpretation of the events of the novel in terms of religious symbology.

27. Other examples of overt representation of attempts to "connect" with the infinite are *Midnight at the Well of Souls* (1977) by Jack L. Chalker, and *Altered States* (1978) by Paddy Chayevsky.

28. E. Hopkins. *op. cit.*, pp. 101-102.

CHAPTER SIX

1. *cf.* B. M. Stableford. "Rockets," in *The Encyclopaedia of Science Fiction*.

2. T. S. Kuhn. *op. cit.*, p. 85.

3. A. Toffler. *Future Shock* (1970), pp. 383-384.

4. M. McLuhan. *The Medium Is the Massage* (1967), p. 124.

5. F. Manuel. "Toward a Psychological History of Utopias," in *Utopias and Utopian Thought*, ed. F. Manuel, pp. 69-100.

6. *cf.* B. M. Stableford. "Colonization," in *The Encyclopedia of Science Fiction*.

7. *cf.* B. M. Stableford. "Ecology," in *The Encyclopedia of Science Fiction*.

BIBLIOGRAPHY

1. SOCIOLOGY OF LITERATURE AND THE MASS MEDIA

Belson, W. A. *The Impact of Television.* London, 1967.

Burke, K. *The Philosophy of Literary Form.* Berkeley, CA, 1941.

Cauter, T. & Downham, J. S. *The Communication of Ideas.* London, 1954.

Cawelti, J. *Adventure, Mystery and Romance: Formula Stories as Art and Popular Culture.* Chicago, 1976.

Defleur, M. L. *Theories of Mass Communication.* New York, 1966.

Dewey, J. *Art as Experience.* New York, 1934.

Duncan, H. D. *Communication and Social Order.* New York, 1962.

_____. *Language and Literature in Society.* Chicago, 1953.

Duvigneaud, J. *The Sociology of Art.* London, 1972 (orig. ed., 1967).

Eastman, M. *The Literary Mind.* New York, 1931.

Escarpit, R. *The Book Revolution.* London, 1966 (orig. ed. 1959).

_____. *Sociology of Literature.* London, 1965 (rev. ed. 1971; orig. ed. 1958).

Fischer, E. *The Necessity of Art.* London, 1963 (orig. ed. 1959).

Goldmann, L. *The Hidden God.* London, 1964 (orig. ed. 1955).

_____. *Towards a Sociology of the Novel.* London, 1975 (orig. ed. 1964).

Hoggart, R. *The Uses of Literacy.* London, 1957.

Kavolis, V. *Artistic Expression: A Sociological Analysis.* New York, 1968.

167

Klapper, J. T. *The Effects of Mass Communication.* New York, 1960.

Laurenson, D. & Swingewood, A. *The Sociology of Literature.* London, 1972.

Lazarsfeld, P. F. & Stanton, F. *Radio Research 1942-3.* New York, 1944.

Leavis, F. R. *Mass Civilisation and Minority Culture.* Cambridge, 1930.

Leavis, Q. D. *Fiction and the Reading Public.* London, 1932.

Lewis, C. S. *An Experiment in Criticism.* Cambridge, 1961.

Lowenthal, L. *Literature and the Image of Man.* Boston, 1957.

_____. *Literature, Popular Culture and Society.* Palo Alto, 1961.

Lukacs, G. *The Historical Novel.* London, 1969 (orig. ed. 1955).

McLuhan, M. *Understanding Media.* London, 1964.

McQuail, D. *Towards a Sociology of Mass Communications.* London, 1969.

Mann, P. *Books and Reading.* London, 1969.

Rand, A. *The Romantic Manifesto.* New York, 1971.

Richards, I. A. *Principles of Literary Criticism.* London, 1924.

Rosenberg, B. & White, D. M., eds. *Mass Culture—the Popular Arts in America.* New York, 1957.

_____. *Mass Culture Revisited.* New York, 1971.

Schramm, W., ed. *The Processes and Effects of Mass Communication.* Urbana, IL, 1954.

Schucking, L. *The Sociology of Literary Taste.* Chicago, 1966 (orig. ed. 1923, rev. 1931).

Steinberg, C. S., ed. *Mass Media and Communication.* New York, 1966.

Waples, D., Berelson, B., & Bradshaw, F. R. *What Reading Does to People.* Chicago, 1940.

Watt, I. *The Rise of the Novel.* London, 1957.

Wellek, R. & Warren, A. *Theory of Literature*. New York, 1949.

Williams, R. *Culture and Society 1780-1950*. London, 1958.

_____. *The Long Revolution*. London, 1961 (rev. 1965).

Working Papers in Cultural Studies. Journal published by the Centre for Contemporary Cultural Studies, University of Birmingham (U.K.).

Wright, C. R. *Mass Communications: A Sociological Perspective*. New York, 1959.

Zeraffa, M. *Fictions: the Novel and Social Reality*. London, 1976 (orig. ed. 1971).

2. SCIENCE FICTION

Aldiss, B. W. *Billion Year Spree*. London, 1973.

_____ & Harrison, H. *Hell's Cartographers*. London, 1975.

Amis, K. *New Maps of Hell*. London, 1961.

Armytage, W. H. G. *Yesterday's Tomorrows*. London, 1968.

Ash, B. *Faces of the Future*. London, 1975.

_____, ed. *The Visual Encyclopaedia of Science Fiction*. London, 1978.

Atheling, W. (J. Blish). *The Issue at Hand*. Chicago, 1964.

_____. *More Issues at Hand*. Chicago, 1970.

Bailey, J. O. *Pilgrims Through Space and Time*. New York, 1947.

Barron, N. *Anatomy of Wonder*. New York, 1976.

Berneri, M. L. *Journey Through Utopia*. 1950.

Bleiler, E. F. *The Checklist of Fantastic Literature*. Chicago, 1948.

Bloomfield, P. *Imaginary Worlds or the Evolution of Utopia*. London, 1932.

Bretnor, R., ed. *Modern Science Fiction*. New York, 1953.
_____. *Science Fiction: Today and Tomorrow*. London, 1974.

Carter, L. *Imaginary Worlds*. New York, 1973.

Clareson, T., D., ed. *SF: The Other Side of Realism*. Bowling Green, OH, 1971.

_____. *Voices for the Future*. Bowling Green, OH, 19776.

Clarke, I. F. *The Tale of the Future*. London, 2nd ed., 1972.

_____. *Voices Prophesying War*. London 1966.

Davenport, B. *Inquiry into Science Fiction*. London, 1955.

_____, ed. *The Science Fiction Novel: Imagination and Social Criticism*. Chicago, 1959.

Day, D. B. *Index to the Science Fiction Magazines 1926-50*. Portland, OR, 1952.

de Camp, L. S. *Science Fiction Handbook*. New York, 1953 (rev. ed., 1975).

Eschback, L. A., ed. *Of Worlds Beyond*. Chicago, 1965.

Extrapolation. Journal published by the College of Wooster, Ohio. Ed., T. S. Clareson.

Foundation. Journal published by the North East Polytechnic. Ed., M. Edwards.

Franklin, H. B. *Future Perfect*. New York, 1966.

Gove, P. B. *The Imaginary Voyage in Prose Fiction*. New York, 1941.

Graaf, V. *Homo Futurus: eine Analyse der modernen Science Fiction*. Hamburg, 1971.

Gunn, J. E. *Alternate Worlds*. New Jersey, 1975.

Hillegas, M. R. *The Future as Nightmare*. New York, 1967.

Hopkins, E. "New Maps of Heaven" in *Theoria to Theory*, October 1966.

Ketterer, D. *New Worlds for Old*. Terre Haute, IN, 1974.

Knight, D. *In Search for Wonder*. Chicago, rev. ed., 1967.

Lundwall, S. *Science Fiction: What it's All About*. New York, 1971.

Manuel, F., ed. *Utopias and Utopian Thought*. New York, 1966.

Moore, P. *Science and Fiction*. London, 1957.

Moskowitz, S. *Explorers of the Infinite*. Cleveland, 1963.

_____. *Seekers of Tomorrow*. Cleveland, 1965.

_____. *Strange Horizons*. New York, 1976.

New England S. F. Association. *Index to the Science Fiction Magazines 1966-70*. West Hanover, MA, 1971.

Nicholson, M. H. *Voyages to the Moon*. New York, 1949.

Nicholls, P., ed. *Science Fiction at Large*. London, 1976.

_____. *The Encyclopedia of Science Fiction*. London, 1979.

Panshin, A. *Heinlein in Dimension*. Chicago, 1968.

Philmus, R. *Into the Unknown*. Berkeley, CA, 1970.

Polak, F. *The Image of the Future*. Amsterdam, rev. ed., 1973.

Rabkin, E. S. *The Fantastic in Literature*. Princeton, NJ, 1976.

Reginald, R. *Science Fiction and Fantasy Literature: A Checklist, 1700-1974, with Contemporary Science Fiction Authors II*, 2 vols. Detroit, 1979.

Rogers, A. *A Requiem for* Astounding. Chicago, 1964.

Rose, M., ed. *Science Fiction: A Collection of Critical Essays*. New Jersey, 1976.

Sadoul, J. *Histoire de la science fiction moderne (1911-71)*. Paris, 1973.

_____. *2,000 A.D.*. London, 1975 (orig. ed., 1973).

Scholes, R. S. *Structural Fabulation*. Notre Dame, IN, 1975.

_____ & Rabkin, E. S. *Science Fiction: History, Science, Vision*. London, 1977.

Science Fiction Studies. Journal published by Indiana State University, ed., D. Suvin & R. D. Mullen.

Strauss, E. S. *Index to the Science Fiction Magazines, 1951-65*. Cambridge, MA, 1966.

Sussmann, H. L. *Victorians and the Machine: the Literary Response to Technology.* Harvard, 1968.

Tuck, D. H. *Encyclopedia of Science Fiction and Fantasy.* Chicago, vol. 1, 1974, vol. 2, 1978.

Versins, P. *Encyclopédie de L'Utopie et de la Science Fiction.* Lausanne, 1973.

Walsh, C. *From Utopia to Nightmare.* New York, 1962.

Warner, H. *All Our Yesterdays.* Chicago, 1969.

Wollheim, D. A. *The Universe Makers.* London, 1972.

INDEX

1. WORKS OF SCIENCE FICTION INDEXED BY AUTHOR

176

182

"Cor Serpentis"/"The Heart of the Serpent," 116
Zamyatin, Yegevny
We, 124
Zebrowski, George
The Omega Point, 139
Zelazny, Roger
"For a Breath I Tarry," 109
"A Rose for Ecclesiastes," 117

2. GENERAL INDEX

ABOUT THE AUTHOR

BRIAN M. STABLEFORD was born at Shipley, Yorkshire in 1948. He graduated in Biology from the University of York in 1969, and was later awarded a D. Phil. from the Sociology Department of the same university for the thesis which forms the basis of the present book. He worked for some years as a freelance writer before obtaining a lectureship in the Sociology Department of the University of Reading. He teaches in several areas of the subject, including the philosophy of social science, the sociology of literature and the mass media, and the sociology of technology. He has also taught extramural courses in science fiction and fantasy literature. His nonfiction books include *The Mysteries of Modern Science*, *Future Man*, *Scientific Romance in Britain*, *Masters of Science Fiction* (Borgo), and *The Third Millennium: A History of the World, 2000-3000 A.D.* (in collaboration with David Langford). He has also written numerous science fiction novels, and has contributed to most of the important reference books on science fiction and fantasy.